KT-179-105

Monster's F.A.M.E. Attitude

Think Like a **F**ree Agent

- Every job arrangement is considered temporary.
- Your ongoing value grows with your relevant skills.
- Relationships count: a strong personal network is good for you and good for business.
- Your resume is your sales tool.

Train Like an **A**thlete

- Training is the only thing that makes you stronger.
- Training builds confidence.
- Your job search is a competition.

Prepare Like a **M**arketer

- Define your personal brand.
- Focus on your target customers.
- Deliver a memorable message.

Work Like an **E**ntrepreneur

- Entrepreneurs put themselves in the way of opportunity.
- Entrepreneurs take action.
- Entrepreneurs lead and get others to follow.

In your career . . .
YOU decide how much F.A.M.E. you will have!
—JEFF TAYLOR

Jeff Taylor

The idea for Monster came to founder (and Chief Monster) Jeff Taylor in a dream.

Head of his own recruitment ad agency, Adion, Jeff was focusing his business on big ideas and technological efficiencies for his high-tech clients. In the fall of 1993, a client said to him, "No more big ideas. I want a monster idea!"

Soon afterward, Jeff says, "I woke up at 4:30 A.M. from a dream that I built a bulletin board system where people could look for jobs. In the dark, I wrote down on a pad next to my bed, 'The Monster Board.' Realizing that in the morning I wouldn't be able to read what I had written, I got out of bed, went to a coffee shop, and at five in the morning designed a lot of the concepts and interface we're still using today."

Recognized as an innovator and visionary in both the Internet and careers industries, Jeff has reinvented the way the world looks for employment. His "monster idea," conceived at the dawn of the World Wide Web, quickly became one of the first dot-com companies (454th on the Web) and has since grown into the world's leading online career site. Today, the Monster global network consists of local content and language sites in nineteen countries and serves over 16 million unique visitors monthly.

Jeff is a frequent speaker at colleges and universities across the country, and at technology, advertising, and human capital conferences hosted by such noted organizations as Forrester Research, 21st Century Workforce Summit, The Partnership for Public Service, The Society for Human Resource Management (SHRM), Fast Company, and The Working Women Network. He serves on both the national and Massachusetts boards of directors of Junior Achievement and is also a board member of Boston's Wang Center for the Performing Arts.

Jeff has an undergraduate degree from the University of Massachusetts at Amherst and a certificate from the Owner/President Management (OPM) Program, Executive Education, Harvard Business School. He also holds an honorary doctorate from Bentley College.

In March 2000, Jeff reached yet another notable milestone: he became the Blimp Waterskiing World Champion.

Doug Hardy

Doug Hardy, a certified job and career transition coach, was the editor in chief of Monster and is currently general manager of Monster Careers. Prior to joining Monster, Hardy directed book, magazine, and Web publishing businesses in New York and Boston.

Both Taylor and Hardy live near Boston.

Trumpasaurus
(ˌtrəm-pə-ˈsȯr- əs)

Monster's mascot was brought to life on June 10, 1994. Trump is big and he's very friendly, always encouraging people to explore their possibilities and realize their dreams.

monster
Careers

>> How to Land the Job of Your Life <<

JEFF TAYLOR, FOUNDER OF **monster**®

WITH DOUG HARDY

PENGUIN BOOKS

PENGUIN BOOKS
Published by the Penguin Group
Penguin Group (USA) Inc., 375 Hudson Street, New York, New York 10014, U.S.A.
Penguin Books Ltd, 80 Strand, London WC2R 0RL, England
Penguin Books Australia Ltd, 250 Camberwell Road, Camberwell, Victoria 3124, Australia
Penguin Books Canada Ltd, 10 Alcorn Avenue, Toronto, Ontario, Canada M4V 3B2
Penguin Books India (P) Ltd, 11 Community Centre, Panchsheel Park, New Delhi – 110 017, India
Penguin Books (N.Z.) Ltd, Cnr Rosedale and Airborne Roads, Albany, Auckland, New Zealand
Penguin Books (South Africa) (Pty) Ltd, 24 Sturdee Avenue, Rosebank, Johannesburg 2196, South Africa

Penguin Books Ltd, Registered Offices:
80 Strand, London WC2R 0RL, England

First published in Penguin Books 2004

10   9   8   7   6   5   4   3   2

Copyright © Monster Worldwide, 2004
All rights reserved

Trademarks: All brand names and product names used in this book are trade names, service marks, trademarks, or registered trademarks of their respective owners. Penguin USA is not associated with any product or vendor mentioned in this book.

The names and addresses of individuals used as examples (on resumes and cover letters, in illustrations and text) are fictitious. No resemblance to any real person, living or dead, is intended. Some organization names (e.g., ABC Co.) are likewise fictitious. Names of some Monster members have been abbreviated, or their online "alias" names used, to preserve their privacy.

LIBRARY OF CONGRESS CATALOGING-IN-PUBLICATION DATA
Taylor, Jeff, 1960–
    Monster careers : how to land the job of your life / Jeff Taylor and Doug Hardy.
        p.   cm.
    Includes index.
    ISBN 0-14-200436-7
    1. Job hunting.   I. Hardy, Doug.   II. Title.
    HF5382.7.T39 2004   2003064785

Printed in the United States of America
Set in Giovanni Book with Gill Sans
Designed by Sabrina Bowers

Except in the United States of America, this book is sold subject to the condition that it shall not, by way of trade or otherwise, be lent, resold, hired out, or otherwise circulated without the publisher's prior consent in any form of binding or cover other than that in which it is published and without a similar condition including this condition being imposed on the subsequent purchaser.

The scanning, uploading, and distribution of this book via the Internet or via any other means without the permission of the publisher is illegal and punishable by law. Please purchase only authorized electronic editions and do not participate in or encourage electronic piracy of copyrighted materials. Your support of the author's rights is appreciated.

>>DEDICATION and ACKNOWLEDGMENTS <<

This book is dedicated to Monster's employees,
job seeker members, and employer customers.

Much of the most original advice in this book comes from the employers who use Monster, and they are quoted in the book. Special thanks to Lynn M. Arts, Brad Barrell, Neal Bruce, Art Coviello, Kate DeCamp, Robin Fischer, Bill Hickmott, Sean Huurman, Bobbie Jeanotte, Kent Kirch, Kyle K. Laverents, Carl Lopes, Barry Mehrman, Dave Morgan, Amy Needleman, Christy Peacock, Alison Rosenblum, Scott N. Santoro, Mike Walsh, Nikki Warren, Eric Winegardner.

A number of world-class athletes contributed their insights about training and competition: James Bregman, Rebecca Barnett, A. J. Mleczko, Jimmy Pedro, Marisa Pedulla, Daron Rahlves. Charles Camiel, Walt Lewis, and Mike Baum added great notes about structuring a job search.

Experts in employment and business topics gave us real-world advice. They are a diverse group, and their insights come from carefully observing the employment process. Many thanks for the expertise they shared so generously: Lou Adler, Carolyn Culbreth Ain, Susan Ascher, Peter Blacklow, Gail Blanke, Krista Bradford, Charles Campbell, John Challenger, Ian Christie, Gerry Crispin, Jeevan Devore, Bruce Dorskind, Robert Dunham, Tracey Esherick, Dennis Finn, Robin Fischer, Rob Galford, Michael Hattersley, China Miner Gorman, John Isaacson, Michael Katz, Richard Knowdell, Rieva Lesonsky, Jeff Lewis, Kristy Meghreblian, Arnie Miller, Julie Miller, Colin Moor, Fred Nothnagel, Pat O'Brien, Tom Osborne, Don Prior, Ginny Rehberg, Alison Rosenblum, Jonathan Rossheim, Max Stier, John Swanson, Kate Taylor, Carol Szatkowski, Dave Trance, Bruce Wain, Robert Wykes.

Monster's Web site features advice about every career subject. These experts shared especially helpful tips: Michael Chaffers, Karen Hofferber, Kim Isaacs, Deborah Knox, Carol Martin, Michael Neece, Kiki Peppard, Barbara Reinhold, Peter Vogt.

The following employees of Monster contributed their time and talent to the book and its companion Web site, **monstercareers.com**. Many others will continue to be involved with the site after publication: Emily Baillieul, Maya Baratz, Erin Barriere, Michael Bennett, Sally Beirschmitt, Paul Bert, Brigitte Burkholder, Jonathan Canger, Brian Corey, David Dellovo, Sue Duro, Jeana Genme, Charles Gerhold, James Gonyea, Donna Guilmette, Vartan Hagopian, Chip Henry, Mike Herzog, Alan Hoffman, Chuck Hughes, Doug Jackson, Carole Johnson, Heidi LaFleche, Kaycee Langford, Marcel Legrand, Ryck Lent, Ericka Malzberg, Danielle McCabe, Carol McCarthy, Ed Melia, Dan Miller, Jessica Miller, Norma Mushkat, Steve Pemberton, Michele Pearl, David Perla, Brent Pearson, Thad Peterson, Becky Richards, Michael Schutzler, Mark Smith, Christine Swiminer, Gillian Tangen, Kerry Testa, April Young.

Peter Ginsberg, a distinguished literary agent and an old friend re-met, understood the book perfectly from the first conversation, and shepherded it through the publishing process seamlessly. Thanks again to Peter and his colleagues at Curtis Brown, Ltd.

Great thanks belong to our excellent editors Jane von Mehren and Brett Kelly, and their team of professionals at Penguin. Every comment, thoughtfully considered and graciously suggested, made *Monster Careers* a better book.

Finally, a million thanks (or rather, tens of millions) to the job seekers who share their experiences with us and each other on Monster every day. May they all land the jobs of their lives!

>> CONTENTS <<

Dedication and Acknowledgments   vii
Introduction: Today's the Day   xi

PART I: THE NEW JOB SEARCH BASICS
1. Never Settle!   3
2. Monster's F.A.M.E. Attitude   13
3. Job Good, Life Good!   29
4. Behind the Scenes at the Recruiter   43
5. People Who Will Help You   53
6. Who Are You?   71

PART II: PREPARING YOUR SEARCH
7. Plan Your Job Search   97
8. Build a Job Search Portfolio   115
9. Your Pitch   145
10. Create a Resume That Sells   157
11. Cover Letters and Cover Messages   209

PART III: INTO THE MARKETPLACE
12. The Power of Research   229
13. Finding Opportunity—and Creating It   255
14. Networking   279

PART IV: LANDING THE JOB
15. The Job Interview   303
16. Negotiating the Best Deal   341
17. Your Transition to a New Job   353
18. Special Situations   361

Afterword   379
Resources   381
Index   397

>> INTRODUCTION: TODAY'S THE DAY <<

here are you in your work life today?

- Are you looking for a job today?
- Are you employed, but wondering if there's something better out there?
- Are you just entering the workforce?
- Are you stuck in a dead-end job?
- Are you happy with your career, but want to move up?

Wherever you are, you need new job search strategies in order to survive and thrive. Today's the day to get started on a new kind of job search.

I don't believe you have to settle into a job you dislike in order to have something called "job security." You don't have to settle for less than a great job because you dropped out of college, or were just laid off, or because you've failed in the past.

I don't believe you have to settle for making less money than you're worth because someone said "take it or leave it."

I'm here to tell you that settling for less than a life of growth and fulfillment at work is a terrible injustice—to yourself, your family, and your future. Your work life can be outrageously satisfying. Whatever stage of life you're at today, you can pursue a new vision of your career, and make your other dreams come true as well.

My challenge to you is *never settle*.

"Never settle" doesn't mean that you can have all the money, fame, power, and love you want by tomorrow afternoon. It means never settle into boredom, resignation, or despair. It means never settle into blaming someone else because you don't like your job. It means never settle back in your chair, thinking nothing will change.

It's a challenge to *you*. It's not up to your employer to make you happy or successful. It's not up to your next paycheck to make your life good. It's up to you.

Your boss, your parents, your spouse, the economy, globalization, the stock market, a recession, or just bad luck—none of these can keep you from pursuing your dream job unless *you* let it happen.

Today's the day. Commit yourself today to doing what it takes to find the right job. If you've had setbacks, or if you have a hard time believing in yourself, you're not alone. We've seen thousands in your situation take control of their lives, and make their dreams come true. Our members write to us every day with stories like this one:

> *Many thanks to Monster for my first time landing a new job through the Internet. I got a promotion and a big raise over my last job where I had been for 16 years! I was unemployed for 6 months. It required much work & persistence . . . Never ever give up faith. Keep up the good fight. Thanks again.*
> —*Monster member Brian B.*

This is a book about finding and landing your dream job. And today your search is very different from what it was even five years ago. You'll use technology as well as job search tools and techniques that have dramatically changed how you look for work and how employers hire people. This book will show you how to use these tools to your advantage. The important point of the *Monster Careers* program: your job should be one of the keys to a good life, not just a way to pay the rent.

This program gives you up-to-the-minute information that comes from the "frontline" experts—employers who told us what *really* works in a job search today. Pay attention to their advice, because they're just like the people who will hire you! You don't have to read this book from front to back to get the benefit of their wisdom, however. Instead, wherever you are in your career, you can find information and tips that will help.

Here's an overview of how *Monster Careers* is organized:

- First, you'll learn about the revolutionary changes in hiring practices that require a new, Internet-powered job search and the four principles, called the "F.A.M.E. attitude," that you must adopt to survive and thrive in the new world of work.

- Then, you'll define your own personal job landscape—who you are, what you want to do, and who will help you in your search. You will complete some exercises and start making critical decisions about the direction of your search.

- Next, you will create a set of professional documents—a resume, cover letters, and more—that will market you to employers.

- Then, you'll enter the marketplace with research, job applications, and networking.

- Finally, you'll learn to conduct a confident job interview, negotiate the best deal, and make the transition into a great new job.

The *Monster Careers* Web Activity Center

A special Web site on Monster acts as this book's interactive companion. It's located at **monstercareers.com**.

Wherever you see the note "**BOOK TO WEB**" or this picture of Trump you'll know you can go to the Web site **monstercareers.com**, and power up your job search. On this site, you'll find downloadable versions of the exercises in the book so you can either write in the book or work on your computer. In addition, the Web site is a gateway to Monster's many interactive resources that we've adapted to work with the Monster career program:

- Professional resume advice

- Interactive self-assessment tools

- Networking tools and techniques

- Relocation tools and advice

- Alternative work arrangements like free agency, contract and temporary work, job sharing, telecommuting, and part-time work

- . . . and updates to the advice in this book!

Wherever possible, I'll refer you to other Web sites that can help your search. Bear in mind, however, that Web addresses can change without notice. We'll keep a list of Web links on the companion site, and update it as necessary, so if you reach a dead end, check **monstercareers.com**.

As you get started on the *Monster Careers* program, ask yourself that question: Where am I in my work life today? Do I want to make it better? Am I ready to work hard to find a great job?

Wherever you are, today's the day to get started. You *can* make your job one of the pillars of personal fulfillment. It's half about a better job . . . and half about a better life!

—JEFF TAYLOR

PART 1

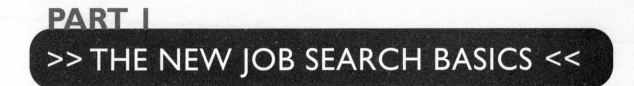

>> THE NEW JOB SEARCH BASICS <<

>> Never Settle! <<

My grandfather worked for Bell Telephone his entire career. He had been in his job for nineteen years when Personnel offered him a different job. He said, "Show me where I'll sit, and I'll take the job." He didn't care what the job was as long as he had one, and he trusted Bell to look after his best interests for his entire working life. That was the way of the work world.

Today, a company is just as likely to say, "Thanks for nineteen years of service. You've done everything we've asked and done it well, but there's a restructuring today and we have to lay you off."

It's a generational dilemma: Growing up, most of us thought that the road to success led upward through one or two organizations. If you were fired, it was because of some terrible failure on your part. No more. Today, you might find yourself saying, "What did I do wrong?" Often the answer is: nothing. Simply to survive, companies place their financial performance first. Employers need to adapt to a fast-changing business climate. Sometimes they have to eliminate 30 percent of their jobs to save the other 70 percent. It's not personal—it's a business fact of life.

21st-Century Work: Change and More Change

Note to all those who think the workplace is changing too fast: Fasten your seat belts. Take a deep breath. Hang on.

Every trend changing the American workplace is accelerating. The best methods for finding a job and prospering at work are also changing with these trends: globalization and the roller-coaster world economy, the Internet, the speed at which companies are born and die, changing employment laws, and the new "free agent" phenomenon.

A few realities about the decline in job security:

- Fifty years ago, the average tenure in a job was 23½ years. By 1996, that number had dropped to 3½ years. If you're entering the workforce now, at age 20, you're likely to have eight jobs by the time you're 32—and as many as twenty jobs in your career!

- The remaking, restructuring, resizing, and consolidation of companies has steadily increased churn—the coming and going of employees.

- In 1900, service industries employed 31 percent of the American workforce; manufacturing and agriculture combined employed 69 percent. Today, that's reversed—78 percent of employed people work in services and 22 percent in manufacturing and agriculture. In 2001–2002 we lost more than two million manufacturing jobs, many of them going to places like China and Malaysia. Even as growth returns, manufacturing is expected to grow just 0.3 percent in employment per year, the lowest increase among all industries. Big companies like General Electric and IBM have stayed in the game by moving into service businesses like finance and consulting, which displaced some workers but created opportunity for others.

- Companies have to compete ferociously to survive and thrive. They have to change and keep costs down, and that combination means your job may disappear because of forces beyond your control. The phenomenon of companies exporting white-collar and customer support jobs overseas is a recent example.

Although traditional job security is under pressure, layoffs are only half the story. There's a revolution raging in the world of work, and it isn't just about employers. It's also about talent (you!) and the increasing importance of people in our corporations, big or small. In fact, there are irresistible trends working in favor of the employee:

- In the next decade, tens of millions of baby boomers will retire. By 2010, there will be a shortfall of as many as five million workers. There

The New Face of Unemployment

Outplacement executive Colin Moor describes the shock wave that hit formerly "secure" employees recently. "There is something fundamental happening to America's workforce," says Colin. "In the last slowdown we saw an impact on job seekers across generations. By 2003 you could walk into any outplacement firm and the first thing you'd notice was the number of white males over fifty strolling in the corridors. We saw a whole generation of baby boomers [who used to be the last standing] getting whacked at all levels and in all fields. What happens to all that talent, ambition, and drive for material well-being?

"Everything now is uncertain, and that puts an enormous amount of pressure on any individual to decide what their career path is going to be. Be prepared for multiple careers."

simply aren't enough younger people entering the workforce to fill the gap.

- Tenure shortening will continue. Short job tenure means more people are moving from job to job, even as the total unemployment rate stays low by historical standards. Some percentage of the workforce is always "unemployed" as people move from one job to another.

- Switching jobs is no longer considered a negative. Ten years ago, people who had three positions in ten years were labeled "job-hoppers," people whose lack of loyalty made them untrustworthy. Now, employers wonder, "If this person is so good, why did they stay in one job for ten years?"

- There are long-term shortages of skilled workers in health care, technology, services, and many other fields. America is already importing nurses, social workers, certain high-tech engineers, and many others because American schools are not graduating enough people in certain fields to fill the jobs. The Employment Policy Foundation in Washington, D.C., has predicted "persistent shortages of qualified employees" during the next thirty years, which translates to high employment and healthy wage increases. Whether there will be an actual shortage of *people* in the workforce is debatable; but the relevant trend for job seekers is a looming shortage of *skills.* Even in recession, these shortages aren't going to go away for long, and recession creates change, which starts the process over again.

- The skills shortage puts pressure on prejudice. For example, says Dr. Peter Cappelli, author of *The New Deal at Work,* "The most important consequence of . . . demographic changes is likely to be the need for employers to change their hiring focus and spend more time courting older workers, who will be relatively more abundant and typically more skilled as well." Corporate diversity programs are also partly fueled by this realization.

- Job growth is not limited to jobs requiring a college degree or advanced skills. The Bureau of Labor Statistics estimates that retail salespersons and cashiers will experience the second- and third-largest growth in jobs from 1998 to 2008. Furthermore, many high-paying jobs do not require a degree.

- America has led the world into the service economy—think Wal-Mart, Citicorp, and Disney. Sixty-four of the Fortune 100 largest companies don't "make" anything; they provide services like retailing, insurance, and entertainment. In the world of small business (under 500 employees), services accounted for about 85 percent of new jobs in the 1990s.

- The traction of the Internet, the usefulness and cost savings of this new mass medium, is fueling a headlong move into e-business. To use the term coined by MIT's Nicholas Negroponte, corporate production is moving "from atoms to bits," that is, changing from manufacturing hard goods (atoms) to trading information (bits and bytes, the building blocks of digital data). North America, Europe, and some Asian countries are creating the "Knowledge Marketplace." In businesses like software development and financial services, the ability to learn, manipulate, and manage information doesn't just help the business, it *is* the business. This marketplace has enormous potential for growth and job creation.

- College graduates age 25 and over earn twice as much as high school graduates. The good news, if you're up to the challenge, is that education pays off at any time in life.

- America's smartest companies recognize and understand what employees want and align their corporate goals with people at the center.

They are committed to the "Obtain, Train, and Retain" cycle, described on page 9.

- More and more people are leaving traditional work arrangements to run their own company that they call "me." The emergence of this free-agent world empowers the individual as never before.

All these trends disrupt lives, careers, and industries, and may even define new economies, but they create incredible opportunities for those who take control of their careers. The revolution challenges the mutual bond of loyalty between company and employees and gives new power and responsibility to the individual. Whatever you do for a living, you are going to have to put a lot more time and thought into career management than your grandparents or parents did, because your career landscape *will* change. President Harry Truman once said, "It's a recession when your neighbor loses his job; it's a depression when you lose yours." I say, if you've prepared for the changes in advance, a bump in the road will turn into opportunity. Let the advice in this book be your guide.

The "Never Settle" Employee Cycle

The new pattern of employment is not my grandfather's straight-line path but a three-stage cycle that turns continuously throughout your career. If you're looking for a job, the new cycle begins with you "matching up" with a new company. You then (1) invest your talents and energy in a new company; (2) enhance your job with constant learning so you can and will outgrow it; and (3) apply advanced techniques to landing your next job.

This cycle, which I call "Earn, Learn, and Yearn," creates confidence because it puts you in control of your own direction and destiny. If you map this process over the course of a single job, it should look something like this:

"Never Settle" Employee Cycle

EARN	LEARN	YEARN
Stage 1	**Stage 2**	**Stage 3**
1. Match your skills, personality, and passion with a new company.	1. Acquire new skills and knowledge on the job and in company-paid training (where possible).	1. Challenge the company to keep pace with your growing abilities.
2. Make a deal with the new company.	2. Learn the company's business . . . not just your job.	2. Review your career progression.
3. Invest your talent in this job/company.	3. Network within the company's industry.	3. Put your resume and skills in circulation.
4. Work smart, work hard!	4. Work with mentors.	4. Move up and/or move on.
	5. Grow your skills with self-inspired training (classes, reading, online training).	

Challenge the traditional definition of job security! (The one that says, "Perform well in your job and the company will take care of you.") Learn to manage your career yourself, because that's the *only* security you have with today's light-speed business changes. "Never Settle" is the mindset that keeps you focused not only on where you are, but where you need to be next!

The Employer Cycle

Employers go through a similar three-stage cycle: (1) Attract the people (skills) the company needs to grow; (2) Train employees in new skills, company culture, and the company's best practices; and (3) Hold on to talent before others try to lure them away. I call this cycle "Obtain, Train, and Retain," and it looks like this:

"Never Settle" Employer Cycle

OBTAIN	TRAIN	RETAIN
Stage 1	**Stage 2**	**Stage 3**
1. Recruit talent.	1. Identify and nurture talent.	1. Promote the company culture.
2. Develop product/ project teams.	2. Increase employee skills and productivity.	2. Offer new opportunities and challenges.
3. Teach the "company way" of doing business.	3. Manage change.	3. Reward the best.
4. Draw growth (fuel) from the employees.		4. Offer longer-term incentives.
		5. Reassign or fire underachievers.

If we imagine this chart laid on top of the previous one, we see that stages one and two match up pretty well, but there's conflict at stage three: An employer, having invested time and money to find and train high-performing employees, now has people who are in great demand . . . by other employers. Those people, having invested their time and learning in that company, find that they're worth more, both to that company and others.

Without the continued mutual promise of reward and loyalty, the best employees leave. Result: a company made up of less talented, less productive employees.

The best employers recognize the tension between the employee and employer cycles, and reward top performers with more than money. Human capital expert Dennis Finn cites that there are sound business reasons for this approach: 53 percent of people who leave companies do so not just to make more money (or because they were fired), but because they're looking for more satisfying work, a better opportunity, more work/ life balance, or other lifestyle rewards. When a prime employee leaves, the company pays upward of $250,000 in lost productivity and replacement costs!

To job seekers, this means aggressive career planning. For employers, this means: pay attention to your employees!

Supply and Demand

All the changes of the last twenty years haven't destroyed the law of supply and demand, and the cycles it creates. In each of the last four decades we've had about two years of difficult times and about eight years of reasonably good times.

Employees take advantage during an economic boom. People move more rapidly from job to job; pay raises and bonuses are more generous. A peak example of this came a few years ago, when an unemployment rate as low as 3.8% tipped control clearly toward the employee. I believe this situation will be repeated a few years from now.

In a recession or slow-growth economy, when more people are actively looking for jobs, employers take advantage: pay raises are lower, signing and performance bonuses decrease or disappear, and workers are asked to do more with less. Hiring slows down and layoffs increase the number of candidates.

Within the overall context of the economy's cycles, there's more fragmentation lately. Technology jobs may be scarce in telecommunications or finance while at the same time those jobs grow in health care and government.

What does this mean for your job search? It takes longer during a recession. You have less bargaining power, and employers can be more selective (because the competition for jobs is more intense). In a boom, you have more bargaining power. You can get better pay, and also training, relocation, or a flexible work arrangement. You have more chance of lining up multiple job offers. You'll get a job quicker. The company may even be willing to define the candidate/job match more loosely.

Whatever the state of the general economy or your field, you will need to rely more on yourself, increase your skills, and be prepared to move into a different job or industry. Your future career aspirations are going to be tied into an environment in which you're going to have more control and more responsibility for your situation. In recession or recovery, good talent is always in demand.

Play a Little Jazz

Career management is like playing jazz. With a solid base of talent you can pick up a tune . . . and then improvise. Great jazz musicians move comfortably off their sheet music into unknown territory. In your career, you will have to change "your tune" when the time comes. You won't always know where you'll finish up, but you can have a great time getting there—and you may surprise yourself, too.

This insight separates the achievers from the also-rans. Achievers give up their dependent attitude. Whether they work in management, on the factory floor, or as freelancers at home, they take a "free agent" attitude. They value the freedom to choose when, where, and for whom to give their time and talents. They understand that managing a career is a second job in itself. Their career confidence comes from knowing the market for their skills and where they stand in that marketplace. They will think one or even two jobs ahead when they plan their careers. They don't belong permanently to a company. They think of work as a service they're going to offer to a customer.

Monster Careers has the tools and techniques that can move your career ahead with a new job. But you have to do the work to make it happen. You have to drop the excuses, put aside your fears, and begin to build the foundation for a more successful career. You can't think that you're not smart enough, or educated enough, or rich enough, or attractive enough, or talented enough. Career management isn't taught in school. If you're really going to get good at it, you're going to have to learn the career management skills, attitudes, and habits that work.

Do you want to start work on Monday with a smile on your face, with your job giving you joy, excitement, inspiration, and fun?

Do you want to find a job where you get respect, money, and a chance to grow?

Do you want to look back on your career years from now and see that it not only fed you and your family, but fed your spirit, helped you make a contribution to the world, and unleashed your most outrageous, inspired creations?

With these tools and the new information in this book, you can master the challenge. And at every step along the way, I'll provide you with new advice from Monster's dozens of career experts, as well as timely input from our customers—the employers, recruiters, and human resource professionals who could hire you. I'll also share the wisdom that Monster's members (there are millions) have given to each other . . . and now to you!

- If you're a student, you'll learn how to spark your resume with internships and build compelling messages around your skills.

- If you've just been laid off, and you're feeling a little unsure of your job search skills, we'll get you working on a systematic, detailed job search program right away.

- If you're not happy in your current job, you can use a job search plan we call "add another day," described in chapter 7.

- If you're re-entering the workforce after an absence of a few years, and you'd like to know the lay of the land before you start, the next couple of chapters will tell you how the world of hiring has changed from the employer's point of view.

- If you're looking to relocate, the chapters on research and networking will help you identify opportunities near your next address. There are tips on running a job search long-distance in chapter 18 as well.

Wherever possible, I'm going to push you to learn new techniques, rather than fall back on outdated advice. You'll learn how to search using a more personal, powerful, and Internet-enabled program. For example, the fundamental work in chapters 7, 8, and 9 will give you a foundation for a personalized job search—one that works with your personal style and situation. If you just "don't know what you want to do," chapters 6, 12, and 13 will help you match your special talents to the job market. If you want to write an effective resume and cover letter, scan chapters 10 and 11. If you get nervous just thinking about a job interview, chapter 15 will help you develop confidence.

More than that, I'll show you how to develop the Monstrous attitude that puts you in command of your jobs and your career. The balance of power is shifting toward the employee (you), and that's good for employees and companies, too. In the new world of work, you are not just an important part of a company—you *are* the company. Now, a talented truck driver is more important than a truck, a good retail sales team is more important than the season's inventory, and a good computer programmer is more important than the latest software program.

At Monster, we've seen that even a recession creates new hiring needs. Companies lay people off because they don't fit the new business or structure, and then (sooner or later) they hire new people to fit the new structure. If they don't, they risk going out of business.

Change is inevitable, and change creates opportunity. If you are alert to the changes around you, if you use some simple methods to harness them in your job hunt, you'll stand out—not only as a candidate, but also in your new job.

Are you ready to join the revolution?

2   >> Monster's F.A.M.E. Attitude <<

We dream, worry, fantasize, agonize about our careers, and yet . . . it's amazing how many people let their careers just . . . sort of . . . *happen* to them. They choose a field because it was the family's wishes or the family business, or because a friend said they'd like it, or because it was the first job they found and they just stuck with it (or got stuck in it).

Most people seem to spend more time planning their vacations than planning their careers. No wonder they wake up ten, twenty, thirty years later longing for a more fulfilling career. People always say that, on your deathbed, you won't think, "I should have spent more time at my job." They're talking about the importance of family and friends, and they're right, but why not pass on to the next world having loved your family *and* your job? You spend almost one-third of your life working; you might as well get the most from it!

There are four fundamental attitudes you need to take command of your job search. Together, I call them Monster's F.A.M.E. attitudes. You need to:

*Think Like a **F**ree Agent*
*Train Like an **A**thlete*
*Prepare Like a **M**arketer*
*Work Like an **E**ntrepenuer*

Monster's F.A.M.E. attitudes will make you stand out among candidates who just bump their way along in a conventional job search, as if the changes of the last twenty years never happened. The F.A.M.E. attitudes bring a new level of professional performance to your work at any time in your career, but in a job search, they are essential. Let's look at how each attitude specifically powers up your job search.

Think Like a **F**ree Agent

A free agent is not traditionally attached to one company. The free agent moves from one job to another, often juggling several jobs at once. That's why people think of free agents as doing "temporary" or "contract" assignments as opposed to so-called "permanent" positions.

Having a free-agent attitude in a job search is key because it makes you view a "permanent" job as a contract by another name. It allows you to move freely among full-time, part-time, contract, and salaried jobs according to your needs and plans. You are not the permanent property of an employer, but you *are* managing a business relationship. The employer doesn't owe you a job, and you don't owe the employer your life. You are partners in a contract that has to work for both of you.

When something upsets that contract, the job changes. You get downsized, fired, transferred to another assignment. Or maybe the job is just finished.

OR

You decide that you have outgrown the opportunity, and you take steps to grow, with or without your current employer. You're finished with the job.

You can break down the term: "free" means able to call your own shots. "Agent"—well, you can be an agent of change or Agent 007. The point is that you're in action, making things happen.

Let's see how the free-agent attitude plays across the new job landscape of "Earn, Learn, and Yearn."

EVERY job arrangement is considered temporary.

Your career is composed of jobs like a movie is composed of scenes. And like movie scenes, your jobs will take some twists and turns as the story unfolds. The average job tenure these days is 3½ years. Odds are that your extended career will involve full-time, part-time, and contract work arrangements.

Because every arrangement is temporary, a free-agent mindset focuses on the current goal *and* the next one . . . and the one after that. A free agent is always prospecting for new business, even while his or her current job is going great. If you're working full-time now, that doesn't mean job-hopping, but learning now where your next opportunity will be—by talking to management in other departments, reading journals, subscribing to targeted e-mail newsletters, talking to experts, networking with peers.

Your ongoing value grows with your relevant skills.

The cold fact is that work consists of applying skills, whether you are handling a backhoe, taking a blood sample, or managing 200 computer programmers.

Skills are ultimately what you offer an employer. Free agents are always growing their skills, so they have more to offer. They also do a better job than their competition at articulating how these skills will deliver success in the job, today and tomorrow.

For many of you, the free-agent mindset is an important way to operate through your entire job cycle, not just when you're looking. How does the free agent in you keep growing?

- *Be nimble.* During your job search, your view of the job market will grow and change. Be ready to adjust your approach.

- *Be an incredible listener.* You have one mouth and two ears. Ask questions and try to listen twice as much as you talk.

- *Immerse yourself in learning.* Turn every job into a chance to acquire new skills.

- *Get organized.* Good job searching is a complicated process and you can get lost easily. In chapter 7, you'll learn how to manage your time, money, and priorities during the job search.

Relationships count. A strong personal network is good for you and good for business.

The relationships that surround your job are as important as your skills. Once you've established your credentials, your actual skill level may be less important (at least at the beginning of a project) than your ability to relate to others, ask questions, build alliances, and gain respect. Leadership, in fact, is one of the core skills you'll be developing without even thinking about it.

In a traditional job setting, your "client" is your employer—and the source of your next paycheck. Does this mean you should think about quitting every time you don't get your way? Of course not. It means you should be *able* to move on if you determine the relationship cannot be saved. Free agents also build a reputation for keeping their commitments and meeting deadlines.

Relationships go beyond your immediate environment. Meet people from other departments. Let the fun part of your personality show through. Someone with a free-agent attitude never misses a networking opportunity. Someone with a traditional work attitude usually does. Advantage: free agent.

Many people worry that keeping up a network of contacts makes them look suspicious. That kind of thinking keeps people down, but great employees are often great networkers. Your network is a powerful tool for business, making you more connected to your coworkers, your industry, and your customers. Not to mention meeting new customers! You'll learn a lot about networking in chapter 14.

With renewed and relevant skills, a clear view of the marketplace, strong work relationships, and a strong network, the free agent takes his or her place as a partner with the employer, ready to grow, adapt, and change with the marketplace. As your free-agent confidence grows, so do your opportunities.

Your resume is your sales tool.

A free-agent mindset sees a resume as the story of your life skills, not just a sequence of positions at companies. Use your resume as a way to document and showcase your skills. Build your case in writing for moving up, citing specific projects or examples. Focus on the growing momentum of your talents and skills. Updating your resume regularly can be a great motivator, too: as you update your resume, you're reminded constantly to update your skills.

With a free-agent mindset, you can regard any employer as your potential next employer. When someone in business asks, "So, what do you do?" spend just enough time on your accomplishments to establish credibility.

Then move to "listening mode": Ask about their business problems, understand their "pain" and, drawing on your work and life experience, begin to formulate solutions to their business problems. Remember this cycle of problem/experience/solution when you update your resume, because it's what employers are hoping to find.

Train Like an **A**thlete

Athletes know that they have to train hard before, during, and after every competition if they want to win. What does training mean in a job search? It means setting clear goals, making commitments, practicing basic moves to gain confidence, learning from mistakes, and keeping your focus. Athletes can teach candidates a lot of lessons.

Training is the only thing that makes you stronger.

I'd like to introduce a Monster employee, Jimmy Pedro. He manages Monster's Olympic sponsorship programs. He is also a three-time Olympian, who won the bronze medal for his judo performance in Atlanta in 1996. Judo World Champion in 1999, he's the most decorated American judo athlete in history. Jimmy's achievements are the result of a lifetime of training. (As this book goes to press, Jimmy is back in training to compete in Athens in 2004.)

"Judo was a full-time job by the time I was in high school," Jimmy says. "I went to the gym earlier and left later than anyone else. I traveled on my own overseas to learn from the best coaches. At competitions, I would do my running, my workout, and my exercises for hours, and then I'd go for a three-hour match."

Are you dedicated enough to work like that in your job search?

A. J. Mleczko, a forward on the gold-medal 1998 U.S. Women's Olympic Hockey team (also a member of the 2002 silver-medal team), cut short her honeymoon to train. Six days after her wedding, she joined her team in Lake Placid, New York, while her husband's job kept him hundreds of miles away. "You won't hit your goal without that commitment to training," she says. "I did it because I loved my teammates and my sport, but the real inspiration was my Olympic goal."

Is your goal of a dream job a big enough goal to require that kind of commitment?

You are in training right now for a great job search. You will have to keep going when you have setbacks on the way to your goal. You'll have to make your training a full-time commitment. Like a power lifter who begins with light weights and builds to heavier weights, you'll build the skills of your job search from the basics. The exercises, practice notes, and techniques from this book will become your workout plan and calendar. The goal: more money, a better time at work, your dream job!

What's your long-term career goal? What's your goal today? They can be different, they can change, but you must have them in mind. If your goal is "I want more money," you have to decide on your 1-, 2-, and 5-year goals, and what you need to do now to make them a reality.

As an early practice run, take five minutes now to think about your job goals (later, in chapter 6, I'll help you with this process in a lot more detail).

Write down a career goal for today. _____

_____

Write down a career goal for two years from now. _____

_____

Write down a career goal for five years from now. _____

_____

Training builds confidence.

You can't be afraid of setbacks when you're in training. Athletes practice the right moves over and over, failing many times before they get it right. Taking that kind of risk creates a critical edge in managing your career. The *Monster Careers* program demands diligent practice before you actually go on a job interview because that training will build your confidence. It's the candidates who lack confidence, who play it safe, who find themselves in permanent also-ran status.

Nikki Warren, human resources manager at Giles & Kendall in Huntsville, Alabama, believes training and practice pay off in the job interview: "Have a friend shoot questions at you. While you don't want to sound rehearsed, you do want to sound prepared."

Enjoy the practice! You can practice the violin for fifteen minutes because Mom and Dad require it, or you can practice for three hours, because you want to. Likewise, you can practice your "pitch" and answers to interview questions once, or you can practice them in front of friends, in front of your dog, in front of a video camera (and then watch the *painful* video and practice again). At first you may sound terrible, but soon you'll be amazed at how good you sound.

Looking for a job, especially in your approach and interviews, tests your nerves. If you practice interviewing with a friend, you will gain confidence in your ability to handle the tough questions. Practice exposes your weaknesses and fine-tunes your strengths. It allows you to regroup and revise your presentation before the main event.

Your job search is a competition.

Some of you are going to be uncomfortable with the fact that there are winners and losers in the job search game. Your search will inevitably have highs and lows. Part of your training is taking your best shot at jobs that are right for you. You have to manage disappointment when someone else scores (or worse—when you don't hear anything at all).

Remember: In managing your career, you win only if you land in the right job. If you land in the wrong job, you lose. Keep this understanding as part of your plan and someday you'll be saying, "I'm psyched I got this job and not that other one that I wanted so much." Both luck and fate come into play in this process.

Prepare Like a **M**arketer

Marketing is the business of making a clear impression. As you move though your career, each job search is an opportunity to develop, enhance, or change your "personal brand," that is, the package of skills and the professional reputation you present to employers.

The first step is learning to communicate what your best qualities are. For example, if you're a go-to person, you want to give examples of times someone brought you a big problem and how you solved it brilliantly. You need to describe tangible actions to establish that credibility. Don't be afraid of putting your skills and personality forward. Most people are uncomfortable selling themselves. You will be forced into the limelight many times in your life. An interviewer asks you a tough question. You make a bid for that high-profile project. The boss has you stand up at the company meeting and describe a recent accomplishment. With the right preparation, you can feel more comfortable.

Preparing a job search is a lot like preparing a marketing campaign.

Define your personal brand.

What is a personal brand? Peter Blacklow, vice president of marketing at online gaming site WorldWinner, defines your personal brand as "a summary of your most important, unchanging attributes, such as work ethic, honesty, leadership, or creativity." To Pete's definition I'll add that your track record of accomplishments helps define your personal brand, especially if you've been working for a while.

In business, branding is sometimes referred to as a company's "commercial reputation." In career management, it's your professional reputation. Do you come to work early and leave late? How do you act under pressure? What are your dress, demeanor, and attitude toward the corporate culture? Are you reliable? Can you keep information confidential? Over time, people paint a picture of who you are. It is incredibly important that you develop a roadmap for the characteristics that you want to project, and that you document your progress.

A reputation isn't words, it's behavior. You have to live the personal brand you want to project. If you're habitually late to meetings, learn to come two minutes early. If you dress a little sloppy at work, cleaning up your look will strengthen your reputation—it will give you a more credible personal brand.

Barbara Reinhold, director of the Office of Career and Executive Development at Smith College, points out that reputation and relationships are everything in business. Inside a company, your reputation determines whether you'll be given a chance to succeed (and your relationships often determine whether you will succeed). When people hire, they use a candidate's personal brand—their reputation—as a predictor of success.

Developing your personal brand's "key messages" (which you'll do in chapter 8) is just the beginning. In the words of Steve Pogorzelski, president of Monster North America, winning brands accept the challenge of:

- being seen (*You have to put yourself out there in the job market every day.*)

- being heard (*Your message has to be clear and sent to the right people.*)

- being remembered (*By featuring your unique combination of skills and experiences.*)

- being desired (*By presenting yourself as a solution, not just a resource.*)

- being respected (*By delivering on your promises.*)

Understand your brand's value. Whether you're in a 3-month project or a full-time position, you need to know what the employment market will pay for your skills. The more you know about the need for your skills at the company and in the marketplace, the more you can price yourself right. (Also, the more you can learn about the personality of a company, the better you can estimate the non-cash payoffs like opportunity to advance and work/family balance. Your feelings about these are part of your personal brand, too.)

Focus on your target customers.

It's not enough to identify a potential employer—you have to know plenty about its business. Today, it's not enough to just know your customer or audience. You actually have to like them! Your passion will come through if it's genuine. Whether you're selling your own skills or an idea for the next project, information is the key.

Thanks to the Internet, it's easy: In ten minutes on a company's Web site you can understand its core products and services, read its president's description of the company, learn about its executives, and read its history. That information is the price of admission, the minimum you need to have a first conversation with a hiring manager.

Amazingly, a majority of job seekers don't do the minimum work. According to a 2003 survey among people who used the Internet for part of their job search, only 35 percent went online to prepare for an interview and just 32 percent researched different companies online.

As you prepare your marketing materials—your resume, cover letters, and interview notes—in part II of this book, you must stay focused on the customer's needs and the benefit they'll receive by hiring you. You will customize your messages accordingly.

Deliver a memorable message.

You have probably watched tens of thousands of ads on television. How many do you remember? The top agencies who make great advertising know the first and last goal is to be memorable.

An employer advertising a position online will often get as many as *fifty resumes an hour.* You have to rise above all this noise. It's not enough that you shoot off a resume with a cover letter. You have to customize them to fit the job.

Peter Blacklow of WorldWinner agrees that customizing your message is the key to being memorable: "Identify the specific needs of your customer, then present the benefits of your product—which in the job seeker's case are your skills, motivation, and fit. Ask yourself, 'What are five or six things about me that are unique?' It might be what you do in your current job—and it might be what you did two or three jobs ago. Then combine those into a unique package."

Preparation allows you to customize your approach to a company and its needs, and that is what will make you memorable. It's not enough that you tell a hiring manager a memorized speech about your fabulous qualities. You have to be prepared to describe how those qualities will solve their most pressing business problems. If you don't invest time in preparation first, you'll lose later, in a long and frustrating search.

Work Like an **E**ntrepreneur

Are you willing to pour all your energy, imagination, and discipline into finding your dream job? Then you're a lot like the entrepreneurs who start their own businesses. Here's my definition of an entrepreneur: when everyone around you thinks you're crazy and you still think you have a great idea—and you will put yourself on the line for that idea. The work habits of entrepreneurs can teach you a lot about how to run a successful job search.

They never quit. Failure is not an option for entrepreneurs. They learn from their mistakes and act immediately to correct them. When you have setbacks in your job search—and everybody does—you must treat them as opportunities to learn and get better. Entrepreneurs by definition are individuals, but I've noticed some additional patterns among them, and how their core competencies can inform your job search.

Entrepreneurs put themselves in the way of opportunity.

To paraphrase Woody Allen, 80 percent of life is showing up. That saying is on the wall of my closet, so I see it every morning. Most people don't "show up" for the opportunities in life, but I believe in doing it, and that's why I get out there, why I accept invitations to speak, why I take an interest in the person next to me on a plane. Everyone is a potential friend, network opportunity, and customer.

Professor John D. Krumboltz of Stanford University advises career counselors to harness this "planned happenstance" for their clients. In a job search, he says, unplanned events create unexpected opportunities. He advises job seekers to become explorers, to place themselves around people, places, and events that will expand their universe of job possibilities.

Rob Galford of the Center for Executive Development puts it another way. "Careers make sense looking back, but almost never follow a predictable path. The most successful people often couldn't predict their career path early on."

Entrepreneurs know that opportunity appears in places where unplanned meetings occur. Go up to someone at a conference, in a cafeteria, in the dentist's waiting room, and ask how they got where they are. In fact, never mind that; just talk. Salespeople say, "When in doubt, get on the phone." The magic starts when you open your mouth and ears.

Entrepreneurs take action.

Successful entrepreneurs are biased toward action. If something doesn't work, they do something else. When conditions change, they adapt their strategy and actions.

You can think your way into total paralysis in a job search, and never really take a powerful message directly to the employer. Entrepreneurs understand the necessity of taking action, reaching out, trying something new. A common mistake: you spend weeks developing your resume, and then things get slightly better at work—so you don't follow through. Make a habit of following through on your actions.

"Ready, fire, aim." Sometimes you have to move quickly. You will never have perfect information, but you have to develop a sense of when to act. This means applying for a job when you know it has the qualities you've identified as appealing to you. It also means developing several job possibilities simultaneously.

While planning your job search and following that plan is the key to success, you'll have to adapt your plan as you go. For example, you may discover that there isn't enough opportunity in large companies in your area—so focus on the small businesses. You may change your focus to a different job title, and that's all right, too. Trying something new relieves the frustration of repetitive job applications and uncovers opportunity. Be inventive, be innovative. Make up new options as you go along. You'll see plenty of ways to do this in parts II and III of this book.

What would adaptation look like in a job search? Here are some examples of new possibilities:

- *Go global.* Expand your search to overseas firms.

- *Transfer skills.* Move from sales or customer support to product design.

- *Transfer industries.* When you search jobs online, leave the industry field blank and use your skills as keyword searches. Then research those companies and industries that are hiring your skills.

- *Change the arrangement.* Offer to work on a contract for three months, so they can "try before they buy."

- *Change the value you offer.* If a recruiter calls to say, sorry, the job is filled, ask if you can start in a different position. Arrange an informational interview through the recruiter, and offer to help the company locate candidates for other positions.

Another action-oriented habit is innovation, and entrepreneurs are constant innovators. Andy Grove, the former CEO of Intel, wrote a book called *Only the Paranoid Survive.* I disagree. I hung my version of that expression on my wall: "Only the Innovative Thrive." Entrepreneurs spend their lives looking forward, not backward. Throughout your job search, I'll ask you to take the path of innovation, because breaking with convention will distinguish you as a candidate.

In the fourth grade, we're all taught that the shortest distance between two points is a straight line, and most job seekers see their careers as a straight line: "I was this . . . so I'll be that." Actually, the shortest distance between two points is a *good idea.* Follow your good ideas, which are not necessarily the straight lines of a conventional career search.

Innovation: The Fosbury Flop

Dick Fosbury was a high jumper with a completely new way to go after his sport—backwards! At the 1968 Olympics, he unveiled his unorthodox technique of taking off and turning in midair, so his body went back-first over the bar. He beat the previous world record by three inches! The judges met for half an hour to decide that his style of jumping was acceptable.

After his amazing success, jumpers started to adopt the technique—but it wasn't the old jumpers, it was the new ones. In 1972 (Munich) three of the sixteen jumpers did it. By 2000 (Sydney) all top sixteen did the "Fosbury Flop."

Never mind if the "adoption curve" for a new idea is slow. Innovation is the way to break through to a new level in your work and life.

Entrepreneurs are relentless in pursuing their goals. They hear the cliché "Work smarter, not harder," and reply, "I know I'm working smart. Now I'm going to work even harder." Prove to yourself how hard you can work.

I'm going to challenge you to work hard at managing your career. If you worked forty hours a week at your last job, or in school, you should work just that many hours (or more) in your job search. When tough times hit a company, the best employees double down and focus. You must do the same through the challenge of a job search. Furthermore, hard work invites luck. "The harder you work, the luckier you get" is one of the credos I live by.

It's easy to say, but hard to do. Can you really put in forty productive hours a week looking for work? I'll show you how in chapter 7. Most people can't handle the "rejection" feeling of working more than a few hours a week in a job search. Use this fact to beat your competition!

Entrepreneurs lead and get others to follow.

Entrepreneurs sell their vision to others, and your job search is, in some critical ways, a sales job. You're presenting yourself and persuading someone to hire you. Successful entrepreneurs don't always start out as salespeople, but along the way they've all gotten good at persuading people to follow them—to give them money, buy their product, or rally around their cause.

My first recruiting job demanded a lot of phone sales, which is a tough job. But sales skills are irreplaceable (especially early in your career). You learn to listen to the customer. You learn to handle rejection—it would take eighteen to twenty calls before I'd get a job order, so I decided that every rejection call was one call closer to my goal. Your job search has the same kind of odds. You get rejected, and move on. On the very next call, you dig deep into customer problems. You customize your product to their needs, and you learn to deliver above expectations. These are great habits for a successful job search.

Entrepreneurs also imagine the future. Their vision allows them to break out of the prison of the present situation and create a new world. Likewise, your vision of your next career move is what you sell to employers. "This is who I am," you say, "and this is what I will do for you. . . ."

So, "Be the ball!" Visualize yourself right into the new job. Only *you* have the power to do that!

Make These Principles Your Job Search Habits

F.A.M.E. is an attitude of lifelong career management. Since the job search game has changed, and will keep changing, job seekers today have to embrace their second job of active career "explorer." Never settle back in your chair and think you have it all figured out. Neither I nor anyone else can tell you exactly what your career landscape will look like in ten years. An open, curious, and active attitude will propel you, years from now, into work you can hardly imagine today.

Why do I call these habits an attitude? If you think like a free agent, you're taking responsibility for your own career. If you train like an athlete, you're pouring energy into productive and exciting work. If you prepare like a marketer, you're building an irresistible personal brand. If you work like an entrepreneur, you will succeed in unexpected ways.

Throughout this book, I'll show you how the F.A.M.E. attitudes give real horsepower to your job search. Going forward, each chapter will begin with a reminder of how one part of F.A.M.E. thinking relates to one part of a job search. It's my hope that these reminders will help you reflect on how F.A.M.E. is not just a set of sayings; it is a point of view.

Taking Risks

I'm particularly proud of Monster's first big commercial, "When I grow up . . . ," that we first aired at the 1999 Super Bowl. Besides breaking new ground as an Internet company advertising on the Super Bowl, we produced a funny, sharp, memorable message.

In the commercial, young children spoke directly to the camera, saying:

"When I grow up, I want to file all day."

"I want to claw my way up to middle management."

"Be replaced on a whim."

"I want to have a brown nose."

"I want to be a yes-man . . ."

". . . yes-woman."

"Yes, Sir. Coming, Sir."

"Anything for a raise, Sir."

"When I grow up . . ."

"I want to be underappreciated."

"Be paid less for doing the same job."

"I want to be forced into early retirement."

Then the words "What did you want to be?" appeared, and finally we closed with a picture of Trumpasaurus, our Monster; our Web address, **monster.com**; and our tag line, "There's a better job out there."

Amid all those ads for cars and beer, it was an outrageously optimistic statement with an ironic twist about how our childhood dreams get compromised. The ad worked because it captured the voice and personality of Monster. We aired that commercial 4,000 times in 1999, and it put us on the map.

In advertising and branding, it's not just about the money you spend; it's about having a good idea. Your approach to an employer, competing with a hundred others, has to stand out. Your future F.A.M.E. lies in the balance!

What would your commercial look like?

3 >> Job Good, Life Good! <<

F.A.M.E. ATTITUDE: THINK LIKE A **F**REE AGENT
Every job is considered temporary.

What are you working for?

Ask yourself: What do you love to do? What do you talk about for hours? Some of these things could be part of your next job. If you don't love what you do, you won't take your career to the next level.

Since every job is considered temporary in the new world of work, a single company won't be as much a center of your life as it was for previous generations. People sense this happening today, and are demanding greater work/life balance. Nevertheless, work is a big part of your life, and you will have to find work that is meaningful to you many times over in your career.

The first thing we need to talk about in getting your life and your work in sync is passion. When we at Monster say, "Job Good, Life Good," we mean that passion in your work builds both success *and* happiness.

You can talk yourself into hard work, but you can't fake passion. It is total commitment—to an activity, a principle, a person, or the results of your work. It's what you mean when you tell a friend, "I got so involved I lost track of everything else."

I'm not talking about ego. The true entrepreneur knows passion will take you to the moon, while ego is a hollow suit. Ego says, "Hey, look at me, aren't I great!" and Passion says, "I would do this whether anyone noticed or not."

Are you passionate about your current (or last) job? Check off how many of these apply to you:

29

❑ I'm angry at my company/boss/coworkers.

❑ I've been doing the same job for three years.

❑ I feel powerless to achieve anything.

❑ Dilbert® is not just a comic strip, it's my life.

❑ My career is derailed.

❑ My company has lost its way.

❑ I'm stuck.

❑ I didn't finish college so I can't get ahead.

❑ I'm sick and tired of _____!

❑ [write yours here] _____!

If you checked two or more of these, you're not bringing your passion into your work life.

Passion and commitment in a job don't happen by chance, however. In fact, you're going to make very deliberate choices along the way. So, I'd like you to begin thinking about seven crucial ways to bring your passion to work: values, culture, learning, satisfaction, vision, relationships, and mission. I'll describe the importance of each below. At the end of this chapter, you'll create a personal list exploring these seven keys to a job you can feel passionate about.

Value More Than Money

Most people would like to make a little more money—or a lot more—and money is a good motivator. People who are really happy in their work, however, are also motivated by values that go way beyond the bank account. You've got to value something more than money in your job.

Job satisfaction matters. In a Monster poll, 73 percent of respondents said they'd accept less money to be happier at work. If you build nonmonetary goals into your vision for an ideal job, you will be compensated in satisfaction as well as money.

For example, it matters to have a job that unleashes your best skills. Kate DeCamp, senior vice president of human resources at networking leader Cisco, finds this value more important than money. She says, "Candidates focus a lot on how much money they should make, rather than finding a workplace where their skills are going to thrive. [However,] there are a lot of companies that just buy you and forget you. You're looking for a company where you get excited, where you start saying, 'What do you want me to do next?' and not where you're just going to get a nickel more."

I would add to Kate's comment that the best companies provide clear direction and let you run with your job, doing what's best to create momentum for you and the company. In those places, you hear the expression "Beg for forgiveness instead of asking for permission!" I like that kind of environment.

What do you value at work? List some of those nonmonetary rewards in the box below. Examples might include:

- achieving—unleashing my skills
- learning or teaching
- independence
- supporting (or getting support)
- work relationships
- security
- recognition
- communicating
- persuading
- leading
- discovering
- creating

What I value about work: _____
_____
_____
_____

Find a Culture in Which You'll Thrive

Every workplace has its own culture. Culture includes traditions, rules, fashions (or dress codes), and language, but ultimately it is the people—who they are and how they act. As I mentioned earlier, my definition of brand is a company's outside reputation. Culture is the company's inside reputation. How do employees feel? The culture of a company is alive. And fragile.

I think a lot about company culture. At Monster, we have thrived on building a "work hard, play hard" atmosphere, and yes, we have foosball tables and pool tables and 8-foot statues of our mascot, Trumpasaurus. But culture is more than the games that make connections easy and fun. I have extremely high expectations: my people not only work smart but also work hard. And in return, we offer an extraordinarily flexible environment. That's culture, too.

Culture is a complicated word. Someone discussing company culture might mean that all employees have the same work ethic or problem-solving style. Others might mean more intangible attributes. A 54-year-old might be lost in the cultural context of a department staffed by 25-year-olds.

In order to know if you will be happy somewhere, you will have to check out the "employee buzz." The truest vision of employee buzz is the party example. What does an employee of the company say about it and his job at a party? Many people would say, "My job stinks," and that's that. But employees who rally around the company's mission and feel compelled to share stories about the company will say, "I love my job." This is critical for companies because the employees become an army of loyal recruiters.

Ten-Second Job Satisfaction Quiz

How's your commitment to your current (or most recent) job?

- ❏ It rocks.
- ❏ All things considered, it's good.
- ❏ Could be better, could be worse.
- ❏ I'm biding my time until a better one comes around.
- ❏ Save me!

If you chose *any* statement but the first, you're in the norm. In this Monster job seeker poll, **92%** of respondents chose an answer other than "It rocks."

List three qualities of company culture you want. Examples might include:

- a strong work ethic

- an easygoing atmosphere

- high expectations and rewards

- encouraging initiative

- teamwork and consensus-building

- exacting standards of service

- a fast pace

- a deliberate, slower pace

Three cultural traits I like: _____

_____

_____

_____

Learn and Grow

I look forward to feeling a little nervous. The more nervous I am, the closer I am to learning something. For example, before I speak to a large audience, I prepare for hours, and if I'm not nervous during that preparation, I know it's not good enough; I'm just coasting. I'm not challenging myself or my audience, and if there's one thing I've learned in business, it's this:

If you coast, you only coast one way, and that is downhill.

A job search is a fantastic opportunity to push yourself uphill. Take the example of Mike Baum, who started as a radar technician in the Navy. Then he worked at General Electric and the Boston Communications Group, companies that encouraged learning. He read user manuals during breaks at work and found mentors who let him look over their shoulders. "I'd insinuate myself into meetings," he says. "I learned in a safe way while earning my spurs." Mike took classes when he could. In a few years he became a senior engineer.

Perhaps you're a registered nurse, considering your next career step. You could get another nursing position and do the same thing you do now, or you might be intrigued by another option: you might choose to become certified as a hand therapist. As a hand therapist, you'll step into a place where you're not the expert anymore. You'll be a little new, you'll be a little nervous, and you'll learn a lot.

Real leaders never stop pushing themselves into unknown territory. Kate DeCamp, Cisco's senior vice president of human resources, suggests to potential leaders in her company, "Go be bad at something! Use a new job to learn things you're not yet good at doing. Very few people know what they want to do at the first shot. The leaders are the ones who can learn the most."

So when you're considering where to go next, choose the place where you'll learn the most. Don't coast downhill.

Book to Web

You can learn more about lifelong learning at MonsterLearning: **monsterlearning.com**.

List three things you'd like to learn in your next job. Examples might be:

- special technical knowledge, such as computer programming languages
- time management or organizational skills
- interpersonal skills, like communication or persuasion
- sales or marketing skills
- industry knowledge, such as how TV cable systems are bought and sold
- physical skills, such as hairstyling
- intellectual skills, such as how to analyze a failed project

Right now, while you're looking for employment, you also have the opportunity to learn new skills—such as networking, research skills, and presenting yourself in public—that will make you perform better in your next job.

Three things to learn at my next job: _____

_____

_____

_____

Find Daily Satisfaction

There's no worse job situation than doing something you hate all day . . . all week . . . all month . . . all year. . . .

What activities are just plain fun for you? Do you love to share information with people? Do you love to teach? Do you love to work with plants or manipulate figures in a spreadsheet, or draw up project plans or persuade people to buy your product? Do you want to be outdoors all the time, or in front of a computer screen in a private office? Do you like to play sports on a team or as an individual?

If you want to love your work, your hands, voice, and mind should be spending at least part of every day doing something you simply know you are meant to do. We'll take an inventory in chapter 8 of your favorite skills—make sure your next job includes them.

List three work activities that you most enjoy.

Three work activities I enjoy: _____

_____

_____

_____

Create a Broad Vision of Your Career Path

What's the biggest mistake a job seeker can make? "Keeping too narrow a focus," says executive coach Rob Galford. "Early in a search, you have to cast your net widely."

We all have blind spots when it comes to work. We say, "That job is only for bossy people," or "I'd never make it in that company." We think, "I've always been a teacher, so it's the only thing I'm qualified to do."

Look for your blind spots. Career options should only be closed off after some careful inspection. While you are in the job search, use all of your research methods—the Internet, the library, interviews, and networking—to think broadly about your options. Think like a free agent, who keeps one eye on the job landscape at all times.

Another common blind spot comes for people who see one track in their job—"up or out." They see work as a series of promotions toward the top of a pyramid, like this:

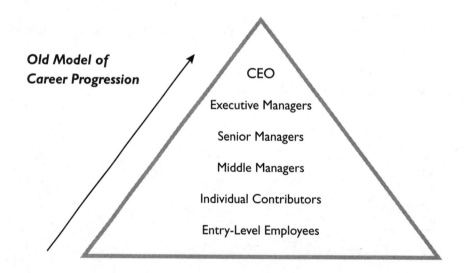

Old Model of Career Progression

CEO

Executive Managers

Senior Managers

Middle Managers

Individual Contributors

Entry-Level Employees

Today's career doesn't usually move in a straight line up that pyramid, and those who pay attention only to their place on the pyramid cut themselves out of many options worth exploring.

Steve Pogorzelski, president of Monster North America, says the modern career path is more like jumping from one rock face to another. You may switch industries, job arrangements, or skill sets. You may make a "lateral move" into another department at a company. For some of your career, corporate work may be the answer, and at another time the free-agent path is right.

List three possible next jobs that (1) interest you and (2) are different from the "traditional" career path. If you're stuck for ideas, make sure you study chapter 12 carefully.

Three alternatives to my "moving up the pyramid": _____

_____

_____

_____

Build Healthy Work Relationships

In a new job, you join a company with its own culture, rules, and systems. Your work might involve customers and vendors. The quality of these relationships can make the difference between spreading your good work far and wide, or spinning out your working life like a hamster on a wheel.

Healthy work relationships help produce results, which is how you'll be judged at work. They require respect, trustworthiness, and commitment to shared goals. Healthy work relationships can handle disagreement and the creative conflict that often produces the most inspiring work in project teams.

Remember that the job search itself is also an opportunity to build good relationships. Your search can lay the foundation of your personal network of contacts. And, most important, create a balance with plenty of friends outside of work!

37

List three good work relationships. Don't restrict yourself to people you've known in paid jobs. You can include anyone with whom you've worked, for example:

- a neighbor
- a member of your church, temple, or club
- a member of a professional or service group
- parents of your children's friends
- members of the PTA or a town committee
- college contacts

Three good work relationships: _____
_____
_____
_____
_____

Fulfill a Mission

Somebody got the idea years ago that you could make any corporate baloney sound meaningful if you said it was about a "mission." Here's what I think it really means:

- your vision for the life you will lead
- your values, which guide big decisions
- the results of your work

Your life's work may be something outside the halls of 9 to 5, or it may be integral to your job. Some people define themselves by their jobs ("I'm a lawyer" or "I'm a sales rep"). Others work to live, supporting their mission outside of work with their job ("I like work, but raising a happy family is my real mission"). Either choice is okay, as long as you keep the perspective that your job is contributing to your life's mission.

Most likely, your career will fall somewhere between these extremes. Most career counselors agree that the happiest people believe their work also serves some cause greater than themselves.

Is there a cause or mission bigger than yourself that you serve? Are you one of those fortunate people who can fulfill that mission at work? Describe that mission here. (And if you don't have a "big" mission yet, don't worry—just remember to consider your vision, values, and the results of your work as you go through the job search.)

Life mission(s): _____

_____

_____

_____

_____

_____

Values, culture, learning, satisfaction, vision, relationships, mission—these seem like a tall order for a job. But imagine for a minute if a job *could* feed all these important parts of your life. I believe it can!

Are you ready to find that good job? Are you ready to give your job search real thought and careful work? Can you make a commitment to something more than the same old job search? With that commitment to your own intrinsic worth, and the job search program described in this book, your job search can make both your job good and your life good.

Summary Exercise

Copy the items you listed throughout this chapter into the form called "What's Important to Me." You'll refer back to this list in chapter 6 as you explore what your perfect job might be.

What's important to me

What I value about work _____
_____
_____
_____

Three cultural traits I like _____
_____
_____
_____

Three things to learn at my next job _____
_____
_____
_____

Three work activities I enjoy _____
_____
_____
_____

Three visions for a good career path (alternatives to moving up the pyramid)
_____
_____
_____

Three good work relationships _____
_____
_____
_____

Life mission(s) _____
_____
_____

You can download this form at monstercareers.com.

Your Value Isn't Measured in Dollars

Back when Monster consisted of twenty people working above a Chinese restaurant in Framingham, Massachusetts, I would eat lunch with everyone else. Some days, I'd go to the sandwich shop across the street to pick up a peanut butter and jelly sandwich.

The counter help at the diner was a woman named Christine Rich. She was a mom, over thirty. She stayed cheerful and warm while performing, let's face it, a tough, low-paying job. There was something special about Chris. I could see that she really thought her job was not "serving sandwiches" but paying attention to all her customers and making them happy. I started to tease her about coming to work for me, and when she told me the diner was closing, I hired her on the spot, first as a receptionist and then for a customer service position. Chris had no computer skills and no Internet knowledge when she started, but she performed fantastically. Customers would ask for her when they had a problem. As the company grew, she just naturally became the "go-to person" for others, who voted her "best employee" several times. Chris embodied Monster's culture, and other people followed. She was promoted to director of customer service.

In 2000 Chris was diagnosed with ALS (Lou Gehrig's disease). She worked long after her diagnosis, facing her illness with incredible courage and even good cheer. She came in to work every day, even after she got so weak she needed a motorized wheelchair to go down the hall. She died in 2001 and hundreds of Monster people attended her memorial service.

I think Chris really was one of my critical hires at Monster because she set a standard for performance and culture that others naturally followed. I didn't have to measure her value to Monster in dollars or even customer satisfaction. Sure, her work made money and increased customer loyalty, but the real point is, Chris lived by her values every day, and she reminded us every day that Monster was a fantastic place in which to work.

4 >> Behind the Scenes at the Recruiter <<

F.A.M.E. ATTITUDE: PREPARE LIKE A MARKETER

Focus on your target customers.

Your "customers" in the job search are the people who make hiring decisions, and their world has changed radically in the last ten years. To market or sell yourself effectively to them—to get that dream job—you need to understand the new realities of their world. Let's walk around to the other side of the desk for a few pages and look at hiring from the recruiter's point of view. (For brevity, I've used the general term "recruiter" in this chapter to indicate many different people, including full-time recruiters, human resource professionals, and hiring managers—anyone who can hire you.)

As Monster's founder, I'm always on the lookout for talent, whether the person appears on CNN or next to me in a meeting. I've personally hired hundreds of people over the last twenty years, and I talk to managers about hiring every chance I get.

Most managers leave their comfort zone when hiring. Even though they invariably tell me that they have a good "gut feel" for candidates, just a few questions reveal that they've had mixed success. They give excuses like "It's tough to fill jobs in my industry." Or, "I just can't seem to find the right candidates locally." Or, they'll openly admit, "I'm not good at hiring people."

Their discomfort is understandable. Hiring is not the job most managers were hired to do. It's a big drain on time. If they hire just a few people a year, there's not much chance to practice and get better at it. If they hire the wrong person, their business will suffer. They may be embarrassed by the professional consequences of a bad hire.

Just as you weren't taught how to manage a job search, most managers were never taught how to hire. Frankly, even most human resources professionals don't receive the training they deserve in the art and science of hiring.

It's easy to hire mediocre people—and get mediocre performance. It's much harder to have the patience, skill, and knowledge to hire high achievers at every level of a team and hold onto them. Managers who are brilliant at selling athletic shoes or building airplanes may become ineffective when they have to hire!

The better you understand the person across the table, the more effective you can be—and the more they can help you. This applies to people who are:

- networking with you
- reading your resume
- interviewing you for a position
- negotiating a job offer with you
- . . . and everyone else in your job search!

You might imagine that the person across the desk is an all-powerful gatekeeper, a sadistic tyrant, or a blank-faced bureaucrat. They're none of those. They are employees themselves, with tasks, deadlines, and bosses to please. They're assaulted by e-mail, phone calls, and to-do lists. They *do* have the power to move your job search along or stop it cold, so it's natural to sit back and let them run the process. That's a low-risk tactic in the short run.

But what if you could actually help them do their jobs? What if you could help them come to hiring decisions with less effort? Wouldn't that make you more memorable?

Most candidates don't even think about the hiring manager's goals. They're focused on selling themselves, and, of course, you will do that, too. But good selling is more than talking about yourself—it's about understanding the customer. Everyone loves finding what they want at a fair price

What No Recruiter Will Tell You

Even if you get a job interview, a recruiter may spend only ninety seconds studying your resume before you walk into the room, and you will probably be judged on your "fit" for the job in a matter of minutes!

when they're shopping. And make no mistake, a recruiter with a job to fill is shopping.

If you mapped the decision curve of a typical interview, it would look like this:

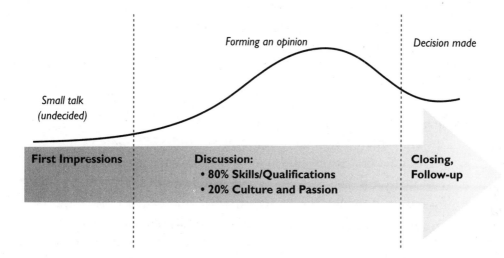

Forming an opinion   Decision made

Small talk
(undecided)

First Impressions   **Discussion:**   **Closing,**
                               • 80% Skills/Qualifications   **Follow-up**
                               • 20% Culture and Passion

For the first three to five minutes of small talk, the recruiter is sizing you up as a person, looking for clues to your character and enthusiasm. For the next half hour or so, the recruiter will ask specific questions about your skills. Finally, if there's time, the recruiter may ask some questions about your values and passion, mostly to confirm ideas he or she has already formed.

I'm not saying this is the best way to hire, but it is by far the most common. I'll show you tactics for dealing with this typical interview in chapter 15.

What Really Matters to a Recruiter

Professional recruiters are judged by the quality and contributions of their hires. (How quickly they fill positions and how long their hires stay is also important in some companies.) Thus, any recruiter is wondering, "How will bringing this person into the company reflect on my performance?" As a result, three qualities about a candidate really matter.

Neal Bruce, a Monster executive who has given deep thought to the hiring process, describes these as the skill match, the culture match, and the motivation match. "In an ideal process," he says, "you would be judged equally on skills [or talent], style [or culture], and motivation [or passion]. Unfortunately, most recruiters assess candidates ninety percent on skills, five percent on style, and five percent on motivation."

Relying on the easy-to-judge skills match, however, is often the *least* reliable predictor of success.

"In my experience," continues Neal, "people who weren't the most skilled, but did fit into the group well and had great passion for their work, were more productive than the people who looked better on paper but didn't have the style or motivation match. That's even more important today, when people have to work in more interdependent groups."

Lou Adler, president of the executive search firm POWERHiring, agrees. He urges hiring managers to withhold judgment for the first thirty minutes of an interview. He also tells them to look no further than the successful people they've promoted to see the criteria that matter.

"A person being promoted or transferred by definition doesn't have the skills or experience to do the job when she starts," he points out. "A high performer shows intelligence, persistence, work ethic, problem-solving ability, motivation—but not always experience in the new job. In other words, the things that get someone promoted are exactly NOT the things that [the] average interviewer hires on."

The recruiter has to take one hundred resumes and narrow them down to twenty. They have to take those twenty candidates and narrow the number to five. Your goal is to lead them to put you in that final five: You need to be an interesting person. You need to be prepared. You have to show them the best parts of you, and prove that you know at least some basics about their company. The more you know, the better. There's no such thing as "overprepared" here!

Most recruiters really have three questions when screening resumes:

Does this candidate have the skills and knowledge to do the job?

This is the big hammer, and it takes place before you get a call, when the recruiter is giving the resume a first quick look. Does this candidate have the experience, training, certification, and school degree I specified in the job description? If no, hit the gong and toss the resume. If yes, maybe take a longer look.

Some qualifications are required by law or common sense. Most are specific to the job and are set by the hiring manager. A manager can assume someone with an MCSE (Microsoft® Certified Systems Engineer) certification will be able to perform a number of tasks with Microsoft systems, so if they need those skills, they'll state "MCSE required."

When applying for a job, you have to know what skills are truly required, and prove that you have those skills. There's usually a gray area between the "must-have" qualifications and the "nice to haves"—call them "ought to haves," which allow you some negotiating room.

But don't think you'll automatically get called to interview for a job, even if your skills are a good match. Employers define skill levels differently, and every job requires a particular mix of skills, knowledge, and experience. (Remember, too, that you will be compared with other candidates throughout the process.) I'll show you how to showcase your skills in chapter 8.

Bear in mind that you might become "qualified" by learning new skills or knowledge on the job, and if you know that, you can still make the case that your experience, cultural fit, and passion are perfect for the position.

Will we like working with this person?

This question comes up in the job interview, and it takes place in that slippery culture zone. Successful recruiters investigate a candidate's personal style: Do they like to work closely with people, or do they work better alone? Do they want a rule book, or are they capable improvisers? Do they like an intense, fast-paced workplace or a quieter, steadier pace?

Culture can vary within a company. A business manager may like aggressive, outspoken, creative, or impulsive people because they spew ideas—but would you want one of those people operating dangerous equipment? That job requires a deliberate and organized person. A company can have different cultures for the sales force and the manufacturing floor, yet create a common sense of mission. The qualities that make your personality unique will come into play here, because it's the essence of what managers mean by their "gut feel" for a hire.

Kate DeCamp of Cisco says, "A good recruiter is a passion hunter—they find the passionate people, put them in the right role, and get out of their way." I agree. If marathon running is important enough that you put it on your resume, I want to talk about it. That's how I'll see what passionate interest looks like to you. If I get you in the right role, I'll get that same energy directed toward the company's mission.

When the answer to the first two questions is "yes," the recruiter asks the third question.

Can we get this person at the right price?

Many factors, from market forces to company budgets to employee benefits, come into play here. If you require twice the amount of money they're offering, it's not a match. Those questions become critical when the recruiter is convinced that you're the right person for the job.

We'll revisit these questions in chapter 15, The Job Interview, and chapter 16, Negotiating the Best Deal.

Six Facts About Hiring Managers

Monster career expert Peter Vogt notes six brutal facts of recruiters' lives, and what to do about them.

THEY'RE OFTEN SKEPTICAL.

Every hiring manager has probably been burned by an applicant who stretched the truth on his resume or lied outright during an interview. So why should they believe you? You can alleviate wary employers' doubts by offering specifics about achievements.

THEY'RE SWAMPED.

All hiring managers have too much to do and too little time in which to do it. Anything you can do to save their time will be to your advantage. Start with a well-written resume and a customized cover message.

THEY'RE COMPARING YOU TO OTHER CANDIDATES.

It's easy to think that a recruiter is comparing you only against the job description. In reality, they're always judging you against other applicants. If you've prepared like a marketer, you can describe your achievements in a memorable way. Then recruiters will compare others to *you*.

THEY AREN'T IN BUSINESS TO TAKE A CHANCE ON YOU.

"If only an employer would give me a chance," you might lament. But it's not a recruiter's goal to give people chances. Their goal is to make great hires every time. So the more you look like the answer to a problem, and the less you ask them to take a chance, the greater your credibility.

THEY'RE UNDER PRESSURE, AND PERHAPS EVEN AFRAID.

Recruiters are judged by the candidates they recommend. If those candidates disappoint, the recruiters will be on the hot seat. So understand that they are feeling some pressure, both internal and external, to make good hires. Keep a helpful attitude. If it's clear that you're not going to be one of the final five candidates, offer to help the recruiter find candidates for other jobs from your personal network.

IT'S A HUMAN PROCESS.

Hiring always hinges on the human factors. The recruiter will judge you the way you judge a new acquaintance at a party—and in those first few moments, your presentation, interest in them, and ability to communicate count a lot.

What Has Changed in the Last Twenty Years

Technology has revolutionized every step in the recruiting process. If you know a little about how recruiters use the technology, you can use it to your advantage.

The essential new tool for recruiters is the database, a collection of information or documents set up so a computer can retrieve just what the user wants. Monster, for example, has a big database where candidates can search for job opportunities and another big database where recruiters can search for resumes.

Internet databases contain millions of resumes, placed there by job seekers (I'll show you how to do this in chapter 10). Recruiters search for resumes in those databases, which also help sort the resumes in various ways—for example, separating the resumes of candidates in Chicago from resumes outside of Chicago. They use the database software to search all these resumes for "keywords." For example, a recruiter looking for nurses may search for all the resumes in Chicago that contain the keywords "nurse," "RN," "Nursing," and so on.

Recruiters may also keep their own databases filled with resumes they've received directly from candidates, and search through them when they're ready to hire. In the hands of an experienced user, these databases are incredibly efficient: they expand the scope of the search while reducing the time searching takes. Think of typing a few commands into a computer versus sorting through 10,000 resumes and you get the idea!

Technology also allows recruiters to spend more time doing the really productive, human tasks: networking, face-to-face interviews with promising candidates, training and managing their own staffs, and getting newly hired employees off to a good start.

But there is a downside: technology bypasses human contact. No database imagines you in a new position, judges your passion for the job, or decides what kind of person you are. You cannot persuade software that you will grow into a leader in the company, yet these questions are still critical.

Another downside: twenty years ago, recruiters knew a lot about most jobs firsthand. Recruiting in today's skills-based economy requires understanding of everything from precision manufacturing systems to database programming—too much for one person to know. It's likely that a recruiter will screen candidates out or in with a set of questions written by someone else. Or, your first screening interview may not be about specific technical skills at all, but you still have to convince that first interviewer you've got the chops.

Bill Hickmott of Ironworks Executive Partners, a human resources consulting firm, points out a new challenge the volume of resumes available poses: "Typically the most experienced person is not reading resumes when they come in. It may be an administrator who culls resumes and sends them to an HR manager for review, who then sends the resumes to someone else. . . . Think of the failure points along this system! You are screened and screened and screened. And nobody has time to study your resume in detail!"

Internet, e-mail, and database technology has made hiring cycles much shorter. In 1990 the hiring process typically took twelve weeks from beginning to end. Now it averages about four weeks, and we've seen many examples of the whole process coming together in three or four days! In the fastest companies, hiring managers expect a choice of pre-identified candidates any time they have a need.

Technology has also changed how you contact an employer. Until recently, sending an e-mail application was considered second-class to mailing a paper resume and cover letter. No more. Every process in business today has integrated e-mail; recruiters would rather not wait for the paper letter to hit their desks.

Now, contrary to some people's assumption, technology has not changed good business etiquette. You must always be courteous and professional with everyone in the process. You must learn professional phone manners. You must send thank-you notes; e-mail or a quick letter is usually fine. And, you must proofread everything. In the end, how you present yourself, in person, on the phone, or in writing, will say a lot about what kind of person you are.

Better, Faster, Cheaper

Like many other jobs, recruiting has grown more demanding in the last twenty years. Here's a snapshot of how the rest of the process has changed in the past two decades:

- "Employers are aiming toward forty to fifty percent of new hires coming from employee referrals," says Gerry Crispin of CareerXRoads. "By giving current employees cash incentives to bring in new hires, they're turning their entire staff into a first-line recruiting machine."

- Testing of technical knowledge, personality type, or "motivated skills" is much more common. Advanced interviewing methods (see chapter 15) have been accepted because they produce good hires.

- Companies are hiring specialty firms ("outsourcing") to do their hiring. The person you contact first may not even work directly for the company!

- Candidates must speak up for themselves when it comes to negotiating their pay, benefits, and work arrangements. With a free-agent mindset, you must be ready to negotiate (see chapter 16).

- Finally, the cost of recruiting has changed. Advertising a position on the Internet costs a fraction of advertising in a newspaper, which means more positions can be advertised for the same dollar amount. Lately, the newspapers have placed much of their job advertising online.

Whether driven by economics or technology, change will continue to rock the people you encounter on the other side of the desk. In the next chapter, we'll talk about the differences among all the people you will work with in your search.

5 >> People Who Will Help You <<

F.A.M.E. ATTITUDE: THINK LIKE A **F**REE AGENT

Relationships count. A strong personal network is good for you and good for business.

Here's the good news: Many people will help you find a job.

Here's the catch: Finding a job is still up to you. It starts with you . . . and it ends with you.

Most job seekers take an apologetic attitude. They don't want to pester their friends and professional contacts with questions. They're uneasy when selling themselves to an employer. To avoid discomfort, they send out resumes day after day, and never really get in front of people.

But going it alone is impossible. In addition to working online and offline, you're going to have to build relationships—personal and professional—that connect you to your next job. There is no substitute for the human connection. Ask yourself during every casual conversation, e-mail, or job application, "What can these people do to assist my job search, and how can I help them do that?"

In other words, "help them help you."

It's as simple as asking a friend at the softball game if they know anyone at ABC Company. It's as professional as asking a full-time recruiter exactly what he or she needs from you to forward your resume to a hiring manager. It's as acceptable as asking an associate if your "pitch" sounds convincing.

To "help people help you" effectively, think about each person's role in your search. Here are the people you may encounter:

- human resources professionals
- hiring managers
- professional recruiters
- counselors, coaches, and outplacement professionals
- government organizations
- business contacts
- friends, family, and community

Any of these people can connect you with a job! Let's go deeper into all the roles, and how you can "help them help you."

Human Resources

It's become a cliché to suggest that human resources doesn't have much to do with hiring decisions. I say, ignore the HR department at your peril. A little history will help you understand why HR is becoming *more* important at the best companies.

Decades ago, most hiring was done by a company's general management. In small companies, it was done by the office manager. Then came the "Office of Personnel," whose job was tactical: the functions were hiring, firing, promotions, and watching over the few benefits offered in those days.

In the 1980s, as business began to recognize that people were key resources, and not interchangeable parts, "Personnel" became "Human Resources." It still handled recruiting, and added employee training, career tracking within an organization, and more complex benefits. HR was responsible for the quality and health of the company's workforce.

In the 1990s, there weren't enough good people to go around, so HR became more focused on strong recruiting. In the slow, uncertain years that followed, recruiting issues were pushed into the background as companies fought for survival. But that won't last. The long-term shortages of skills I discussed in chapter 1 mean that people, not products, are not just key resources—they're the most precious assets of all. The head of human resources now often reports directly to the president or CEO, and carries a title like "Chief People Officer."

In my experience there are three typical varieties of HR recruiter:

- *"Button poppers"*—You know who I'm talking about. They've been in the biz thirty to fifty years. The first thing you notice is the buttons on their shirts, stretched over a big stomach, about to fly out and hit you during an interview! They probably are not technically savvy; they may not even use e-mail. Maybe they don't have any formal HR training. They are, however, well entrenched at the company and excellent gatekeepers. Treat them in a traditional way and get moved along as soon as possible to the hiring manager.

- *"Company generalists"*—Every start-up once had an office manager who did the accounting and the billing, talked to customers, and hired new staff. As the company grew, functions like finance went to specialists, and the generalists fell into HR, without real training. Their job is to move you along without making mistakes. They use e-mail and basic recruiting technology. They tend to know the company culture well.

- *"HR experts"*—Nowadays, many companies have this new generation of top managers, with executive power and high expectations. Most will have degrees in Human Resource Management. They're technically savvy. They have detailed knowledge of job requirements as well as the big picture. They may walk you through the hiring process personally. They will also have a say in your compensation, the makeup of your job, and your mobility around the company.

The quality of the HR professional has gone up dramatically in the past ten years. The first two characters—button poppers and generalists—were 80 percent of HR twenty years ago. Now, HR professionals are more likely to be in the "expert" category, with a graduate degree in HR and special training in recruiting.

When you meet with HR, make a quick assessment. Ask, "Will you be my only contact, or will I also talk to my potential manager, people in other departments, and potential colleagues?" If they say, "You'll work with me all the way through and I'll make the recommendation," you have to invest more of your sale in that individual. If they make it clear that their job is to move you along, help them do that by focusing on your skills and how you fit the job description.

Hiring Managers

The hiring manager is ultimately the person who has to agree you're the right person for the job. They may be line managers, product directors, department heads, executives, or specialists. Recruiters work closely with them. In Monster surveys, recruiters say that close work with hiring managers shortens their recruiting time.

It's common to think of the hiring manager as a blind date who will judge you quickly, but you must transform that person from judge to advocate. Give them reasons to invest in you. This blind date could be worth $500,000 to you over the next ten years (if your salary is $50,000). Think about your long-range opportunity.

Remember this when dealing with hiring managers: ninety percent of their time is spent *managing* people, projects, information, objects, and money. This simple fact implies differences between your approaches to the hiring manager and professional recruiters or human resources staff:

- Your approach to the hiring manager will be more disruptive to their job than your approach to a recruiter. You have to create interest in the first few minutes by focusing on their specific objectives.

- Hiring managers have less time for individuals than recruiters. Ten minutes for an initial phone call is a lot of time. A 45-minute job interview is a big commitment.

- Personal networks matter to hiring managers. If you reach them through a referral from a colleague, acquaintance, or friend, you will have the advantage. Remember, though, that networking only gets you in the door. *You* have to take it from here.

- While HR is focused on the whole company, a hiring manager is accountable for the performance of a much smaller group. If you don't have what they need right now, they may lose interest. Don't take it personally.

- For the same reason, the pain of a bad hire is much worse for a hiring manager. The recruiter wonders, "Does this person have potential for the company?" The hiring manager wonders, "Will this person screw up and cost me time and money?"

You have a much greater stake in the relationship with a hiring manager. You may see your company's human resources director a few times a year. You're likely to see your manager several times a day. Because they are ultimately responsible for your performance, hiring managers usually have the final say. When others may have their doubts, hiring managers who want you will put their own prestige behind the hire. That's why I say, make them your advocates.

Outside Recruiters

Outside recruiters are matchmakers between a candidate and a company. There are many different kinds of outside recruiters, and they can be critically important or downright dangerous. Most job seekers think a recruiter can help them. That's partly because—let's face it—we'd all like someone to do the hard work for us, and partly because recruiters work on the "inside track" to jobs.

You are likely to interest an outside recruiter if:

- You are easy to sell to their clients. This means you have relevant experience, proven results, and a background that suits the recruiter's specialty.

- You have management or advanced technical skills.

- Your work style (full-time, temporary, contract) is right for the recruiter's clients.

- You fit for a position that's open right now.

You may not be right for recruiting firms. If you are considering a career change or just starting out in an entry-level job, focus on direct approaches to employers and networking. Recruiters aren't career counselors and few can make money placing entry-level people.

Even if recruiters don't have a job for you today, they may find a match later. This is where resume databases have made all the difference. In the past, your resume was stuck in a manila folder somewhere, and the chance of you being called back nine months later was zero. Now, a recruiter's resume database may find you two or three years later when the right job comes into their sights.

If the recruiter is impressed by you, he or she will say, "Hey, I like that person, I'm going to place them somewhere." This is called running with an applicant. For example, Sally the technical recruiter may be looking for a database analyst, and meet an awesome systems programmer (you). She calls her client and asks, "I know you need a database analyst, but do you also need a systems programmer? I know a phenomenal one." The company may say, "In fact, we'll need one in three weeks." Bam! The recruiter sold you into the company. She gets a big fee, and you get a job that was never advertised. This kind of dream scenario doesn't happen every day, but highly skilled talent combined with highly skilled recruiters makes it possible.

Types of Recruiters

The major differences among professional recruiters boil down to who they work for and how they get paid:

- *Inside recruiters* work for the company on salary. They will generally give more time to learning about the whole candidate—skills, culture, passions, and long-term prospects. They tend to specialize in difficult-to-fill positions within the company.

- *Contract recruiters* lease their services to a company on a short-term basis for specific needs (often to find candidates for difficult-to-fill positions or for a quick ramp-up of staff). They are not paid to judge your passion or cultural fit but look strictly at a checklist of your skills. They are on the clock, so expect less personal investment in you.

- *Third-party recruiters* are employed by independent companies, which include Staffing firms, Temporary and Contract agencies, Contingency Search and e-Recruitment firms, and Executive Search firms. There are important differences among these:

  - *Staffing firms* supply skilled part-time or full-time employees to their clients. They are paid by the client, and the employee is paid by them. They want candidates with proven skills who can hit the ground running.

  - *Temporary and contract agencies* fill jobs for preset periods of time. For example, they place persons with accounting skills into firms at tax time. Temp agencies place for a week at a time; a contract is a placement for 1- to 6-month jobs. Again, clients pay the agency and the agency pays the employee. Sometimes, your full-time job may grow out of your part-time or contract placement, but the client will have to pay a large fee to the agency. In effect, you'll be more expensive to hire than a comparable nonagency candidate.

- *Contingency search and e-Recruitment firms* generally find candidates for full-time positions. They're paid a percentage of the successful candidate's first-year salary (as much as 25 percent in boom times). Success for them comes from making the most matches with the most companies, without too much prequalification or evaluation. They are more likely to work with managers or technically skilled candidates.

- *Retained search firms,* often called Executive Search firms, find candidates for top leadership positions. They are paid a flat fee not only for identifying candidates but for a long-term consulting relationship with a company. They're a special breed, and we'll describe them in the next section.

Companies use third-party recruiters because, as specialists, they save time and money, and often supply candidates the company can't find with its limited resources. An outside recruiter's goal is solving a problem for the client, not you. The recruiters need to find the right candidates *now,* and if they don't have a position for you this week, they can't give you much time.

The outside recruiter's relationship to the company is not always obvious, so if you can, determine which type of recruiter you're dealing with. On the phone, use a strategically placed question to assess whether they work for the company: "I've learned a lot from the company Web site. Can you tell me more about . . . Oh, first let me ask if you actually work for the company, or have they hired your services?" If the recruiter says, "No, I'm just here on a four- to six-week assignment," you can drop the cultural questions about the company and focus on how your skills can get the job done.

What can you do to help third-party recruiters participate in your job search? Get their interest with a top-notch resume and cover message. Highlight your skills with keywords in a cover message. Add one distinctive achievement story as an attachment to your resume. Even if they have nothing for you today, stay engaged. Offer to connect a recruiter to people in your personal network who are actively looking. Say thanks and keep in touch. Their next client may need you.

Don't send resumes indiscriminately to every recruiter in America. Choose a few agencies to work with and spend your time developing relationships with your recruiters. The better others know you, the better they will be able to represent you.

Remember, they have probably just taken a job order from a company. They may be reluctant to tell you who it is until they feel they have you in their clutches! If a recruiter places you, you are "money" to them. Very likely you will work with this recruiter again as your career progresses. Don't expect them to recruit you away from your employer in six months, though—that's not ethical behavior toward the company that hired you. Just stay in touch and they'll be there when you're ready to make a move.

Retained Executive Search

Retained search firms place executive talent, usually in positions paying more than $150,000 a year, so the stakes for everyone concerned are high. An executive search typically takes longer than other searches, and is conducted discreetly, because most of the candidates are already working in executive jobs. The best firms are really business consultants, deeply involved in a client company's strategic issues, and they're "retained" by the company with a consultant's fee.

If you are so accomplished that an executive recruiter takes an interest, you may go through multiple interviews and much preparation before the recruiter puts you forward to the client. Executive recruiters are concerned with your career at a company, and a good one will ask your manager a month after you're hired, "Hey, how's that person doing? Was she right for the job? Do you want more candidates like her?" They'll also check in with you, because they know that the person they placed yesterday may give them additional business tomorrow.

Inside a Headhunter's Head

Executive recruiter John Isaacson says that finding candidates is the easy part—but great recruiters are more like management consultants. "Clients often feel that headhunting is the search. It counts, but by itself, it doesn't count enough. It's not hard to come up with a collection of plausible candidates, most of them wrong. The trick is to figure out what aligns with strategy. . . . I ask my clients, 'What constitutes victory? How will you know you hired the right person one year after you have hired him or her?'"

Bad Headhunter Tricks

Some recruiters are less ethical than most. Here's how to prevent the most common tricks.

RESUME CREATIVITY: Many recruiters will retype your resume to highlight certain items: skills, education, and so on. Their interpretation may not be comfortable for you.

PREVENTION: Ask to sign off on their interpretation and provide your own resume once you are in the "real" interview—with an employer!

RESUME RANSOM: The recruiter broadcasts your resume all over, and then demands a fee for a connection you made by yourself. Result: the company won't touch you.

PREVENTION: Present the companies you will approach to the recruiter, and require that they tell you in advance when they are sending your resume to a client.

REFERENCE POACHING: The recruiter feigns an interest in you, asks for your references, and then recruits those references. Result: your reference is annoyed at you. Another version: asking for the names of frustrated executives at your (former) employer, which in effect asks you to betray insider information.

PREVENTION: Tell your references in advance that you are working with a recruiter. Withhold references until a recruiter delivers a job interview. Don't discuss your other contacts except those looking actively for work. Remember, your most important references are at the heart of your network; treat them with care.

WEAVING THE DREAM: The recruiter hard-sells a job that isn't right for you, with no regard for your real career direction.

PREVENTION: Never settle for anyone's vision of your career but your own.

SUCCESS INFLATION: Check out claims like "Eighty percent of our candidates are placed within two weeks!"

PREVENTION: Talk to the people they've placed (they should supply names; try to find someone in your field and at your level). Ask how much time the recruiter spent with the candidate, how much they knew about the company, and how long the placement took.

Remember: **The employer, not the candidate, pays the recruiter.** Without careful consideration, *don't* sign up with a search firm that asks you to pay—either up front or after you're hired.

An executive recruiter may match you with several jobs over the years. Thus, you are even more concerned with the relationship. It's really a long-term business partnership, so keep in close touch after you get a job. A recruiter can expand your professional network enormously. If you don't keep that good impression fresh, you won't be remembered when the next good opportunity comes along. Take the time to cultivate your relationships when you are not in search mode, and your job search will be that much easier when you need to kick things into gear.

Counselors, Coaches, and Outplacement

Career counselors and coaches can work wonders if you need help kick-starting a job search or working through the transition from one job to another. The difference between them is focused on your needs:

- A career *counselor* focuses on your thoughts, feelings, ambitions, and life decisions. Through the counseling process, you become more aware of the choices you need to make. Career counselors hold advanced degrees such as a master's degree in counseling. They're appropriate to use at a crossroads in your career, or if one of your job search goals is greater self-understanding.
- A career *coach*, like any coach in sports, is focused on the concrete steps that help you win the game. They get you into the game with training and practice. A coach will also cheer you on, challenge you to do better, and knock down barriers to progress.

Career counselors and coaches are paid like any professional, most often an agreed-upon fee for a selection of services you want. These might include counseling you about various options you haven't considered, helping you write a resume, interview coaching, career interest assessments, and so forth. (For more on career assessments, see chapter 6.)

Career expert Barbara Reinhold points out that counselors and coaches also offer an objective point of view: they can see your "blind spots," question your assumptions (like pleasing your parents or seeking job security), and suggest options you haven't considered.

Check out a counselor or coach carefully before paying any money. Are they offering a systematic program of job search or a more open-ended process? Do they specialize in your field or in your particular situation (for example, re-entering the workforce after a long absence)? Ask their clients how effective their services were for the goals you have in mind. You are giving them money, time, and trust, so choose carefully.

You must also be willing to work hard. Career counselor Kristy Meghreblian suggests that, "Job seekers need to manage their expectations. No career counselor or coach is going to wave her magic wand and tell you what you're going to be for the rest of your life."

You will find career counselors and coaches at state-run employment centers, in employment agencies, and in private practice. Two helpful Web directories are located at the International Coach Federation (**coachfederation. org**) and the National Board for Certified Counselors "Counselorfind" service (**nbcc.org/cfind/**). If you're a student or a recent graduate, take advantage of the coaches or counselors available through your college's alumni/career office. They should be a great source of encouragement, information, and maybe job leads (many of them use Monster as a source of open positions).

As with recruiters, beware of coaches or counselors who guarantee results. Some job seekers shell out thousands of dollars to career services that implied instant employment, only to be disappointed.

> I asked other career counselors, "When you were eighteen, did you know you wanted to be a career counselor?" Not one of them said yes.
>
> —*Career counselor Peter Vogt*

In the last twenty years a counseling specialty called outplacement became popular. These firms are paid by a company to provide career services to executives and managers who have been laid off. They counsel and coach, teach job-seeking skills, administer career tests, and sometimes offer office space, voice mail, Internet access, and career libraries to their clients. Some—like Lee Hecht Harrison, Challenger Gray and Christmas, and DBM—have many offices, and some offer sophisticated online services for their clients. If you are laid off, find out if you are eligible for outplacement.

Government Organizations

Government help for job seekers has become more sophisticated, with trained employment professionals offering free job search services at state centers. Services vary from state to state, but they may include such help as:

- access to child care
- career guidance
- career resource library
- computer learning lab
- education/training opportunities
- e-mail access
- employer recruitments
- employment services for unemployment insurance recipients
- employment services for ex-offenders
- employment and training for workers dislocated due to imports
- food stamp and other government benefit information
- Internet access
- job referrals and placement
- job search libraries
- job search training
- labor market information
- personalized veterans' services
- psychological counseling
- resume development
- self-assessment and career testing
- tax information and assistance for employers
- unemployment claims assistance

You can locate a career center at a federal-state partnership called CareerOneStop at **servicelocator.org/**. Most help for job seekers comes from the state governments, and you can find their services on the Web at your state's home page. The U.S. Department of Labor also lists resources at

doleta.gov/programs/adtrain.asp. A list of state unemployment offices can be found at **jobsearch.about.com/library/blunemploy.htm**.

Business Contacts

If you have spent any time in the workforce, you already have a circle of business contacts. These are coworkers, former heads of departments, people down the hall or in the lunchroom, people you did business with, or even vendors such as the computer sales representative. Executives know that their most potent source of job leads may be their former customers. Even former competitors can be a rich source of contacts and information.

If you've relocated, you can contact professional acquaintances, asking if they know anyone in your new town. You can also start generating new contacts right away in town halls and local businesses. Reporters will tell you that the richest source of information in a town is often the president of the local bank. Give him or her a call!

Even if you're just entering the workforce, your circle of professional contacts can expand quickly, for example:

- landlords
- local services such as print and copy shops
- local newspaper staff
- community chest members
- the chamber of commerce
- local service organizations (Elks, Lions, Rotary, and so on) that attract local business participation
- Junior Achievement
- service professionals like tax or financial advisors

We'll cover the details of networking in chapter 14. For now, your goal is to understand how wide your circle of professional acquaintances really can be.

65

Recently, professional networking groups have come into their own. Their purpose is to help their members find work or customers. If you are specific and diligent with your questions and generous in passing along your contacts, you will be impressed with how quickly they can expand your network, especially early in your search. You'll find a directory of job-networking groups at the always-helpful Riley Guide (**rileyguide.com/support.html#nema**).

In recent years, I've realized that I have no good source for remembering who I know, and when I'm asked, I struggle to come up with only a dozen painfully obvious "members" of my professional network. So, I began a list called "People who matter" on my Blackberry handheld computer. It's great to see that list grow and to come up with many names any time I'm asked to recall my professional network.

For those of you who are working, begin your list today! Start with people at work who matter, people in your community who matter, people in business who matter . . . and you're on your way to developing a networking database.

Friends, Family, and Community

I've saved the best news in this chapter for last. Everybody has a personal network of people who are ready to help, whether or not they know anything about searching for a job.

You can build a personal network. The loneliest newcomer to a big city can begin a job network on his or her first day, even if it's just people in the market downstairs. If you belong to a club, a religious organization, a support group or social organization, you know people who are willing to talk about your job search. Your friends and family will want to help. Neighbors, if they know you are looking, can offer connections or share experiences.

Don't forget your wider circle of acquaintances—shop owners, members of a school committee on which you serve, your dental hygienist, or the technician who fixes your home computer. People who deliver services to local businesses can be fantastic sources of information and contacts because their customers are your potential employers.

Where can you find that wider circle? Everywhere. To get you started thinking, here are twenty-five places where you can start connecting to people who can connect you to jobs:

- bank office
- career fair

- company open house
- job-networking group
- library
- college recruiting drive
- coffee shop
- soccer field
- alumni meeting
- support group (of all kinds)
- church, temple, and so on
- book club
- unemployment service office
- school play committee
- Parent-Teacher Association
- service club (Rotary and so on)
- interest association (Sierra Club, VFW chapter, and so on)
- real estate agency
- parties
- roadside cleanup volunteer group
- restaurant counter
- neighborhood bar (if you do that sort of thing)
- college alumni organization
- online buddy groups
- community group (choir, amateur theater, and so on)

The various professional helpers in your circle of acquaintance—such as ministers and other religious workers, community volunteers, and town government employees—also know about employers that might be right for you. Talk to them.

Many of your acquaintances may work at companies that pay a referral bonus when an employee introduces a successful candidate. Find out who does, and give them your resume—they're motivated to get you a job!

Your child's soccer coach (or the parent standing next to you on the sideline) can connect you to jobs as well. But like everyone else in this process, their help can't be effective unless you provide the details they need.

Help from friends and family members isn't limited to connecting you with an employer. Your personal network also generates ideas and supports you throughout the job search.

Here are just a few ways families and friends can help:

- Listen while you describe your ideal job.
- Rehearse your presentation and "key messages."
- Proofread your resume.
- Connect you to someone in a company you've targeted.
- Help you research people, places, and locations for work.
- Remember old acquaintances who are doing the work you would like to do.
- Let you cry on their shoulder.
- Listen while you rant about the company that laid you off.
- Ask others for help on your behalf.
- Help you remember and describe your achievements.
- Remind you what traps you tend to fall into (for example, choosing the wrong boss over and over).
- Keep an eye out for job opportunities.
- Do a reality check on exercises you've done in this book and on Monster.

You can probably think of a dozen other ways your personal network can help you. As a starter exercise, list three now:

1. _____
2. _____
3. _____

Start a Networking Grid

In chapter 14, you'll begin a networking program in earnest. For now, let's get a preview of your personal network with the following simple networking grid. Don't worry about completing it perfectly; I just want to get you thinking about all the support available right from the start.

NETWORKING GRID

ROLE	NAME(S)	E-MAIL AND CONTACT #	HOW THEY CAN HELP	WHAT YOU HAVE TO ASK
Former work colleagues				
Business acquaintances				
Former clients or competitors				
Church or club members				
Networking groups				
Online acquaintances				
Friends				
Family members				
Schoolmates				
Military service contacts				
Neighbors				
Other				
Other				

You can download this form at monstercareers.com.

List at least five people you can contact in the next week who might be able to help you, how they can help, and what you have to ask. (Save this list for more action in chapter 14.) And when you're done, add three more!

Book to Web

As your network expands, you may want to download this grid in an expandable form at **monstercareers.com**.

There. Your own professional network of people who will help you get a job is well under way. Continue to add names to this list as you work each step in your job search. Remember, you are not alone in this. When you reach into your network for help, good things will happen.

6 >> Who Are You? <<

F.A.M.E. ATTITUDE: PREPARE LIKE A MARKETER

Define your personal brand.

Who are you?

It's a question you must ask yourself many times in a job search, because the more you know about yourself, the more effective your search will be. You'll find the jobs that are a good match for your personality, skills, interests, and values.

Even if you think you know who you are and what you want out of work, don't skip this opportunity for further self-discovery. You may be surprised by the new possibilities that appear as you define that personal brand I discussed in chapter 2.

Your personal brand—that unique combination of your attributes and your achievements—is what employers will hire. I hope that, when you've tried the exercises and tools I'm about to describe, you'll know a lot more about what you really want out of your next job.

In the list called "What's Important to Me" on page 40 in chapter 3, you started to define seven factors that connect a good job and a good life. Refer back to that exercise as you read this chapter. We're about to go deeper into defining your personal brand—the "you" that employers will meet.

At Monster we ask, "Who are you?" (it's easy to remember: W.A.Y.) to highlight the choices we make every day about our work, behavior, and attitudes. Every day at work is filled with those choices, and you must be alert to them. Here are the kind of "Who are you?" questions you should ask yourself during a job search:

- Who are you—the kind of person who seeks new challenges in the next job, or someone who is just coasting? (Remember, if you coast, you only coast one way, and that's downhill.)

- Who are you—a curious person who looks for opportunities to network with new people, or a person who says, "I'm too busy to network" or, "I could never do that, I'm too shy"?

- Who are you—a person who wants to solve a difficult situation right away, or a person who says, "I want to give this more thought before I act"?

I'm going to challenge you to ask yourself this question throughout your job search, especially when you're frustrated or feel like taking the easy way out of a task. It's more important that you be honest than that you "look good."

Who are you? Are you someone who just dreams about career goals—or are you someone who will think a little deeper, train a little harder, prepare a little better, and work a little more to achieve them?

Self-assessment

In this chapter, you'll learn about ways to take on the process of career discovery, a process that career counselors call "self-assessment." Self-assessment helps you know more about your:

- **personality** (unique character, behavior, emotions, and preferences)

- **skills and talents** (what you're good at learning and doing)

- **interests** (what you enjoy learning and doing)

- **work-related values** (what's important to you at work)

Some job and career changers avoid self-assessment because it seems to be overwhelming, difficult, and even scary. But self-assessment is the most useful and potentially rewarding investment you can make in yourself when you're thinking about changing jobs or careers.

There's no instant answer in self-assessment. You must honestly consider your strengths and weaknesses. As your understanding grows, so does your ability to connect your personal brand to the right jobs. In fact, you already know a lot about yourself, but chances are you haven't applied this knowledge to a job search. The point of a search is not fitting yourself to a job; it's finding the jobs that fit you.

In this chapter, I've drawn from the latest thinking about self-assessment and innovative ways to help you gain insights about yourself. At the end of this chapter you'll find eight exercises to get you started (and more at **monstercareers.com**). Most should take no more than fifteen to twenty minutes to complete.

Before you do any of them, create a file folder named "Interactive Assessment Materials" or I-AM. When you've completed an exercise, put your worksheet in that folder. Keep a copy of the "What's Important to Me" exercise in there as well. As you develop more insights about what you like and dislike, write them down and keep them in your I-AM folder.

Then, whenever you come to a crossroads in your search (like deciding whether to change professions, move locations, or focus on a different set of work values), keep asking yourself the question **Who are you?** Often, you'll find that the answer lies in the folder marked I-AM!

Intersecting Worlds

Good job matches are found at the intersection of a person's skills, interests, and values, all within the context of a unique personality. Your ideal work would be found where all these came together, like this:

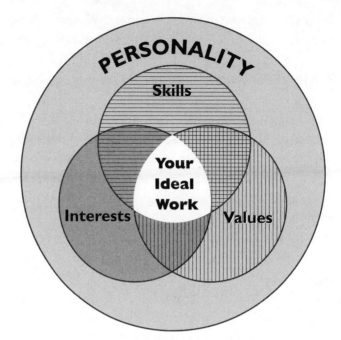

As you identify the details of each circle, compare possible jobs with your unique combination of qualities in all four circles. Jobs that include the best set of overlapping details deserve deep investigation.

Personality

You need to look for jobs that work for your personality. You need to find that sense, perhaps buried under a lot of other expectations, that a job suits your character, behavior, emotions, and preferences.

Psychologists have created several reliable models of personality as it relates to work. You may have heard of their names: RISEAC, Myers-Briggs types, Enneagrams, and others. The models describe personality as a set of preferences among related characteristics. For example, assessments can measure a person's natural tendency between being extremely extroverted (outgoing, energetic) and extremely introverted (private, reserved). Research suggests that measuring these factors can successfully lead to predictions of a person's "fit" across a wide range of jobs and organizations.

The Monster Career Fit Indicator is an example of such a research-based assessment, developed by a team of experts under the direction of Charles

Gerhold. You can use it as a platform for thinking about your work personality. It is based on the following five ranges of personal qualities.

EXTROVERTED VS. INTROVERTED

Extroverted individuals tend to enjoy being with people, have an abundance of energy, and often experience positive emotions.

Introverted individuals tend to be somewhat quiet, reserved, and reflective; their energy is directed inward and is less obvious to others.

CREATIVE VS. CONVENTIONAL

Creative individuals are intellectually curious, appreciative of artistic expression, and open to a wide range of experiences.

Conventional individuals are practical, traditional, conservative, and relate well to factual information and familiar experience.

TRUSTING VS. SKEPTICAL

Trusting individuals place a high value on cooperating with others; therefore, they are considerate, generous, and helpful. They tend to be less competitive.

Skeptical individuals see themselves as fair, objective, and independent. However, others may view them as unsympathetic and stubborn.

PLANFUL VS. FLEXIBLE

Planful individuals like to follow schedules and find pleasure in being organized. Typically, they are very goal-oriented and methodical.

Flexible individuals are easygoing and casual, preferring to not make plans. Others may view them as rather impulsive and unpredictable.

CALM VS. TENSE

Calm individuals are usually optimistic and self-confident, and they do not get upset easily.

Tense individuals are likely to worry about unpredictable events and things that they can't change.

Personality is expressed as a set of degrees to which a person tends in one direction or the other. So, a person with a high tendency toward the qualities labeled extroverted above would likely possess a low level of the introverted qualities. They would probably be well suited to jobs that reward lots of contact with other people, abundant energy, and an outgoing manner. That doesn't mean they never have a quiet moment, but that their preference is toward the extroverted.

Most people do not fall completely on one side or the other of these factors. You might, for example, be strongly inclined toward two of them and somewhere in the middle range for the remaining three. As for a middle range result, it indicates the importance of a situation to your response. For instance, someone in the middle range between "Trusting" and "Skeptical" might be quite willing to trust others at first, but actively skeptical toward people who have been untruthful in the past.

At their best, personality assessment results lead to suggestions of jobs or professions that suit a personality. For example, a person whose strongest tendencies are toward the Creative, Extroverted, and Planful scales might explore jobs in sales management, marketing, advertising, strategy consulting, or public relations, which all value a combination of imagination, communication, and organization.

Who are you? Do you have a gut feel for where you fall on these scales? What does that mean for the type of work you are looking for?

Book to Web

The Career Fit Indicator

You can complete the Career Fit Indicator at **monstercareers.com**. After answering the assessment's questions, you'll receive instant access to a number of resources that will help make your job search more targeted than ever before, including:

- A detailed description of your personality

- An inventory of your most important work values

- Suggested occupations for your type (linked to Monster's job search)

- A list of questions to ask during job interviews, based on your type
- Keywords to include in your resume and cover letters

Remember, the purpose of these tools is to give you a better sense of your preferences. Personality is not destiny. According to career counselor Kristy Meghreblian, a major misconception about personality typing is that the results will tell you what you should be. "Believe me," she says, "there is no fairy that is going to wave her magic wand and say '*Poof!* You should be an architect!' You're going to need to do some research before you get a better grip on what you want to do."

Skills

There are several kinds of skills:

- A *technical skill* is specific and must be learned, like operating a backhoe, computer programming, or using American Sign Language.
- A *motivated ability* is a nontechnical skill that engages you—an ability, talent, or personal quality like listening, persuading, or pattern recognition. Sometimes these are called *aptitudes.* You may learn this or just be "born with it."
- A *specific knowledge* is detailed understanding of a topic, like restaurant health regulations, Spanish literature, or geology. It's not really a skill, but employers often refer to it this way, so it's okay to place it on your skills lists.

As you go through job descriptions, you'll see that many jobs have skills in common, especially the motivated abilities. These "transferable skills" are important when you change jobs; they make the case that you have acquired experience in one field that's relevant to another. For example, skills you developed as a customer service representative—communicating clearly on the phone, listening, problem solving, and empathy—are highly useful in a sales position.

Just listing what you do best isn't always the ticket to an ideal job. You may be skilled at something you don't like to do. For example, you may be technically good at creating a computer spreadsheet, but get no pleasure from working with numbers all day. Richard Knowdell of the Career Planning and Adult Development Network labels these your "burnout skills," and focusing a job around burnout skills is a one-way ticket to an unhappy work life.

Are there skills you are motivated to improve? You may already know what some of these are based on your last performance review. If you have to learn new skills to move on in your career, consider whether you can get on-the-job training in your next position.

Interests

Interests are easy to spot: What energizes you? What activities or subjects engage you for hours? We've talked about the importance of passion; here's your chance to think about what turns you on.

Your interests can lead you to many different professions. A person with a passion for music may be happy as a musician, but also as a producer, choir director, music teacher, promoter, disc jockey, or music retailer.

Make a list of your top interests (as many as you like) on the "Twenty Questions" self-portrait at the end of this chapter. You can include activities or subjects you seek out in books or online. Think about your hobbies and those subjects you love to talk about with friends. Then look for patterns in these interests. The key to translating interests into a career direction is seeing how they may relate (in surprising ways) to work. The Career Directions Inventory™, a career interest assessment, breaks down work interests this way:

Realistic/Practical: People with these interests like physical activity, working with their hands, and practical work such as mechanics or sewing.
- *Job examples:* police and firefighting work, landscaping, construction, product assembly, transportation work

Enterprising: People inclined toward enterprising interests like to lead and persuade others. They are confident, assertive, and adventurous. Money, power, and status are important to them.
- *Job examples:* management, sales, retail, business owner or entrepreneur

Artistic/Communicative: Creative work appeals to people who want to express themselves and their ideas, especially through visual art, music, dance, acting, and discussion or debate. Many subjects interest them, and they don't like routine work.

- *Job examples:* photography, editing, design, broadcasting

Social/Helping: Helping is the key word for these interests, which include teaching, health care, religious or other people-centered work. People with these interests value their qualities of responsibility, sympathy, and kindness.

- *Job examples:* nursing, child welfare work, physical therapy, counseling

Investigative/Logical: This work is for people who like a puzzle. This range of interests includes mathematics, technology, science, and related fields. Curiosity about the physical world motivates people with investigative/logical interests to get satisfaction from a job well done, rather than the approval of others.

- *Job examples:* computer programmer, engineer, business planner

Conventional: This includes a range of interests that demand detail work and logical routine, such as supervising processes or working with numbers. People with these interests are comfortable in big organizations, especially in business; they generally do not like rigorous or dangerous physical work.

- *Job examples:* financial management, accountancy, administration

Serving: These interests focus on the well-being of others, like the social/helping interests, but they are more focused on the comfort and well-being of a wide range of people.

- *Job examples:* restaurant and hotel work, travel agency, personal grooming, clothing care

You might also make a list of activities and topics that *don't* interest you. If you really do not like working with your hands, for example, you can rule out a whole range of careers, such as carpentry, construction, landscaping, and so on.

Book to Web

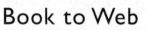

If you're "entry level" and wonder what you can do with that sociology degree, see MonsterTrak's Major to Career Converter: **monstertrak.com/ mtcc/index.html**.

You might look to your favorite recreation or hobby to identify your interests. For example, a pet lover might research what kind of jobs take place in an animal hospital. Someone who loves computer simulation games might explore architecture (design interest), reporting (storytelling interest), or advertising (video production interest) in addition to computer programming.

There are several fine online exercises for helping you determine your interests. See the Resources appendix for a list.

Work Values

The fourth area of assessment is work values. You began thinking about this when you wrote "What's Important to Me" at the end of chapter 3. In fact, research has shown that individuals are much happier in jobs that match their work values. Monster's Career Fit Indicator defines six groups of work values. Try ranking them from 1 to 6 below, starting with your most important value at #1. (We've included a few examples of jobs, all very different, that relate well to each, but remember that jobs are individual situations; to what degree they relate to these values depends on the company culture, job objectives, and so on. Use your chosen priorities as attributes of your personal brand.)

____**Achievement:** To have this value satisfied by your work, you should work in a job that lets you use your best abilities, what you are good at and/or trained to do. In your job, you should see the results of your efforts, and get a feeling of accomplishment through frequent new projects and rewards.

> • *Job examples:* biologist, doctor of medicine (MD), lawyer, managing editor, economist, grant coordinator

____**Independence:** To have this value satisfied by your work, you should look for jobs where they let you do things on your own initiative and where you can make decisions on your own.

- *Job examples:* political scientist, composer, toxicologist, IT manager, instructional coordinator, coach

_____**Recognition:** To have this value satisfied by your work, you should look for jobs with good possibilities for advancement, prestige, and potential for leadership.
- *Job examples:* college administrator, music director, labor relations specialist, airplane dispatcher, producer, technical director, sales manager

_____**Relationships:** To have this value satisfied by your work, you should work in a job where your coworkers are friendly. The job should let you be of service to others, and does not make you do anything that goes against your sense of right and wrong.
- *Job examples:* labor relations manager, language teacher, dentist, orthodontist, public health teacher, athletic trainer

_____**Support:** To have this value satisfied by your work, you should look for jobs where the company stands behind its workers, the workers are comfortable with management's style of supervision, and the company has a reputation for competent and fair management.
- *Job examples:* underwriter, surveying technician, transformer repairperson, chemical engineering technician, insurance agent, utilities manager, radiation protection specialist

_____**Working Conditions:** To have this value satisfied by your work, you should consider pay, job security, and good working conditions when looking at jobs. In addition, look for work that suits your work style, such as being busy all the time, working alone, or having many different things to do.
- *Job examples:* actuary, chiropractor, printer, counseling psychologist, judge, accountant, budget analyst

These values will be useful as springboards for discussion in research, networking, and job interviews. You need to probe how closely a job matches your values, because they're as important to happiness in your job as personality, interests, and skills.

"Don't compromise your values," says career counselor Kristy Meghreblian. "While you should care what others think and want for you, ultimately you must make your own decisions in order to be truly happy." In chapter 3, we discussed values in terms of what you want out of life. Review the values section of your "What's Important to Me" list. Do they agree with some of the priorities you just chose? What jobs might express the values you named?

"Just Remember the Pain"

Want a one-way ticket to career hell? Then take a job for the wrong reasons, says Rob Galford of the Center for Executive Development.

"What are the wrong reasons?" he asks. "Money. Prestige. Revenge. Vindication. Right out of business school, I turned down some really interesting jobs to work at a financial institution. I did it for the money. But the job was so boring it was actually physically painful being there every day. I remember writing 'Just remember the pain' on a piece of paper and sticking it in my wallet. I kept it there for years, as a reminder not to take another job just for the money."

Professional Career Assessment

Professional career assessments compare your personal qualities to those of people in various jobs. If your interests are similar to those of people satisfied by a particular occupation, there's a good chance that you will also be interested in that occupation. Career assessments differ in their focus (personality, skills, interests, values) and in their methods. Some can be taken and the results understood alone; others require a career counselor's interpretation. Some are free and some require payment. You'll find some of the best listed in the Resources at the back of this book. Career assessment has several benefits:

- Assessment results can get you thinking and discussing your real preferences, strengths, and weaknesses.

- Like good career counselors, good career assessments provide some objectivity to your job search.

- Assessments may open your mind to job possibilities you hadn't considered, or help you rule out jobs you wouldn't like.

Why take a career assessment? "It's difficult for candidates to be honest with themselves—everyone wants to think they're the best at everything," says Charles Gerhold. But as useful as assessment can be, says Gerhold,

"You have to take the information more as a guide than as gospel. For example, in the world of career assessment, sales and ministry are actually related. Eventually you have to choose." All these assessments, and the exercises that close this chapter, are meant to get at the timeless truth that you must "Know thyself." As you go through them, and study the results, remember the **Who are you?** question: Are you someone who will settle for a vague idea of what you want, or do you have the courage, dedication, and self-respect to dig deeper?

"I-AM" Exercises

The following Interactive Assessment Materials or I-AM exercises can be taken in any order. Scan them first, and start with the ones that feel right to you. The exercises range from simple to complex, and their main purpose is to provide food for thought. Only you can decide which are most relevant to your job search.

Growing self-awareness—getting real about who you are and what you want—is the emotional foundation of your job search program. Your confident description of your own skills, interests, and values will:

- sharpen your resume,
- light up your networking,
- punch up your interviews, and
- make your F.A.M.E. apparent.

So let's do this!

The Shower

Turn an everyday activity into a brainstorming session.

Don't let anybody tell you how long you can be in the shower. You can reinvent the world in a half-hour shower!

Try thinking about what you want to do with your life while you're in the shower. It works! So take dry-erase markers or china markers into the shower, and if you get a good idea, write it down. Write all over the tile wall!

I know this has happened to you. . . . You're in the middle of your shower and all of a sudden you can't remember whether you washed your hair or not. You look around and make sure no one is looking and you wash it again. Your mind is somewhere else. There's no scientific study to confirm this, but I think both sides of your brain—the creative right side and the logical left side—talk to each other in the shower.

What do you want to be? Write it all out in the shower!

You can download this form at monstercareers.com.

Signature

How much have you changed since you were a child?

I enjoy doing this exercise with individuals or small groups.

Write your signature exactly as it appeared in the fourth grade:

_____

Now write your signature as it appears today:

_____

That fourth-grade signature represents your personality as a kid and your first train-ing. Your signature today represents who you've become. You've changed since you were ten, and it's time to think about those changes.

List five important changes in your values, behavior, or beliefs since you were a kid:

1. _____
2. _____
3. _____
4. _____
5. _____

Do you remember deliberately changing your signature? Why did you change it?

Free Career Counseling

Your family and friends may know you better than you know yourself.

Career expert Barbara Reinhold invented the following shortcut to career counseling.

You probably have a cadre of **free career counselors** within earshot or calling range, anytime you want to listen to what they have to say. Your friends, selected family members, coworkers, coaches, clerics, and supervisors have seen you in action enough to have some ideas about how and where you might do really good work. So make a list of at least ten people you think you could approach, and set to work asking them the following simple questions:

1. If I could magically have whatever skills, experience, or training I would need, what kinds of work could you see me doing well and enjoying?
2. Why? What about me would make me good at those things?
3. Do you know anybody else doing that work?
4. If yes, would you be willing to set me up with an informational interview with that person?

As you can imagine, this is a terrific way to begin making a list of possible fields or jobs for you and, in many cases, a chance to build a list of contacts for eventual informational interviews. These leads are based on the best data in the world: what people think of you.

You can download this form at monstercareers.com.

What Did You Want to Be?

Trace your changing ambitions for clues to your true work.

As our first television ad asked, "What did you want to be?" List some of the ambitions you had as a child:

_____

_____

_____

_____

_____

_____

Now list your ambitions when you were twenty:

_____

_____

_____

_____

_____

_____

List your ambitions now:

_____

_____

_____

_____

_____

_____

Have they changed? How and why? Are these deliberate decisions? What do your growing ambitions mean for your next job?

You can download this form at monstercareers.com.

Heroes

Why do you admire certain people? The answers may guide your ambitions.

Write the name of the living person you admire most:

_____

Write the names of persons from history you admire most:

_____

Now answer the questions below. Try not to judge your answers or the persons you picked. Henry Ford, Mel Gibson, your parents, Wayne Gretsky, Abraham Lincoln, and Mother Teresa are equally valid choices for this exercise.

Why do you admire them?

_____

Would you like to emulate them?

_____

How did they make a living?

_____

What talents, skills, or values do you share with them?

_____

What doubts, fears, or obstacles did they overcome?

_____

What motivated them in their life's work?

_____

How did they feel about money, prestige, power, or autonomy?

_____

What lesson from their lives can you apply to your career?

_____

You can download this form at monstercareers.com.

Twenty Questions

If you like to write, try this career expert's simple self-exploration tool.

Career expert James C. Gonyea, who pioneered online career guidance at America Online in 1987, offers these twenty questions to consider. Write down your answer to each.

1. What subjects do you most enjoy reading about?
2. What television or radio programs do you most enjoy?
3. What are your favorite types of movies?
4. What are your favorite hobbies or pastimes?
5. What type of volunteer activities do you prefer?
6. What subjects do you enjoy discussing with friends?
7. What subjects come to mind when you daydream?
8. What have been your favorite jobs?
9. What were your favorite school subjects?
10. What are your pet peeves?
11. If you doodle, what do you often draw?
12. If you ran the world, what changes would you make?
13. If you won a million bucks, what would you do with it?
14. What are your favorite kinds of people?
15. How would you like to be remembered after your death?
16. What are your favorite toys?
17. How would you describe your political beliefs?
18. Who do you most admire in life and why?
19. What tasks have brought you the most success?
20. What tasks do you think you could do well that you haven't yet done?

Examine your answers. Do you see a certain behavior or belief in more than one aspect of your life? What information do you see repeated that seems to reveal a behavior pattern? What are your long-lasting interests?

Using this information, complete the following statements:

- I am mainly interested in . . .
- I believe most in . . .
- I most value . . .
- For a good life, I feel I need . . .
- I can do the following well . . .

Now ask yourself if your current job helps you achieve the things included in these five statements. If it does, you're probably in the right career. Chances are, however, that the nagging voice means your current career is not satisfying your core. If this is the case, then it's time to find a better fit.

You can download this form at monstercareers.com.

How Much Is Enough?

Balance can be a key to happiness at work. Identify the size of your ambitions for money, power, achievement, and more.

This exercise is about clarifying your life goals. How much money would it take for you to stop worrying about money? How much fame or independence would satisfy you? Would you trade more money for less independence? Would you sacrifice a prestigious job for a more satisfying one with lesser status?

Never settle on someone else's idea of how much you need . . . of anything. Your priorities may change, but you have to make them (or someone else will make them for you).

Describe your "enough" thresholds for the following, and be as specific as possible. Then compare them, and write down which goals you really want to focus your career on achieving.

- Money
- Job satisfaction
- Property (of all kinds, from houses to clothes)
- Security (financial or emotional)
- Prestige
- Mission fulfillment
- Leisure time
- Autonomy/Independence
- Approval (be specific about whose)
- Love

You can download this form at monstercareers.com.

Overcoming Objections

You may have misguided beliefs, assumptions, and perceptions about what you can and can't do. Often, people make career decisions based upon unquestioned assumptions such as, "Careers in finance are more stable" or, "You'll never get a job with an art history degree" or, "People who work on an hourly basis don't get rich." Which ones are standing in the way of you finding your ideal career? Uncover them with the following exercise.

Write the word BUT in the center of a notepad. On the left, write a couple of jobs you wish you could have. On the right, write the reason you can't have it—your objections. Then, answer the following questions about those reasons on the right:

- Where did I first learn this objection? Who told me this?
- What objective proof confirms this objection? Do I know for certain this is true?
- How could I overcome this objection in three years? five years? ten years?
- What related profession is immune to the objection?

Here are two examples:

I want to be a doctor.—BUT—I don't have the education.

What facts do I know about becoming a doctor? Are there longer and shorter training paths? Would other medical jobs (nurse, physician assistant) give me the same satisfaction? What objections might I have to those—prestige, money, ability to help?

I want to write for a leading sports magazine.—BUT—That's the kind of job only well-known reporters can get.

Have I spoken to a writer at one of those magazines about his career path? What were they doing early in their careers? How did they connect with their current job? How do I know I only want to write about sports? Which is critical—writing for a living or being involved in sports for a living?

You can download this form at monstercareers.com.

As you work through the job search program that makes up the rest of this book, I suggest you return to this chapter from time to time to bring your job search back to its center—who you are and what you want in your working life. It's easy to get lost in the details and get off track. When that happens, return to that all-important question, **Who are you?**

PART II
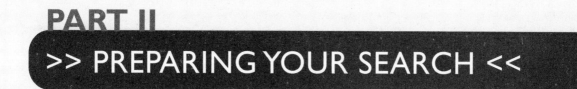
>> PREPARING YOUR SEARCH <<

The easy way out usually leads back in!

By that I mean, if you want to find a great new job, you need to work hard at it. Taking the easy way out—for example, applying for jobs you know you're not qualified to do—will lead you back into the same situation you hoped to leave: unemployed or unhappy at work, and looking for another job. I suspect you're anxious to apply for jobs today. You're already studying online job listings. Maybe you've sent off a few resumes. But . . .

If you really want a better job, do what it takes to perform a better job search. After you land a job, you're going to spend a lot of time at work—30 to 50 percent of your waking hours. That's worth an investment of time toward finding the right job. Make that investment because a little extra effort now will pay big dividends later.

You need to do this because employers' expectations are higher today than ever before. Kent Kirsch, global director of recruiting for Deloitte, the professional services firm, notes that even though Internet recruiting has shortened hiring time from three weeks to a few days, in some cases, candidates are still expected to be fully prepared to make their case when an employer calls. Are you really ready to win this competition if the call of your life comes tomorrow afternoon? What if it comes two minutes after you apply for a job online? Can you stand out from the other fifty candidates in less than a minute?

In part I of this book, you learned the lay of the land—the facts that shape today's job market, the decisions only you can make about what you want in a job, and the people you'll meet in a job search.

Part II is all about preparing for that better job search.

- You'll learn to create a real job search timetable, budget, and goals.

- You'll prepare critical documents like a resume, cover letter(s), and a list of work achievements.

- You'll learn how to train like an athlete to ace the job interview.

In part III, you'll learn how to take that knowledge and preparation to the job marketplace, as you research the job market, apply for jobs online and offline, and network to find new opportunities.

In part IV, you will get in front of employers with a more compelling case than your competition. Once you land a job, you'll swing into the art of negotiating the best deal, and you'll plan a transition that gets your new job off to a successful start.

Most job seekers start their search with a lot of activity . . . for two days. Then they run out of ideas, and wonder if they're doing everything they can to find a job. You will not have that problem. Follow this plan, and you'll be running your search like a full-time business. And by the way, you'll get a job a lot faster.

7 >> Plan Your Job Search <<

I t's time to plan your search and work that plan like an entrepreneur building a business. Whether your search takes two weeks, two months, or even longer, the steps in the *Monster Careers* program will show you how to approach employers with confidence and power. Raise your expectations; go for your dream job—but don't just dream about it. Get yourself into high gear—*now* . . . and make it happen.

A Model Job Search Plan

There are three phases to a job search: preparation, getting up to speed, and going after job opportunities. The following ten-week model gives you two weeks to get ready, three weeks to enter the marketplace, and five weeks of daily routines that keep the right job opportunities flowing through your job search "pipeline."

Ten weeks is a suggestion, and you will adjust your own timetable as you go. Your job search may take more or less time based on uncontrollable factors like a changing economy, your level of experience, and the number of qualified applicants in your local area. You might want to adjust the time for each step based on your financial needs or level of seniority.

Plan for your search to take longer than you think, and you'll be pleasantly surprised if you get a job quickly.

You are your own boss now, so set yourself a tough schedule. Most job seekers seem to start at 9:00 and run out of ideas by 10:30. But if you're unemployed now, looking for work is your full-time job. Ten weeks give you 400 hours, and you can get a lot done in 400 hours.

Prepare—two weeks.

Give yourself two weeks to get organized and create the documents you'll need for your search. If you haven't completed the I-AM exercises in chapter 6, this is also the time to do them.

- **Chapter 7:** This chapter contains practical advice on how to manage your time, budget, and priorities. Whether you're unemployed now or "just looking" while you have a job, the information in this chapter will help you get to that dream job as quickly as possible.

- **Chapter 8:** Here, you'll prepare documents that help you create a memorable message to employers about your skills and experiences. These will become the basis for preparing your resume in chapter 10 and cover letters in chapter 11.

- **Chapter 9:** Eventually, you have to convince people face-to-face that you're right for the job, and practicing your "pitch" builds confidence. You'll create a framework for delivering your pitch, as well as a unique document for networking. You will be able to walk into a job interview or a networking meeting feeling strong and self-assured.

- **Chapter 10:** Your resume is your selling tool, and there is no substitute for a good one. I'll show you how to write a compelling resume, customized to your particular situation and formatted in the necessary print and electronic versions.

- **Chapter 11:** Your job search is a competition. You have to stand out among a huge numbers of candidates. A powerful, three-part cover letter or e-mail message gets attention when you apply for a job.

Don't skip the exercises in chapters 7 to 9! You may be tempted to jump ahead to the separate chapters about resumes, cover messages, research, applying for jobs, networking, and job interviews, but chapters 7 to 9 are the building blocks of a great job search, and you'll be better at all the other steps if you go through these three critical chapters first.

Get up to speed—three weeks.

When your documents are prepared, you're ready to find out which jobs are available, which employers interest you, and how to approach them. During the next three weeks, you'll start applying for jobs online and networking with others who can connect you to jobs.

- **Chapter 12:** Knowledge is power, and when you're a candidate, research gives you the edge over less well-prepared competition. I'll show you where and how to find out about jobs, employers, and industries on the Internet, in the library, and in informational interviews.
- **Chapter 13:** You will apply for the best jobs you can find at Internet job sites, company Web sites, and other places. Then, you'll go beyond the listed jobs to go directly into the "hidden" job market.
- **Chapter 14:** Networking may be the most powerful technique in your job search. Build a strong personal network, and you'll connect to jobs in ways you never imagined.

Go after opportunity—five weeks.

They say that twenty-one days of practice makes a habit, so after three weeks of this job search, you're really working at full throttle. Now that everything's running, it's a step-and-repeat process until you're hired. During the next five weeks, fill your pipeline with a set of companies, job possibilities, and networking contacts that you diligently explore. Your research and networking expand your web of contacts, sharpen your presentation, and locate promising companies and jobs. You apply for jobs, interview, and follow up.

During these weeks you'll continue to research, apply for jobs, and network. As you approach the finish line, you need to know about three more steps:

- **Chapter 15**: The job interview is the big show, the time all your work comes together in a face-to-face meeting with an employer. I'll show how your preparation turns a scary interrogation into a confident conversation.

- **Chapter 16:** You got the job offer! Before you say yes, discuss all the details. You can get the best possible deal with some easy, professional negotiating tactics.

- **Chapter 17:** Your first one hundred days in a new job can make the difference between success and so-so job performance. Here's how to plan for success.

People make the mistake of slowing down their program as soon as they get two or three "hopefuls"—but you must keep filling your pipeline. As a busy candidate, you'll get employers' attention, and the only thing better than a job offer is multiple job offers!

Follow the "add another day" plan.

Are you working *and* hunting? Whether you are currently working twenty or forty hours a week, or have responsibilities that cut back your available hours, the ten-week plan above may be too ambitious. The plan that follows is equally viable and will help you get the job you want!

In this situation you have to "add another day" to your working week to find a better job. That doesn't mean you have to work all day Saturday, but that you devote eight hours every week to the search. You could, for example, work this program two evening hours each Tuesday and Thursday and four hours on Saturday. "Add another day" will test your commitment to your career. It takes discipline to carve those hours out of your nonwork time. This process may take more weeks to complete than a full-time job search, but if you stick to your commitment, you'll get that momentum!

Can you add more than eight hours? Sure, but you'll need to determine where to find them. Open your calendar and mark down what tasks you will do and when. Making a big to-do list and then not getting to it, or filling a calendar and ignoring it, won't get you anywhere. If you identify the hours that you have and actually work this program in those hours, you will be astonished at your progress.

In the "add another day" plan, you should not let your ambition to find a new job contaminate your current job. This also means you shouldn't steal eight hours a week from your current employer. While respecting your current employer with a full day's work, respect your own privacy by doing the following:

- Center your job search from home. Don't leave job research notes scattered around your workplace.

- Set up private e-mail separate from work e-mail (just taking this deliberate step may signal your seriousness of purpose to yourself).

- Don't search online through the company network. A huge number of companies legally monitor employees' Internet use (although they rarely tell employees this).

- Give your cell phone or home phone number for contact information.

Arrange job search–related calls and meetings well in advance. If you have to take a search-related call during your workday, ask to call back from a private location. This is one of those times a private cell phone really helps! Even if you have to go across the street to call from a public phone, make the effort. Your prospective next employer should respect your need for privacy.

Plan your time.

Whether you're searching full time or part time, you need to plan and organize those hours. If you've recently been laid off and need time to clear your head before a job search, take it. Don't overdo it, though—a lot of job seekers say they regret the three months they took off after losing a job. That fact should inspire you to get started. You have to get back into the game as soon as you're ready.

Writing a resume, networking, researching, and applying for jobs all take time. It helps, even at this early stage, to start a to-do list of tasks and mark time in your calendar to complete them. For example, you may need one or even two full days to prepare your resume (see chapter 10). Give yourself the time you need up front to write a great one; that investment will pay off in job interviews later.

If you use a handheld computer or notebook-style planner, use it to plan your time and keep track of your tasks. You can use any time-management tool you like—the important thing is to use it. When you write down a time to do a task, think of it as a significant appointment, as important as a job interview. Especially if you are currently unemployed, with a whole "empty" day confronting you each morning, you will have to generate this kind of discipline to keep the job search moving.

You will find a number of exercises in chapters 7 to 12 that build your job search up to a steady rhythm of activity. Soon you will be busier than you imagined! Many people find that their estimated time to prepare their materials—resume, cover letters, and the like—changes from a few days to a couple of weeks. That's okay if it means you are improving the quality of your search. It's a smart move to re-estimate your timeline once a week or so, as you learn how long some actions actually take. But don't be intimidated. Writing it down will jump-start your process, and set the tone for the rest of your search.

This is the time you really have to buckle down. If your plan calls for your resume to be ready Tuesday, ask yourself on Monday morning if it's done. If not, get yourself in the chair and get writing.

Plan your expenses.

Your job search will cost time *and* money, and the sooner you get real about both, the more effective your plan will be. A job search doesn't have to be expensive, however. For someone who's unemployed, the much bigger worry is lost income. Money worries can complicate a good search plan because, frankly, the more time you put into a quality job search, the longer you'll go without bringing in money. If you're unemployed, check your situation with the simple worksheet on page 103.

Now look at #5. If it looks like bad news, you're not alone. In a Monster poll, 70 percent of respondents told us their savings would last less than three months if they lost their jobs. Only 15 percent could hang on for more than six months on their savings alone.

Financial professionals have long advised their clients to save at least six months of living expenses for emergencies. During a slowdown or recession, one year or even eighteen months seems more prudent.

But if you are unemployed now, and don't have much savings, you still have choices:

- Decrease your expenses.
- Increase your earned income, either by finding temporary work in your field or with a "Plan C" job, whose only purpose is to support you while you look for work (see page 112). One common tactic: find a part-time "Plan C" job and use the rest of your time to hunt for the right full-time position.
- Gain support from another source.

BUDGET WORKSHEET

1.	Your monthly expenses (everything you know: food, transportation, entertainment, taxes, rent, insurance, debt payments—all of it)	$$$ amount
2.	Your monthly income now (from severance, unemployment insurance, rental income, temporary job, and all other sources)	$$$ amount
3.	Subtract #1 from #2. This is how much it costs you each month to be unemployed.	$$$ amount
4.	How much savings are you willing to spend to support a full-time search? (Include your best estimate of out-of-pocket expenses, like getting resumes printed or paying dues to a networking group.)	$$$ amount
5.	Divide #4 by #3. This is how many months you have to look full-time without bringing in additional income (and without creating too much burden on your family, your financial future, and so on).	time

You can download this form at monstercareers.com.

Recognizing trade-offs is the key to sound budgeting, so go through your expenses item-by-item and decide if you need to cut back. Making a few cuts in expenses, even small ones, might signal you're taking this process seriously. Make the most of free help from libraries, government employment services, and friends (we'll cover these in chapters 12 to 14).

If you've been laid off, check with your state's office of employment services to find out your eligibility for unemployment benefits. It's astonishing how many people incorrectly think they are not eligible for these state-mandated benefits. Even if you got a severance package, chances are you can collect unemployment money. Some states also provide supplemental money for health insurance plans. This can amount to hundreds of dollars a month!

If you're currently employed, your income can sustain a longer job search. Time to search, however, is harder to find. To get in gear, see the "add another day" plan on page 100.

The basic items needed for a job search aren't expensive, but you should budget a little money for business cards, printed resumes, and investments in your appearance such as a haircut and a nice suit.

M any job search expenses (even driving to and from job interviews) are tax-deductible. Save your receipts. You may not collect the money until next year, but it can end up being a surprising sum. Detailed information is available from the IRS. Go to **irs.gov/formspubs/** and search on "unemployment benefits."

Set up a place to work.

"One of the hardest things about a job search is creating a center for it," says John Rossheim, Monster senior contributing writer. "You need a place and time in your day where other to-do lists won't intrude." Look into the possibility of setting aside a room in your house or apartment as a home office. This may provide you with tax benefits along with a place to focus your efforts. Your work space doesn't have to be large. Anywhere that is free of distractions will do. A room with a door is good (work with the door shut!). If that's not available, a quiet corner, a kitchen table, or the desk where you pay the monthly bills can be the right space. At a minimum, you must have the following:

- a filing system (paper and/or electronic)
- an e-mail account (today you cannot afford *not* to have one):
    - from a free Web service such as AOL, MSN, or Yahoo!
    - from your college
    - from a professional organization
    - from an Internet Service Provider
- a telephone with answering machine or voice mail
- a way to take notes
- a calendar, handheld computer, or PDA (personal digital assistant)
- a way to keep track of addresses such as a Rolodex, card file, or electronic equivalent
- stationery and envelopes

Everything else falls on a sliding scale of cost, convenience, and sophistication. The following are enormously productive in a search:

- a personal computer and printer
- a home Internet connection
- common office supplies such as a stapler, dictionary, thesaurus, and calculator

Internet-connected computers are generally available in libraries, schools, and government centers. Don't shell out $2,000 for a cool new laptop unless you can afford it. (Besides, there's a glut of used equipment at Internet auction sites or in the local want ads that can provide all you need at a fraction of the cost.)

It was common in the last ten years to recommend a home fax machine, but e-mail has made faxes much less important, and recruiters tell us that faxing resumes should be a last resort.

April Young, who runs Monster's phone support group for job seekers, tells us she gets calls from all sorts of places: "People call us from libraries; they call us on their cell phones from anywhere; they call us from career centers and state job offices and cyber-cafes." As long as you are organized, technology has made it possible for your search to be mobile.

Keep track of everything.

Monster senior contributing writer John Rossheim points out that keeping good records gives you a competitive edge. "Recruiters tell me this nightmare happens all the time," say John. "They get a resume, call the candidate, and the candidate asks, 'What was that job? Which resume did I send you?' This is a killer. If they hear that, they'll use it as a way to eliminate you. . . . You are memorable to the extent that you can recall specific approaches you used with an employer. You need a simple record of what you did—a journal or file that documents who you approached, and when, and which version of a resume or letter you've used."

As you build your job search, keeping information organized becomes critical. I'll remind you as you work through your job search where to make files. It only takes a few minutes a day to keep these files organized, and the payoff is a shorter, more productive job search.

If you are already an organized person, feel free to adapt your files to best suit your style. If you're the type who "just can't stay organized," you may need to give this step some extra effort. By all means use whatever organizational tools work best for you. Some people like a lot of paper—folders, files, paper forms, napkins with scribbled notes. Some only keep electronic files in their PC or handheld computer.

These files will give form to your search, and you'll return to them over and over. Sometimes, when you're wondering what to do next, just looking through your files can get things moving again. When a recruiter calls, you should be able to scan your folders and casually open your conversation, whether you keep your computer desktop open or use a file system.

Dave Trance of the IT consulting services firm CTG points out another reason to keep good records: you may need that documentation to qualify for unemployment payments, because they are proof you're actively looking for work (which can be a requirement for collecting unemployment benefits).

Stay productive.

China Miner Gorman, president of global outplacement firm Lee Hecht Harrison, describes three key behaviors that bring a job search to success. "Our data show that the people who are most successful [in the job search] are highly organized, are focused on getting face-to-face with decision-makers, and diligently follow up with those decision-makers." It follows that the activities that drive you toward face-to-face meetings are the most productive.

Don't surf the Internet all day. Automate tasks to save time. During your search, use self-discipline, priority lists, and routine to avoid diversions. Online, you can automate the job search with tools like those found in "My Monster."

Monster Member Michelle: Do Whatever It Takes

Michelle posted this fantastic program on our message board. It shows what a solid job search program can do.

"I created a job log and I began networking with everyone! I also created a 'brag book' about myself. Finally, I created files on each company with all the information I could find.

"The job log was important in so many ways. First, it made me see on paper that I was doing all I could to get a job. Second, it helped me keep track of my progress, any rejection letters I had received, what companies I had sent information to, whom I spoke with, what dates and how much time I spent at the job service center printing off information about every company, what newspapers I purchased, and when and what jobs I applied for from each newspaper. Best of all, it ended up helping me a great deal once I got interviews.

"My brag book contained several copies of my resume, a copy of my degree, a list of all my activities, sports, and awards from high school on. I also included letters of recommendation for past jobs. I even included 2 letters from physicians [because] I was trying to become a pharmaceutical representative, and both letters of recommendation from the physicians stated they would like having me in their offices as a rep. In the end, the brag book I took to interviews was 17 pages long.

"The result: I had 2 job offers and had to withdraw myself from a final interview for a third!"

Book to Web

Go to **monstercareers.com** for tools described in this book. Go to **my.monster.com** for additional job search tools and services.

The key is getting to the most important items first, every day. So much of a good job search is time-intensive work (interviews, customizing a resume for a particular job, self-assessment, and research) that anything you can do to get to those priority items first will shorten the length of your search.

Have a routine.

Friends who work at home tell us that establishing a routine really helps. Try to start at the same time each day, and figure out a time when you're at your best. If you work best from 1 to 5 in the morning, more power to you. If you're used to working on a 9-to-5 schedule, work 9 to 5. Make sure you give yourself a routine that's realistic and stick to it. Good things happen if you stay in that chair.

Monster member Charles Camiel discussed how the power of routine helped his search. "To stay productive, I had a standard agenda: Get up every morning just like when I was employed, shower, have breakfast, and get to work." He adds, "How did I keep up with my industry in my last job? Read *The Wall Street Journal* or check an online site. Do that first. Then make some calls, check your online job search agents, or go to an information interview."

If you have to conduct your search outside your home, you should still keep your schedule. Routine can be honored in the library, too.

Manage your time.

There's no way to know exactly how long your search will take; only ways to make each hour count. To get there as fast as possible, you have to manage your time well. Many people think that only means getting more to-dos checked off their list, which usually results in trying to do two things at once. Instead, says Robert Dunham, founder of executive consulting firm Action in Management, you need to focus your attention on *results*. "The key is to get clear what outcome you want from your actions," he says.

Ask yourself each morning:

- What do I want to accomplish by the end of this day?
- What actions must I take to accomplish this?
- How long will each action realistically take?

Dunham continues: "After you lay out what results you want, actually track what you do and what gets produced. Write it down. Then say no to everything else that gets in the way."

Focus on the most productive activities first, or maybe the things you find hardest to do, like cold calling companies on your target list. For many people, this is the hardest part of a job search.

Finally, when your workday is almost done, learn what worked. Ask yourself:

- What did I want for an outcome today (a resume written, a connection made, a good job interview)?

- Was I focused on the right tasks?

- Did I waste time on the wrong tasks?

- Am I balancing my job search with the rest of my life (no matter how urgent my search)?

Getting more of the wrong stuff done in a day is a waste of a life, and that goes double for a job search. It's unlikely you can create strong, thoughtful applications for twenty jobs every morning. Two or three a day is more realistic. Whatever number you pick, stick to it or be tough on yourself—make up the shortfall the next day!

Set priorities.

Listed below are the actions you will learn in the next few chapters of this book. I've grouped them here by importance. Priority 1 items are key elements of the Monster career program. They're the fastest route to a new job, so do them first. Priority 2 items are also important but less time-sensitive. For activities you haven't done yet, I've listed the chapter where you will learn about them.

PRIORITY 1

- Completing self-assessment exercises (chapter 6)

- Completing the job search documents (chapter 8)

- Preparing your "pitch" (chapter 9)

- Writing a resume and drafting cover letters (chapters 10 and 11)

- Sending a customized job application and cover letter (chapter 13)
- Sending a resume requested by a recruiter (chapter 13)
- Posting a resume in an online database (chapter 13)
- Following up on calls and letters (chapters 13 and 14)
- Networking (chapter 14)
- Completing a job interview (chapter 15)

PRIORITY 2

- Administration—filing, organizing, time management (chapter 7)
- Job and company research (chapter 12)
- Automating job search tasks such as setting up an online job service to e-mail job opportunities to you automatically (chapter 13)
- Completing an information interview (chapter 14)
- Receiving a referral name (chapter 14)

The following items are very common in a typical job search, but they have little value. Don't give in to the temptation to do these time-wasters.

LOW/NO PRIORITY

- E-mailing or faxing resumes indiscriminately
- Sending "to whom it may concern" cover letters
- Applying to long-shot jobs
- Surfing the Web without a specific goal

And on those days when you just can't seem to think of anything to do, remember the entrepreneur's bias toward action. Take this advice from a Monster member who uses the name yonder910: "If your resume isn't getting you the interviews you need, revamp it. If you're not making it to the second interview, figure out why. If you want a job, you're going to have to give it your all, 24/7—weekends included."

Have a "Plan B"

What happens if jobs in your "first-choice" category are just too scarce? What if your "first-choice" jobs don't pay enough, or are mostly located in another part of the country? You need to have a "Plan B."

When you're just starting a job search, you don't know what you're going to discover about a new job you're considering. You also don't know what the future will hold in terms of economic growth/recession, or the rise and fall of different businesses. That's why, just as you invest considerable time and effort in developing a "Plan A" for your job or career change, it's wise to spend at least a little time and effort developing a "Plan B."

Your Plan B job should work well with the skills, experience, and work values you explored in chapter 6. I-AM exercises such as "What Did You Want to Be?" on page 87, and "Twenty Questions" on page 89 may already have suggested alternatives. Examples of a Plan B include:

- deciding to relocate
- finding the job you want in a different business from the one you expected
- identifying other jobs that need your skills and experience
- deciding to change careers entirely

For many, Plan B isn't a complete change in job outlook but an adjustment. For example, they decide to be more flexible on the *where* part of their roadmap by considering relocation. Lynn M. Arts of Johnson Controls, Inc., a large manufacturing firm, points out that this may evolve into your Plan A. "Relocation is critical to our business," she says. "In order to find the right long-term career here, you have to be open to it."

Plan B may just be a "backup" career that you would enjoy. For example, Gail's ambition was always to pursue a career as a university career counselor. She field-tested the idea through volunteer work and eventually got a degree in counseling, and a series of positions. Now she's a career counselor at a midwestern university. All the while, however, she explored and kept her eye on a Plan B: real estate sales. She obtained a real estate agent's license, which she continues to maintain as an insurance policy. She's ready to start a new career if that becomes necessary.

Keep that Plan B simmering on the back burner until you start your new job. You will have more leverage in negotiation, expand your contacts, and broaden your long-term career vision. You'll also feel more secure.

Do You Need a "Plan C"?

If you're out of work and don't have much money in the bank, you may have to consider the "Plan C" job, a situation that is meant only to pay the bills while you continue to search for the job you really want.

Plan C jobs are like working your way through school. Some candidates attach a sense of failure to this, but there's no shame in supporting yourself. Going to Plan C doesn't mean you're settling for a second-rate career path, either. And it doesn't tell employers you're desperate. On the contrary, it shows you are active and embracing your responsibilities.

It helps, of course, if the job is related to your chosen field or takes place at one of your target companies. Sometimes, Plan C leads directly to Plan A. For example, a candidate for an account management job in a packaged goods company may find a first job as a customer service representative at the same company.

Another version of Plan C is short-term consulting, and it's an exciting alternative. You may be able to help a company—especially a target company—with a specific problem on a contract basis. Some candidates turn this into a "try before you buy" opportunity and, if they do a good job, they'll have the inside track for the next open position.

The cost of taking a temporary, contract, or consulting assignment when your real goal is full-time employment is that it will extend the time your job search takes. A more subtle risk is that this work can occupy so much of your attention that your job search just stops. In the end, Plan C is another time-cost-quality trade-off.

Again, Work Like an Entrepreneur

This is hard work, and you have to work hard. It's not easy to plan, prepare, and produce a great job search, but it's much harder work to keep looking fruitlessly for a job. And it's misery to spend one-third of your life in a job you don't like, so think big!

If you embrace the hard work up front, you'll soon find that this job search will pay off. Most jobs keep you focused on one set of responsibilities and tasks. The work of a job search keeps you focused on a world of possibilities. You will discover new interests. You will learn an enormous amount. You will gain skills that can make you better at *all* your activities. And your self-knowledge and curiosity about the world of work will make you a more dynamic person—exactly the kind of person a company wants and an employer wants to hire!

Career Management Will Make You a Stronger Employee

There's another benefit to really working a job search plan. Since most schools don't teach you how to look for work, you don't always develop these talents. Those talents and techniques are highly transferable to your work. In fact, career management while you work can make you better at your job.

Here are some of the skills you'll practice in a really great job search that will make you a better employee, one more likely to get the really great opportunities:

- Present ideas clearly.
- Research a marketplace.
- Persuade people to talk to you.
- Discuss shortcomings openly.
- Put a positive spin on negative information.
- Persevere through difficulties and dry spells.
- Become a self-starter.

8 >> Build a Job Search Portfolio <<

F.A.M.E. ATTITUDE: PREPARE LIKE A MARKETER

Deliver a memorable message.

Now that you have planned your search, it's time to get moving. In these first few days of your plan, you will create the most important materials in your job search: a master collection of documents that will showcase your best work and the full range of your talents. Your resume and cover letters will grow easily out of these documents. Your "sales pitch" in job interviews will grow confidently out of what you create in this chapter. Together, I call these documents your Job Search Portfolio.

Your Job Search Portfolio will include the following documents:

- key messages
- employment history
- achievement stories
- skills
- personal story
- references
- certifications

Book to Web

To make your job easier, every document in the Job Search Portfolio is available at **monstercareers.com**. You can copy each as a formatted document to your computer, and fill in the blanks with as many words as you require. You can then edit the document like any other.

This chapter contains blank forms for each document. If you choose to make copies of your documents, create a Job Search Portfolio file and keep it handy. You will refer to these documents many times during your search.

Your Job Search Portfolio is central to your ability to land the job you want, so take the time to write it carefully. The documents it contains will identify your strengths and weaknesses and turbocharge your search. For example, you will need specific examples about your achievements to make a strong impression in a job interview, and you'll prepare them in the "Your Achievement Stories" section on page 127. If you want to write a powerful resume, you must identify your strongest selling points. Do you *really* know what they are? Your Job Search Portfolio will make them stand out like a neon sign. Finally, your Job Search Portfolio continues the path of self-discovery you started in chapter 6. The very act of listing your skills, achievements, and interests will boost your confidence and confirm your decisions about your perfect job.

The first step is to develop the most important statements about you, called your key messages.

Key Messages

As we've seen, time-stressed recruiters can't absorb complex messages about you in the early stages of hiring. You won't get your foot in the door without a set of clear, consistent messages describing who you are and what you do. In the world of marketing, these are called key messages; they're the powerful statements that distinguish one brand from its competition.

For example, a key message of Volvo cars is that they are safe. Whatever Volvo's marketing says about an individual model, it also says, "this is a really safe car." Other cars carry different key messages—"fun to drive," "tough," or "economical," for example—but when people are thinking of buying a really safe car, they often think of Volvo.

An employer wants to know what you promise as a candidate. They may be looking for "reliable," "creative," "a go-getter," or any of the qualities you possess, but they won't find those qualities unless you clearly state them and prove them. They ask, "Who are you?" and you answer, "This is exactly who I am. . . ."

Actually, you could give a hyper-condensed answer to that with just four key words, but if I ask you to capture yourself in four words right now, you'd likely be paralyzed. So let's build a roadmap of your key messages first, and from there we'll get it down to four key words.

Writing Your Key Messages

The first step in writing your key messages is to answer the classic reporter's questions: Who, What, Where, When, How, and Why. Think of an employer asking those questions in this way:

Who are you?

What are your skills?

Where do you want to work?

When and **How** have you done your best work in the past?

Why should I hire you?

Answer those questions by following the instructions below. I'll give you examples of answers, but writing a key message is very personal, so go ahead and write what you need to customize *your* job search. If you've completed the I-AM exercises in chapter 6, reflect on some of those statements as you write.

When you're done, you'll bring all the answers together on a single form on page 122, a ready reference of your best selling points throughout your search.

Who: Complete the sentence *"My name is _____, and I'm a(n) _____."* It's easy enough to use a job title (*"My name is Patricia Kidd, and I'm a marketing manager"*) but it's much stronger to put forward your personal brand with a colorful description of your work. Create your own reputation! For example:

- [marketing manager] *My name is Patricia Kidd, and I'm an inspired builder of great brands.*

117

- [sales representative] *My name is Lois Delgado, and I'm a classic closer.*

- [landscaper] *My name is Robin Stein, and I'm an artist who works in plants.*

You can take another tack, stating the results of your work:

- [911 dispatcher] *My name is Chris Eifler, and I get the right help where it's needed—fast.*

- [hotel manager] *My name is Maryellen Wilson, and I make people feel comfortable when they're far from home.*

- [court reporter] *My name is Robert Bellonci, and I create quick, accurate records of complex legal proceedings.*

Emphasize your most important selling points. For example, because speed and accuracy are the critical skills for court reporters, the last example above stresses speed and accuracy.

Write your **Who** statement here:

My name is _____,

and I'm a(n) _____.

What: Complete the sentence *"My strengths are* _____.*"* This is the place to showcase your top skills, abilities, and expertise. In your roadmap, feature both your skills and expertise that are most in demand as well as those that are most important to you.

- [computer programmer] *My strengths are programming in PERL, ASP, Java, and other Web-building languages, as well as team leadership.*

- [interpreter] *My strengths are simultaneous translation in Russian and French, with special expertise in the vocabulary of business.*

- [social worker] *My strengths are gaining trust and cooperation from individuals in crisis, with special knowledge of domestic abuse issues.*

Another powerful approach is to state clearly what kinds of problems you solve:

- [administrative assistant] *My strength is that I solve managers' most difficult time-management problems.*

- [quality-control manager] *My strength is preventing errors in manufacturing.*

Write your **What** statement here, either your strengths or the problems you solve:

My strength is _____

_____ .

Where: Complete the sentence *"I want to work in/at _____."* Write as many particulars about the location, size, and culture of your ideal company, and your ideal job's working conditions.

Here is an area where *you* need to stay flexible. Carolyn Culbreth, executive vice president of The Corporate Source Group, points out that being open to several locations powers up your search. She says, "If you broaden your search, even in tough times, you can be in a position to have more than one employer interested in you. That boosts your confidence and raises the perception of your value."

- [architect] *I want to work in a small, privately owned office (fewer than ten associates) within 20 miles of Indianapolis. The practice will focus on high-end residential properties.*

- [power distributor] *I want to work in a large, publicly owned power facility in the Midwest that runs on a three-shift schedule.*

- [customer service representative] *I want to work in a profitable financial services company within thirty minutes' drive of my home that values work/life balance.*

- [range manager] *I want to work for a state (first choice) or federal (second choice) conservation agency. Roughly 75% of my working time should be spent outdoors in the Rocky Mountain region.*

Write your **Where** statement here:

I want to work in/at _____

_____ .

When and How: Complete the sentence *"I've achieved the following: _____."* Fill in highlights of your work achievements. You can add achievements outside of work if they are relevant to your next job. Write as many statements as you can, and use numbers wherever possible.

119

In the section called "Your Achievement Stories," page 127, you'll create a document that will go into greater detail about these. You will need that document later, when you rehearse your sales pitch. For now, however, just identify your best achievements, as in the following examples:

- [commercial driver] *I achieved a perfect safety record and a 90% on-time record over 5 years of handling transportation and delivery of hazardous liquid materials.*

- [nurse manager] *I was able to decrease rehabilitation staff turnover by 50% in 18 months, while meeting patient-care standards.*

- [events planner] *I directed 22 volunteer coaches in a rotating schedule of 14 youth soccer teams in Lynchburg.*

- [product manager] *I directed the development and marketing of Spingy organic breath freshener, with sales of $8.7 million in 2003.*

Write your **When and How** statement here:

I've achieved the following: _____

_____ .

Why: Complete the sentence *"The benefit to you (or your customers) is* _____." Why should they hire you? Describe the main benefit to your employer (or their customers) of hiring you.

You want to give this statement some thought. Fred Nothnagel of career counseling firm R. L. Stevens Associates tells beginning job seekers that there are only five business reasons to hire someone. "You must do one or more of these," says Fred:

- Improve product quality.

- Improve customer service.

- Cut cost of doing business.

- Create new products or services.

- Sell or market the company's products and brand.

I'd add a couple of wild cards to Fred's list. These are critical questions any employer will ask:

- Would I like working next to this person?

- Would I follow this person?

- Does this person show leadership? Are they not only convincing but also compelling?
- Is this person a cultural fit with my company?

Again, write as many statements as you can, such as:

- [product inspector] *The benefit to you is a satisfied customer, because I assure the flawless operation and quality of your products before they leave the factory.* [Improve product quality.]

- [customer support phone representative] *The benefit of my friendly and patient advice to your customers is that they have a good experience with your company even if they have a problem using the product.* [Improve customer service.]

- [technical writer] *The benefit of my clarity and thoroughness is decreased calls to the customer service 800 number.* [Cut cost of doing business.]

- [product development manager] *The benefit of my team leadership is a steady stream of new products for your customers.* [Create new products or services.]

- [warehouse manager] *The benefit of my experience managing inventory is more efficient use of your existing delivery fleet.* [Cut cost of doing business.]

- [graphic designer] *The benefit to you is an outstanding reflection of your brand message in every product brochure, resulting in increased sales.* [Market the company's products and/or brand.]

Write your statement about **why** an employer should hire you here. If you have several benefits, write them all in your statement:

The benefit to you (or your customers) is _____

_____ .

Putting Them All Together

Now that you've written your Who, What, Where, When/How, and Why statements, consolidate them all into a single page using the form on page 122. Your key messages are now ready to use, but you don't have to think of them as "finished." You may think of additional statements as you go through your search; write those down, too.

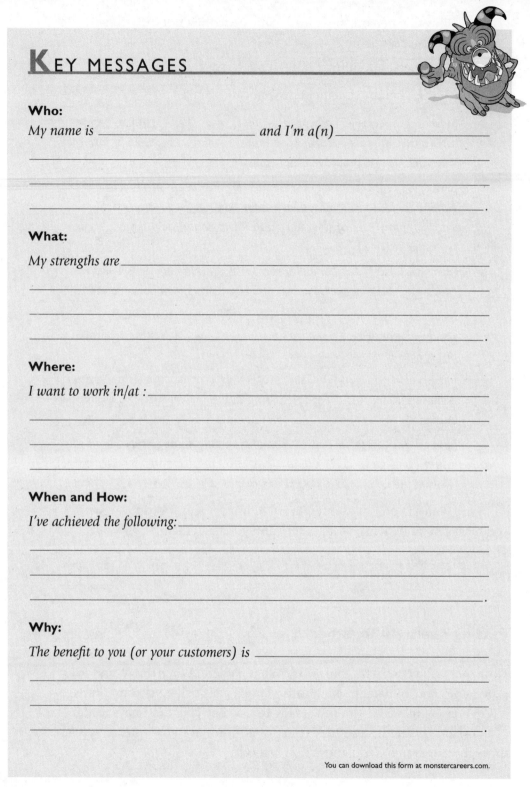

KEY MESSAGES

Who:

My name is _____ *and I'm a(n)* _____

_____

_____

_____ .

What:

My strengths are _____

_____

_____

_____ .

Where:

I want to work in/at : _____

_____

_____

_____ .

When and How:

I've achieved the following: _____

_____

_____

_____ .

Why:

The benefit to you (or your customers) is _____

_____

_____

_____ .

You can download this form at monstercareers.com.

Key Words

Now you're ready to consolidate your key messages into four key words, which help you focus yourself and your message. One minute before you go into a job interview, you won't have time to remember all the answers to all the questions that may be asked, but you can repeat to yourself the four words that capture the essence of your personal brand. When the recruiter who found your resume in a file calls unexpectedly, you can rely on those four key words to get your message across.

It may seem like a contradiction, but the first step in boiling your messages down is to broaden your thinking about them a little. Look for patterns among your key messages. Do certain qualities come through in all of them? What does each key message say about you? Are some messages stronger than others? Grab a notepad or sit in front of the computer and begin to write about each key message in detail. Maybe they say you are reliable, technical, diligent, a cost-cutter. Maybe they say that you're sales-minded, a leader, an "out of the box" thinker. Maybe they say you are focused on results, or efficiency, or great teamwork. Write as much as you like. Keep the pencil on the paper or your fingers on the keyboard for thirty minutes or more.

Show your key messages to your best friends, parents, partner, kids, boss, or peers, and ask, "What's the pattern here? What does this say about me? How would you describe me?" Write down what they say as well. Then study everything you've written and do the following:

1. Consolidate the best of what you wrote into four paragraphs about yourself. Write one paragraph each for your What, Where, When/How, and Why key messages. (Your Who key message, containing your name, stands alone as your introduction and isn't part of this exercise.)

2. Summarize each of these four paragraphs with one sentence.

3. Choose one word in each sentence that will remind you of the key message.

Now, write your four words in this grid (it's okay if some are two or even three words long—but no longer!).

These are your key words, the essence of your best work qualities. Your key messages sit behind those words, ready to impress someone in an interview or a phone call. The paragraphs you wrote in step 2 sit behind those key messages, supporting them with details and proof of your abilities. Congratulations, you've created the core of your message to employers! Most people barely have one core idea—you've got four!

Here are mine:

Leadership	Marketer
Entrepreneur	Confidence

If a magazine or television interviewer asks me to talk about myself, I think: "Leadership—Marketer—Entrepreneur—Confidence." Those are my key words. I have key messages based on each word. I have stories behind each key message. The result of this preparation is a great interview, because I'm ready to tell my story and also to listen, to learn, to be genuine, and to make my stories relevant to each particular interview. I'm relaxed.

Public Relations

There are mountains of products at Monster. I can't mention them all in a press interview, especially for radio or television. But in those five minutes before I'm on the air, I have my key messages all set, with a word or two for each at the back of my mind. For example:

- How many people are looking for work today? (Key Word: *unemployment*)
- How many jobs are on Monster today? (Key Words: *Monster jobs*)
- Which sectors of the job market are hiring? (Key Word: *sectors*)
- Come visit us at **monster.com**. (Key words: *visit us*)

My Key Words are *unemployment, Monster jobs, sectors, visit us*. Whatever the interviewer asks, I'm going to remember those words to get my key messages across sometime during the interview. It's the same for you. Whatever questions you answer in your job interview, you'll also get across your key messages. That's how you'll be remembered.

Write your key words on an index card, and make that card the last thing you look at before you walk into a job interview. Tape a copy of that card to the monitor of your home computer. Re-read it before an informational interview. This is the essence of your personal brand, and it should become second nature to you during the job search.

In the next sections, expand the proof that backs up these statements. You'll describe your employment history, achievements, skills, and other evidence that you are exactly the person your key messages describe.

Employment History

Your employment history is a critical component of your resume, and it will also be questioned closely in every job interview. You will customize and expand this information in the following chapters, so in this exercise just make a complete list of everywhere you've worked.

Use the form on page 126 to describe your jobs, starting with the most recent. You may want to include volunteer work, internships, and other significant commitments, especially if your career is just getting started, or you want to return to work after a substantial break.

In the spaces provided, list:

- The job's beginning and end dates. If you have been working less than five years, use months and years. If more than that, just listing years is sufficient up to your two most recent jobs.

- The job title.

- A few words describing the job's most important responsibilities.

Avoid these mistakes:

- Try not to leave unexplained gaps in the chronological order of your history.

- If you have had more than one job title with a company, make sure that's easily understood.

Be accurate, but don't worry about writing brilliant prose at this point. We'll cover style and other issues related to writing an effective resume in chapter 10.

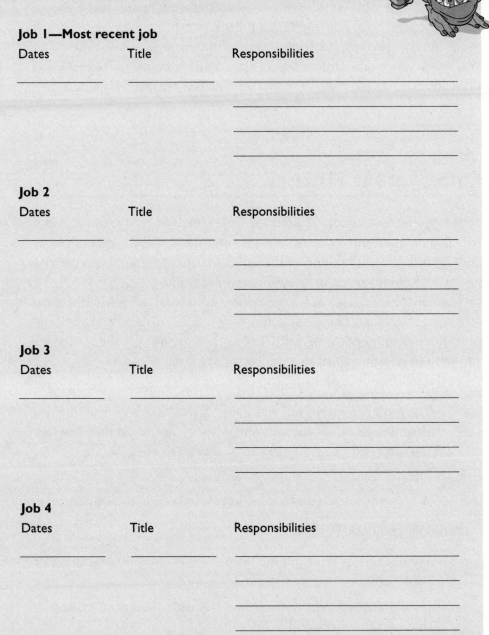

Employment history

Job 1—Most recent job

Dates   Title   Responsibilities

_____   _____   _____

                                                  _____

                                                  _____

                                                  _____

Job 2

Dates   Title   Responsibilities

_____   _____   _____

                                                  _____

                                                  _____

                                                  _____

Job 3

Dates   Title   Responsibilities

_____   _____   _____

                                                  _____

                                                  _____

                                                  _____

Job 4

Dates   Title   Responsibilities

_____   _____   _____

                                                  _____

                                                  _____

                                                  _____

You can download this form at monstercareers.com.

Your Achievement Stories

Job candidates who offer proof of their skills have a dramatic advantage over candidates who don't. If you can describe your achievements—even those outside of a regular work environment—you're in the running.

You will use your achievement stories to strengthen your resume. They are also absolutely essential in interviews. "Employers believe the best predictor of performance is past behavior," says career consultant Julie Miller. "So they ask for specific examples that mirror what goes on in their company." Bobbi Jeanotte, vice president of human resources at health-care company Matria, Inc., notes that the strongest candidates connect their past achievements to the job they're currently seeking, for example: "The R&D engineers often jump in and illustrate how they could help in specific situations."

Start with the **When and How** statements of your key messages in the previous section of this chapter. Write them on the Achievement Stories form on page 130.

How to Write Your Achievement Stories

As a candidate, you want to communicate quickly what each achievement says about you. Just stating an achievement, though, won't make you memorable. For example, here's a boring description of an achievement: "I increased efficiency at a wallboard manufacturing plant." What does that tell an employer specifically about your problem-solving talents or leadership abilities? Not much.

An effective way to describe an achievement is to tell it in this order:

Problem: What was the key problem(s) you faced?

Action: What actions did you take to overcome the problem?

Result: What was the result of your efforts, and how did your performance benefit the company?

If you change "I increased efficiency at a wallboard manufacturing plant" to a problem-action-result format, it might sound like this:

Problem: A construction materials manufacturing line was beset with mechanical failures causing downtime of 30 to 35%.

Action: I brought managers and line workers together to identify several hundred small problems causing downtime, each of which could be addressed individually.

Result: Within three months, downtime went below 1%—and the extra time allowed the team to build and operate an additional line six months ahead of schedule.

This says a lot! It shows talents for problem solving, leadership, and putting solutions into action. It shows dramatic, measurable results.

Achievement stories have great impact with employers if they are backed up by numbers. Numbers feel like proof, not opinion. Most businesses are run "by the numbers." You don't have to be an accountant, though, to quantify your achievements. There are many ways to express results of your work in numbers.

Think money. When did you earn, save, or manage money in your work? Here are examples of achievement stories that are expressed in terms of money:

- Identified, researched, and recommended a new Internet Service Provider, cutting the company's online costs by 15%.

- Wrote fund-raising letter that has brought in more than $25,000 in donations to date.

- Managed a staff of eight with a budget (including payroll) of $386,000.

Think time. Companies and organizations are constantly looking for ways to save time and meet deadlines:

- Assisted with twice-monthly payroll activities, ensuring that employees were paid as expected and on time.

- Attended high school basketball games, interviewed players and coaches afterward, and composed 750-word articles by an 11 P.M. deadline.

- Suggested procedures that cut the average order-processing time from ten minutes to five minutes.

Think amounts. In business, numbers that measure how much you do are highly relevant:

- Recruited 25 members for a volunteer environmental organization.

- Trained five new employees in restaurant operations procedures.

- Introduced 17 service-improvement proposals to the help desk.

You don't have to draw all your achievement stories from past jobs. Activities outside of work demonstrate personal qualities that employers seek. Persistence, diligence, insight, persuasiveness, loyalty, enthusiasm, responsibility, helpfulness, and other qualities of character are highly valuable to employers, and can be illustrated by personal achievements.

Dave Morgan, a recruiting manager at Ford Motor Company, recalls a candidate whose achievements outside the 9-to-5 got him a job. "We had a recent graduate who had organized a Habitat for Humanity house in Detroit," recalls Dave. "The individual did it on his own, talking to friends, neighbors, family—organizing people just because it was a worthwhile thing to do. We saw that as leadership ability—not formally sanctioned by a job title, but evident in life experience."

In the Achievement Stories form on page 130, write about your best achievements. Use numbers and problem-action-result statements wherever you can. Note what personal qualities, like leadership or problem solving, you believe your achievements demonstrate. In chapter 10, you'll learn how to use these on your resume.

What If You've Never Had a "Real Job"?

Just getting out of school? Entering the workforce after raising a family? What if you've been out of the corporate workforce for fifteen years?

You may assume you cannot list achievement stories without having worked in a traditional setting. Pat O'Brien, author of *Making College Count*, offers this perspective on personal achievements:

"EVERY job is a real job," says Pat. "If you were delivering papers, you were developing behavioral traits (like delivering on time), attitudes (like being concerned that your customers and the newspaper were both happy), and skills (like managing your route and still getting to school on time). In your school work, you displayed behavioral traits, attitudes toward learning, and skills. And what qualifies you for the next job is some combination of—guess what?—behavioral traits, attitudes, and skills!"

You may have had internships, been a church volunteer, or done nontraditional jobs. You may have coached soccer or directed a school play. You may have managed your aging parents' household budget. Your life is full of stories that prove you will be a great employee!

ACHIEVEMENT STORIES

Achievement 1

_____

_____

_____

Personal qualities demonstrated

_____

_____

Achievement 2

_____

_____

_____

Personal qualities demonstrated

_____

_____

Achievement 3

_____

_____

_____

Personal qualities demonstrated

_____

_____

Achievement 4

_____

_____

_____

Personal qualities demonstrated

_____

_____

You can download this form at monstercareers.com.

List Your Skills

Now that you know what you want to say (key messages), can relate your experience (employment history), and have proof of your abilities (achievement stories), you're ready to list your skills in greater detail.

Employers always say they focus on a candidate's "skills," but it's hard to know exactly what they mean by that word. For some, it's *intuitive abilities*, like a knack for making people feel at ease or a talent for working with numbers. Others mean *specific information or expertise* required for a job, like knowing a programming language. Still others mean the *degree* to which a candidate is expert, as in "She's a very skilled analyst."

For job-hunting purposes, a "skill" is *any quality or knowledge you possess that helps you get the job done.* We'll use that loose definition because it's how employers use the word.

There are tens of thousands of skills used in the workplace. How do you start listing all of yours? Once again, study your key messages and achievement stories. What abilities or knowledge prove your key messages? What abilities or knowledge helped you?

Here are four examples we saw in the section on achievement stories, and some of the skills that they would demonstrate.

> **Achievement:** Managed a staff of eight with a budget (including payroll) of $386,000.
>
> **Skills:** managing teams, budgeting, communication, leadership
>
> **Achievement:** Identified, researched, and recommended a new Internet Service Provider, cutting the company's online costs by 15%.
>
> **Skills:** business research, technical knowledge, cost-consciousness
>
> **Achievement:** Attended high school basketball games, interviewed players and coaches afterward, and composed 750-word articles by an 11 P.M. deadline.
>
> **Skills:** writing, interviewing, ability to handle deadlines, reliability
>
> **Achievement:** Trained five new employees in restaurant operations procedures.
>
> **Skills:** training, spoken communication, knowledge of restaurant operations

Study the following broad categories of skills. For each skill category, ask yourself, "Do I have skills like this? Can I prove it?" Write the names of several categories in the spaces marked "Major skills category" on the skills list, page 134. (If you'd like more information, you can find detailed de-

Skill Categories

Accounting and Finance	Environmental	Medical and/or Dental
Administration	Facilities Management	Money Management
Advertising	Graphic Arts	Motivation
Analysis	Health Care	Multimedia Creation
Animal Care	Health Care Administration	Negotiation
Automated Testing	Health Care Specializations	Operating Systems Knowledge
B2B Integration Tools		Organizational
Biotechnology	Human Resources	Patient Care
Change Management	Insurance	People Management
Communication (written and oral)	Internet	Physical Demands
Computer Office Applications	Interpersonal	Problem Solving
Construction	Journalism	Product
Consulting	Laboratory	Professional Knowledge
Creative	Language	Public Relations
Customer Service	Law Enforcement/Security	Quality Assurance
Desktop Publishing	Leadership	Resource Management and Logistics
Driving	Learning	Sales
Electronics	Legal	Statistical Analysis
Emergency Preparedness/ Safety	Listening	System Administration
Engineering	Management	Telecommunications
Engineering Tools	Manufacturing	Thinking
Enterprise Resource Planning	Marketing	Training and Education
	Mathematical	Web Marketing
	Mechanical	

scriptions of major skill categories at the Department of Labor's "Skill Search": **online.onetcenter.org/gen_skills_page**.)

When you have selected major skill categories, name specific skills you possess under each category. Since it's impractical to list 10,000 possible skills in this book, you'll have to identify them from your experience and research.

If you have a hard time naming your specific skills, even with your key messages, employment history, and achievement stories documents at hand, you can ask for outside help. Ask your colleagues, instructors, supervisors, and friends what they see as your most important skills. Review your performance evaluations from previous jobs. What skills powered your performance? Which skills and knowledge do you most enjoy using?

For example, if you listed good communications skills, you might list one or more of the following:

- American Sign Language
- Communicating to children
- Creating illustrative stories
- Creating presentations
- Developing forms
- Instructional writing
- Interviewing
- Languages spoken
- Listening
- Persuasive writing
- Phone manner
- Public speaking
- Radio announcing
- Teaching
- Technical writing

Under computer skills you might select specific software programs at which you're expert, or some of these specifics:

- Application Server
- Computer Networking
- Computer Programming
- Database Management
- Data Processing
- Development Tools
- e-Commerce
- Information Security
- Mail Servers
- Protocols and Standards
- Software Development
- Technical Management
- Technical Support
- Technical Writing
- Web Server Administration

SKILLS LIST

Major skill category: _____

Specific skills in this category: _____

_____

_____

_____

Major skill category: _____

Specific skills in this category: _____

_____

_____

_____

Major skill category: _____

Specific skills in this category: _____

_____

_____

_____

Major skill category: _____

Specific skills in this category: _____

_____

_____

_____

Major skill category: _____

Specific skills in this category: _____

_____

_____

You can download this form at monstercareers.com.

Your skills inventory is a living document. Keep adding to it, whether as a result of a casual conversation or a skill you see in a job posting.

Your list of skills might get quite long (you have, after all, been acquiring skills since you were born), so you may want to circle your most marketable skills—the ones employers most often seek. The National Association of Colleges and Employers ranked the top groups of skills that employers want this way:

1. Interpersonal
2. Teamwork
3. Verbal Communication
4. Analytical
5. Computer
6. Written Communication
7. Leadership

Be honest about which skills you possess. According to executive recruiter Arnie Miller of Isaacson, Miller, one of the most powerful statements from a candidate can be a frank admission of what they don't know. For example, you may be brilliant at delivering off-the-cuff presentations, but agonize over written presentations. It's fine to say so.

Finally, make a habit of updating your skills list after you get a new job. As you learn and grow in the job, write down your achievements and new skills, and update that list regularly. The list will give more power to your next resume.

Your Personal Story

"Why did you leave your last job?"

It's an unavoidable question. You need a strong story explaining why you're available.

If you are unemployed right now, future employers will naturally be concerned about the reason. Did you quit? Were you fired? Did the company have layoffs or go out of business? If you're employed now but looking for something better, expect a more subtle version of the question in job interviews: "Why do you want to leave your current job?"

Write why you are looking for work on the first line of the Personal Story form on page 139. If you're unemployed, write a description of why you are no longer working where you were. Here are a few examples:

- *Skyrocketing fuel prices forced my trucking company to cut costs. I was laid off along with twelve other drivers.*

- *My company relocated to another state, and family obligations, including my spouse's job, caused me to accept a severance package.*

- *My department did not hit its sales budget, and I was let go.*

- *My boss and I had a series of helpful, honest conversations, and mutually agreed that the job was, in fact, not the right fit for me. There was nothing else available at the company.*

- *State budget problems forced the school district to cut back funding for my job. I am teaching part-time while looking for a full-time position.*

Be careful to position your statement in the positive, and don't get personal. If you were laid off to make room for the boss's nephew, just say there was a restructuring in your department and your job was eliminated.

While staying positive, you must be honest in your statement, because an employer may verify your story with your last employer. If you lost your job in a way that doesn't reflect well on you (for example, if you were convicted of a crime or failed a drug test), it's best to be frank: "I made this mistake. . . . This was the consequence. . . . Here's what I've done to correct the mistake and prevent it from happening again." This demonstrates accountability, honesty, and candor, which is what the employer is really wondering about. Your decisions from the past will come back to haunt you if you roll the lie forward. The right employer will handle your news and move on.

If you are currently employed, your statement can be simpler. Simply explain why you may want to leave your current job. For example:

- *I think I can earn more in a better job.*

- *I'm looking for a bigger challenge.*

- *I have decided to relocate to your (the employer's) area.*

Now, Add an Upbeat Message

As a candidate, you also want to connect your recent experience to the next step. This is true whether you're unemployed or employed but looking for something better. Expand your first statement on the form with an additional sentence or two that projects a positive message. Using the examples above, I'd add the following:

"Unemployed" positive messages:

- *Skyrocketing fuel prices forced my trucking company to cut costs. I was laid off along with twelve other drivers.* **I've since thought a lot about cost-cutting ideas my next company can use when fuel prices spike again. Here are a few:** [give examples].

- *My company relocated to another state, and family obligations, including my spouse's job, caused me to accept a severance package.* **Your company's long commitment to the St. Louis area makes me hopeful that it values roots in the community. You can see from my local volunteer work how important commitment is to me.**

- *My department did not hit its sales budget, and I was let go.* **That's why I'm really interested in finding a team where everyone knows that goals can be hit if we all go the extra mile.**

- *My boss and I had a series of helpful, honest conversations, and mutually agreed that the job was, in fact, not the right fit for me. There was nothing else available at the company.* **I'm really glad we're being careful here to make sure the job and I are a great match. I've learned how important it is to be thorough, whether you're finding out about a job or learning about a customer's business problems.**

- *State budget cuts forced the school district to end funding for my job. I am teaching part-time while looking for a full-time position.* **I hope that shows you how motivated I am to teach reading to younger students.**

"Employed" positive messages:

- *I think I can earn more in a better job.* **Your company is known for rewarding great performance, and I believe I can be one of your best performers in a job like this one.**

- *I'm looking for a bigger challenge.* **My current position does not offer room for growth, and I have been doing the job for three years. It's time for me to find a position that allows me to make a greater contribution to a company's success.**

- *I have decided to move to the Denver area.* **And I'm not looking for just any job in Denver. After a lot of research, I've singled out your company for the following reasons . . ."**

137

Your positive statement may also include a forward-looking finish, telling employers and networking contacts what job(s) you have in mind. They won't know unless you tell them. You don't have to restrict yourself to one job title, but it helps to give a description that includes some detail, as in the following examples:

- [marketing manager] *I am looking for an opportunity to introduce new brands or bring new life to aging brands at a company doing more than $50 million in sales.*

- [sales representative] *I would like to know more about opportunities to improve sales in retailing electronics or recreational goods.*

- [home appraiser] *I am looking for an entry-level position as an appraiser at a company in the Twin Cities metro area.*

Write a positive, forward-looking statement in the second section of the Personal Story form on page 139. It may grow or even change entirely as you go through your job search, and that's okay. In fact, seeing new possibilities is one of the benefits of a good search!

Your References

President Ronald Reagan was fond of saying this about the Soviet Union: "Trust, but verify." Employers feel the same way about you. Before they offer you a job, they will want an objective second opinion.

The time and care you invest in choosing and even coaching references might very well determine whether you're offered the job. Most employers aren't going to rely on your word or even their own judgments of you. They simply haven't known you long enough. They haven't seen you in action.

Early in your search, you need to secure permission from at least three people to act as your professional references. When you're deep into a job search, you should have five to seven references available. This makes it easy for an interested employer to reach at least one or two in a short time.

References should be trustworthy, they should have seen you work, and they should be willing to take a call from a prospective employer. Many people might suit these purposes:

Past Employers: These are your best references because they can discuss your skills and performance credibly. They are likely to speak the same

PERSONAL STORY

Answer one of the following questions, depending on your current work status:

If you're employed: Why do you want to leave your current job?
If you're unemployed: Why did you leave your last job?

_____
_____
_____
_____
_____
_____
_____
_____
_____

Now, expand your statement with a positive, forward-looking message:

_____
_____
_____
_____
_____
_____
_____
_____
_____
_____
_____
_____
_____

You can download this form at monstercareers.com.

language as the employer who's considering you. A work mentor can be ideal. If you haven't changed jobs in decades and your past employer was twenty years ago, see "Been in One Job a Long Time," page 376.

Colleagues: People with whom you've worked in the past, especially if they are in management positions now, can be particularly effective. They probably know you and your work better than the human resources department. Fellow members of a professional organization can also help.

Professors and Advisors: If you've graduated recently, professors and advisors may be suitable. While professors may not be able to speak to the skills you gained in an employment setting, they can describe your academic abilities and your skills in areas like research, written communication, and oral presentation.

Other Supervisors: If you've done any volunteering in your community, you've probably worked with at least one person who has overseen your efforts. That person can talk about your level of commitment and maybe your creative skill and follow-through habits as well.

Make your references effective by showing them your resume (references make great proofreaders, by the way). Share your key messages and coach them on what achievements and qualities you'd like them to mention. Notify your references if you know they are about to be contacted by a prospective employer.

Do not list a reference's contact information on your resume or give it out without their permission. Unfortunately, broadcasting your references' contact information can result in their receiving unwanted calls or e-mail.

Personal References: Personal references are less important than they used to be, but they're useful if you haven't been in the workforce for a while. People who know you well can vouch for your work ethic, character, and other traits. They might include friends, clerics, and members of civic organizations or clubs. Bear in mind that their ability to vouch for you is limited to the personal, not professional. Do not offer family members or partners as personal references. And be aware that personal references cannot substitute for professional references. In a Monster poll, fewer than half of recruiters said they use personal references.

After you've secured permission from your references, write their names and contact information on the References form on page 141.

REFERENCES

Reference 1:

_____

_____

Reference 2:

_____

_____

Reference 3:

_____

_____

(Optional)
Reference 4:

_____

_____

Reference 5:

_____

_____

Reference 6:

_____

_____

Reference 7:

_____

_____

You can download this form at monstercareers.com.

Your Certifications

Certifications are similar to achievement stories; they prove a point you want to make. It's one thing to say, for example, "I'm good at financial management." It's another to have a degree from a top school specializing in finance, where you had to prove your abilities. Recent graduates might bring in a diploma, academic honors, or a description of an honors thesis. If you've completed a certification program in a technical skill such as programming or mechanics, your certificate confirms your proficiency.

A certification doesn't have to be as formal as a diploma, however. To prove your writing skills, you can present copies of a column you wrote for your student newspaper or the brochure you wrote for a volunteer organization. It could be a newsletter describing one of your accomplishments. Awards from an employer are powerful testimony to your effectiveness in a job. Membership in a professional group implies you're networked and ambitious.

List two or three certifications you could show a potential employer on the form below.

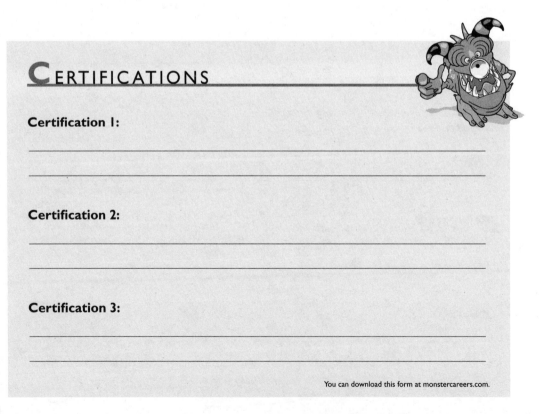

CERTIFICATIONS

Certification 1:

_____

_____

Certification 2:

_____

_____

Certification 3:

_____

_____

You can download this form at monstercareers.com.

Putting Your Portfolio to Work

If you have completed the seven documents in your Job Search Portfolio, the foundation of your job search is firmly in place. The more care you put into creating this portfolio, the bigger your payoff will be for the rest of your search.

You now have serious advantages over other candidates: You can deliver a short, memorable statement of your value with your key messages. You can talk about your skills and prove your abilities with achievement stories. You can give a confident answer to the question "Why are you looking for work?" in a job interview. Most candidates never get to this level; you're already there.

You don't have to wait for a job interview, however, to reap the benefits of this effort. The portfolio goes to work for you in the next three chapters. In chapter 9, you will turn these statements into a polished "sales pitch," and in chapters 10 and 11, you'll draft a resume and cover letters from statements in your portfolio.

9 >> Your Pitch <<

F.A.M.E. ATTITUDE: TRAIN LIKE AN **A**THLETE

Training builds confidence.

Your completed Job Search Portfolio highlights the reasons you should be hired. Now, like the athletes we discussed in chapter 2, you need to train. You have to develop and practice a compelling presentation for interviews and networking, and this chapter will focus on the training you need to deliver a smooth pitch, that is, a concise, persuasive statement of your candidacy. You will find not only that this makes you more effective, but also that diligent practice of your pitch will build your confidence. When you feel confident, good things happen.

The documents you created in the last chapter provide the foundation, whether you're networking for leads, talking to a recruiter on the phone, or interviewing for your dream job. It's imperative that you be able to drop your key messages effectively into those kinds of conversations. Whether or not your dream job involves sales, you will need to sell your vision.

Outplacement executive Colin Moor points out the reality of job interviews and job networking. "You don't get much time—thirty minutes to an hour for a meeting," he says. "So you have to cover a lot of ground quickly and efficiently. You have to clarify the networking conversation or job interview: What are the key points you want to get across? What value do you bring as a candidate?"

In this chapter, you will create your pitch on a short document, and then memorize it. It's a whole new way to present yourself.

You haven't seen this document before. It's a new, powerful addition to your resume and cover letters. It is superior to the resume as an informal "discussion guide" for networking, because it quickly presents your key messages, skills, and achievements without the resume's extra information. The people with whom you network often miss your key messages because they focus on the resume's description of your work history.

When you are networking for job leads, your pitch will help your contacts think of likely employers. If you show your resume, they'll focus the conversation on where you have been; if you show your pitch, they'll focus on where you are going—and how they can help you get there.

For a recruiter, the pitch document breaks through the frustration of reviewing hundreds of resumes. Frankly, it makes their job easier, because it is shorter than a resume, presenting only the information that persuades them to take a closer look.

Before you build your pitch, page 147 has a sneak preview: a completed pitch for a candidate looking for a sales job. As you read this pitch, imagine you are meeting this person for the first time.

Right away you know Pat's strengths, experiences, and key skills. She has placed key messages both in her summary and in the section called "Highlights." You know her style and what job she's seeking. You know she has results to prove her claims.

To begin writing your own pitch, see the template on page 151. At the top of the document, you should write your name and supply simple contact information (e-mail and phone are fine—you'll list full contact information on your resume). You can add a job title if you know exactly what job you seek, as in the example above.

Write Your Summary

You have ninety seconds to make a first impression. What can you say that will grab their interest and make them ask for more? You need to relate your key messages, plus just enough additional information to get them hooked. When marketers want to describe their brand in ninety seconds, they create a crisp highlight of what the brand stands for and why you should be interested. Your summary will do the same for you.

Pat Jones—Sales representative
(512) 123-4567
pjones@1mail.com

Summary:
My name is Pat Jones, and I'm a classic closer! I've increased sales dramatically in several lines of business, including consumer goods, business services, and software. I've accomplished this by acting as a "consultant" to customers, using exceptional business analysis skills. Most recently, I've held sales positions at ABC Co., where I doubled new client accounts AND raised existing client sales an average of 15% per year. I am seeking a senior sales position in a leading business-to-business services or software firm in central Texas.

Highlights:
- I act as a "consultant" to my clients, focusing on value, not just price.
- I've increased sales dramatically at several firms, in different business lines.
- My exceptional business analysis skills convince clients I know their business—because I do!
- I am looking for a new opportunity in business-to-business sales.

Key skills:
- Communication: Phone, written, and in person.
- Persuasion: Applying problem-action-result scenario to win business.
- Business analysis: I sell my clients on value, not price.

Key achievements:
- ABC Co.: Doubled new client accounts to $1.4 million in one year.
- ABC Co.: Increased sales 15% on existing accounts.
- XYZ Co.: Closed an average of 8 new accounts per quarter, producing yearly gain of 12% (*50% over quota*).

To write your summary, select the best parts of your Job Search Portfolio and blend them into a smooth paragraph. Here's how:

1. Start with your name and your key messages.

2. Add a statement about your experience and what you have to offer. You can use experience from your employment history or your skills list.

3. Mention your best achievement stories (you don't have to go into detail) as examples of your work.

4. Finish with the forward-looking statement from your personal story form.

You may want to read the three examples that follow before you write. When you do write, try to merge the statements into a smooth paragraph. Read it aloud. Does it sound like conversation? You're on your way.

You should be able to say the whole paragraph in ninety seconds or less. You may have to shorten your paragraph to fit the time limit, but in the case of the summary, ninety seconds of speaking in a slow, natural voice is the limit.

Summary Examples

Here's an example of a summary for a product manager at a packaged foods company. [Relevant Job Search Portfolio documents are in brackets.]

My name is Mary Jones, and I'm a builder of premium brands in packaged foods [key message]. *My strongest skills are brand development and market planning, extending markets for existing products, and strong financial management* [skills]. *At ABC Foods, I expanded institutional sales of frozen prepared foods by 300% in two years, to yearly sales of $9 million, while simultaneously cutting delivery time and costs* [achievement story]. *I am looking for an opportunity to introduce new brands or bring new life to aging brands at a company doing above $50 million in sales* [forward-looking statement].

Note what *isn't* in this statement: the size of Mary's staff (it was only five, so size alone isn't a selling point); a long list of skills (she'll get to that on her resume); demands like *"I won't relocate"* (that discussion takes place much later in the process). It's also not too long: Mary selected the most exciting selling points from her Job Search Portfolio for her pitch.

Mary captures her listener by stating strong results (300% rise in sales), describing actions (developing new markets such as institutional sales), and putting her best strengths up front (planning, getting more out of existing products, and watching the bottom line). She's actually hit three of the five reasons a company would want her: she **makes money** by expanding markets, she **saves money** by getting more out of old products, and she **sells the company's products** through marketing programs.

Here's another example, a retail sales manager starting a networking conversation:

> *My name is Bob Smith, and I have an award-winning record* [certifications] *leading retail sales teams. I am skilled at merchandising operations, measuring customer experience, and motivational training* [skills]. *Most recently, I increased off-price clothing net revenue by 23% across six stores with a combination of programs including sales incentives, loss prevention, sales rep coaching, and customer loyalty* [achievement story]. *I would like to know more about similar opportunities to improve sales in retailing electronics or recreational goods* [forward-looking statement].

Bob has only included one number—and it's a good one. He's decided to emphasize leadership and initiative, and he confirms that with a four-part program he ran to increase sales. He's positioned a move out of clothing stores and into other popular categories. He's also included a lot of strong phrases in his statement, such as *award-winning, leading, measuring, motivational, loss prevention, coaching, loyalty,* and *net revenue.*

Here's a pitch from someone returning to the workforce after devoting eight years to full-time parenting:

> *My name is Cynthia Halliday, and I am an ASA-certified* [certifications] *appraiser of residential real estate properties. I offer accurate, friendly, and efficient service to residential property owners—the service that leads to word-of-mouth business* [key message]. *Previously employed at Tom and Jean Carter Appraisers* [work experience], *I am returning to the workforce after a period of full-time parenting. As a director of a charitable organization for the last three years, I sharpened management skills by organizing 25 volunteers at monthly events* [achievement story]. *I look forward to combining those skills with my experience in a position as appraiser at a company in the Twin Cities metro area* [forward-looking statement].

Cynthia has gone right after the first question she thinks she'll encounter: "How do I know you're qualified to be an appraiser?" She kept up her certification with the American Society of Appraisers while she was a full-time parent. Next, she says she'll project a positive image to customers, which is critical to her business. She points out that she's worked in the business in the past, and demonstrates that, even as a full-time parent, she saw volunteer work as an opportunity to grow her skills.

Chapter 10, Create a Resume That Sells, has a list of Action Phrases and Power Verbs. Check it out if you'd like to add some sizzle to your pitch.

Finish Your Pitch

When you have a summary you can repeat in ninety seconds or less, write it at the top of the Create Your Pitch form on page 151. Then, use your key messages, key skills, and achievement stories from your Job Search Portfolio to complete the form. This is a simple task of consolidating the highlights of three documents:

- Write your strongest sales points in the "Highlights" space. Adapt your key messages or additional high-impact statements, as Pat did in the example on page 147.

- Copy your major skills categories (or specific skills, depending on which you think are more effective in a pitch) in the "Key Skills" space.

- Write highlights of your top achievement stories in the "Achievements" space.

When you get to informational interviewing and networking, I'll suggest you use a printed version of your pitch as a conversation-starter. If you choose to fill out the form in the book today, that's fine, but if you want to use this as a separate document, either copy the form or download it from **monstercareers.com**.

Keep your pitch document handy. A printed copy can also serve as an effective addition to a resume in many situations. You can even attach your pitch to your resume and leave it with an interviewer or networking contact to make yourself more memorable.

- It will be a reliable reminder of your "talking points" before any job interview, similar to the "Key Words" index card you made in chapter 8.

CREATE YOUR PITCH

[name and job title]

_____
_____

Summary:

_____
_____
_____

Highlights:

- _____
- _____
- _____
- _____

Key Skills:

_____
_____
_____

Achievements:

1. _____
_____

2. _____
_____

3. _____
_____

You can download this form at monstercareers.com.

151

- When a recruiter calls, glancing at your form will "re-center" your attention, helping you make your strongest sales points.

- When you are networking for job leads, your pitch can focus the discussion on your strengths and skills better than a resume, which focuses mostly on your previous work experience.

If calling this document a "pitch" doesn't suit your style, simply refer to it as your summary or outline. Place it in front of a networking contact and say, "Before I show you my resume, please have a look at my summary. It should tell you everything you need to know for this conversation."

Book to Web

Since your pitch is likely to improve as your search progresses, it is an especially good form to download from **monstercareers.com**. This will enable you to rewrite it many times, if you wish.

Now, Train Like an Athlete

Your pitch is like a gymnast's routine or a quarterback's game plan. Like an athlete, you must plan your strongest "routine"—all the moves you want to include—and then practice it. Creating a routine and practicing it is part of training like an athlete, and you will be amazed at how it creates confidence.

MEMORIZE YOUR PITCH. Be able to recite its words as effortlessly as you recite the Pledge of Allegiance. You must know the details of your pitch in order to impress an employer in a job interview. If you are groping for answers, trying to remember what to say, you can't listen. You can't pay attention. You aren't able to think. And you're not very impressive.

If you memorize the different parts of your pitch, you will have ready answers to critical questions:

- Your summary will capture the attention of employers and networking contacts.

- Your key messages will spring to mind as you answer interview questions.

- You will drop the names of your top skills into answers, even when the questions aren't directly about skills.

- You will be able to relate your best achievements, harnessing the particular power of "telling a story" to make yourself stand out from the crowd.

If memorizing is difficult for you, use this trick taught to professional actors: Repeat the first sentence five times, then add the second sentence and repeat them together five times. Then add the third sentence, and so on. This is how kids learn to sing "The Twelve Days of Christmas," and it works!

Memorize your pitch, and then PRACTICE!

- Practice in the shower.

- Practice while you do the dishes.

- Practice during your commute.

- Practice in front of your friends.

- Practice in front of your references.

And if you really want to excel, practice in front of a video camera!

Don't worry about nailing down a "final" script for your pitch. It will grow and change. Athletes, actors, and musicians know that as you practice something you've memorized, an amazing creativity is released. You will find yourself adding interesting remarks, discovering fresh ways to describe yourself, remembering people or companies you should contact, recalling new achievement stories to add to your arsenal.

This is the heart of your training. Practice every day, and don't be afraid to upgrade your ideas. When you find a better way to tell your story, memorize that!

Practice Your Phone Skills

At some point in your job search, you'll have to pick up the phone, so you also need to practice your telephone "door opening" skills, which are the same skills you've just practiced, adapted for the phone. Whether you are calling to set up an appointment, network, or have a telephone job interview, you need to step up your phone power. Avoid the common mistakes of job search phone work by developing some simple habits:

Stand up and smile. This is common advice for sales representatives, and it's a shame more people don't adopt it for every professional phone conversation. If you are standing and smiling while you talk on the phone, your energy and positive attitude come right through your voice.

Slow down. If you're a little nervous, your voice tends to rise, get louder, and speed up. Take a deep breath and slow down; a phone call isn't a race.

Listen. Give the other person time to finish his or her statements. Don't panic over a few seconds of silence.

Avoid multitasking/distractions. Look away from your computer screen. Close your instant messenger. Turn off the TV/radio. If you're at home, move to a quiet spot where you can focus. Have your pitch and your resume handy, but mostly, try to be present. Having your mind fully on the call will produce better results.

Don't forget your goal. Spend a few minutes before the call jotting down exactly what you want to say and what you want to get out of the conversation, whether it's an appointment, information, or a face-to-face interview.

Adopt a bottom-line attitude when it comes to the phone: make the call. When you doubt yourself, pick up the phone. When your job search is stalled, pick up the phone. Good things will start to happen. (For more on telephone job interviews, see chapter 15.)

Next Steps

Your pitch document is a fresh, focused marketing tool. Recruiters and managers haven't seen it before. It stimulates conversation. It focuses your networking and interviews on your selling points. It makes other people more effective at helping you. It helps you practice an expert presentation. It is strategic as well, because it tells employers that you're a more thoughtful, focused candidate. Your pitch is one critical difference between a traditional job search and a *Monster Careers* search. You will use your pitch, both memorized and written, in the chapters to come on resumes, cover letters, research, networking, and job interviews. All of these require you to present yourself clearly and quickly.

If you have put enough time and thought into creating your pitch, you will beat the competition for the job. You can be confident that employers will see you as a whole person, not just another resume. You have thought through important questions about who you are and what you want—and you have woven the answers into a compelling story. You are ready to impress potential employers. Now that you have that foundation, it's time to create the documents that allow you to enter the actual job marketplace. It's time to write your resume and cover letters.

10 >> Create a Resume That Sells <<

F.A.M.E. ATTITUDE: THINK LIKE A FREE AGENT
Your resume is your sales tool.

Maybe I've got a romantic view of this, but your resume is much more than data. It's your life document. It stays with you across your career experience. A great resume is a vivid and accurate portrayal of you at your most promising. As you gain work experience, it becomes an ongoing document of what you've accomplished. It sets the stage for your entire presentation. For that reason, the free agent attitude sees a resume as an ongoing sales tool: it markets you, establishes your credibility, and represents you when you're not there. In fact, a resume will not "get you a job." A resume will get you a job *interview.* A resume documents your past; you use it to move yourself forward.

If you turned to this chapter first, you will see a few new terms that were introduced in chapters 7 to 9, such as "Job Search Portfolio." The Job Search Portfolio is the *Monster Careers* foundation of a great resume as well as job interviews, networking, and other actions. Even if you want to read this chapter first, I recommend you complete the documents in chapters 7 to 9 before you consider your resume really polished.

If you've completed your Job Search Portfolio, you're ready to go. We'll refer back to those documents throughout this chapter, because they are the building blocks of the best possible resume you can write.

The Durable Document

I sit on panels in the United States and abroad, with experts who say the resume or CV (*curriculum vitae*—in some countries this is another name for a resume) will disappear in a few years. Don't believe it. There is no clearer, more complete way to exhibit one's skills, work history, and potential.

Predicting the end of the resume is like predicting the end of the book. Both have proven incredibly durable, whether they're in print, in electronic form, or online. In technical jargon, the resume is a common standard across the world. Everyone agrees to follow the same broad formats, which makes resumes easy to read and share.

A few years back, two university archives provided a Monster team with resumes from each decade of the twentieth century. We pinned them all on the wall and stepped back ten feet, and they all looked alike. All contained:

- Name and contact information
- Job Objective or Summary
- Current job
- Previous jobs
- Education

Over the decades, as jobs and skills became more complex, the print got smaller and the resumes got denser. A few cultural changes were reflected as well: Education used to come first, now it's generally last. Personal information was explicit—we saw "Happily married with 3 children" on resumes from the 1940s, which in many instances is too much information today! Hobbies and interests changed (we had a resume from the 1920s that listed "fox hunting" under hobbies).

The big resume story of the last few years has come from technology. Everything about how resumes are found, analyzed, and handled has changed:

- Early in the job search process, it is likely your resume will be read electronically in a database. Even if it's a paper document, it will probably be scanned by a computer and placed in a database. That said, a lot of companies still keep resumes stored in manila folders in file cabinets.

- Resume databases may contain a few hundred resumes (in a small company) or hundreds of thousands of resumes in Internet databases (as of this writing, Monster has more than 30 million). Recruiters have never had such a wide choice of candidates.

- It's there, in the database, that recruiters also try to cope with the limitations of the search engine (software that helps search the database documents). A resume with the job title "Executive Assistant to the President" may come up in database searches for an Executive, an Assistant, and a President. Search engines are getting better, but they're not perfect.

- Listing your job skills as keywords is critical to having your resume show up in a recruiter's search for candidates. The more you can help the software target you exactly, the more likely a recruiter will find you.

- A busy recruiter makes the first decision about the quality or relevance of a resume in about ninety seconds. Great resumes get a big YES notation. Bad ones get lost. Many get printed out and placed in a folder. This is a terrible place to be—the folder gets put in a stack, then onto another stack, and then filed . . . and lost forever.

- Finally, the next resume in a database is just a click away. Forget competition from lousy resumes—there will be plenty from strong ones. Any athlete knows you have to win in the early rounds to be around for the finals.

Resume Formats

Because of the technology just described, you need an electronic version of your resume. You will bring old-fashioned printed resumes to job interviews, and you may mail printed resumes to companies from time to time as well, but to participate in the new world of work there is simply no way around having a computer-based resume. If you do not own a personal computer, use one in your school or library to create your resume. Yes, it is that important!

You need to create your resume file two ways. The printed "Presentation Resume" belongs in a standard manila folder. Always keep at least ten copies at hand. The electronic versions of your resume will live in a folder on your personal computer or, if you are using a public computer (in your library or career center), on a floppy disk, CD, or other storage medium.

You should format your electronic resume in at least three ways, which will be adequate for 90 percent of uses. When your resume is completely drafted, you will need to save three versions of it as follows:

1. **Microsoft Word or other common word-processing format.** This format is for printing out paper resumes and also for many e-mails. I'll call this the "Presentation Resume," the one you bring to interviews.

2. **ASCII format with line breaks.** ASCII (American Standard Code for Information Interchange) allows databases and character-recognition software to read your resume without the confusion caused by formatting. In Microsoft Word, use the "Save As" command, save your resume (name it differently from the first version), and save the file as Plain Text. In the dialogue box that appears, choose "Other Encoding" and select US-ASCII. Also click the "Insert line breaks" checkbox.

3. **ASCII format without line breaks.** This is often convenient for uploading a resume to an online database, where you will likely have to cut and paste the information into fields with preset lengths. Follow the directions in number 2 above, but skip the last step.

Two additional formats that you may want to have available are:

- **Rich Text Format:** Occasionally your resume may be requested in Rich Text Format (RTF). Using the "Save As" command in your word processor, select Rich Text Format. This preserves type treatments.

- **.pdf format:** This is the format used by Adobe Acrobat Reader, which preserves the look of a printed document. It's useful for designers and other creative occupations in which really advanced design is part of the package. (If you're good enough to need this format, I don't have to tell you how to create it.)

If you're using AppleWorks on an Apple computer, use the "Save As" function to save your resume as a Microsoft Word document.

You don't have to write your resume three times to have the proper formats. Write it once in a word processor, and save the files as I've described above.

Let's get writing!

The Anatomy of a Great Resume

If you've created a Job Search Portfolio in chapter 8 and a sales pitch in chapter 9, you have more than enough to create a resume that will get you

Are You Writing a Resume or a Suicide Note?

I f you're sitting down one night to write your resume quickly because you're mad at your company, you won't write a good resume. Everyone starts by writing the same generalities about themselves in the first draft.

Good writing is hard work. People approach me at conferences and say, "I get no response to my resume on Monster." And I'll get their name and go look at their resume on Monster, and it looks like they wrote it in ten minutes.

Make a life investment. Spend three, five, ten hours—whatever it takes—to write a great resume.

job interviews. Keep those documents handy now, because you're about to use them to build that winning resume.

Let's go through one from beginning to end. The categories below include all the information required on a typical resume, the kind modeled in the Monster resume builder. You may choose a different design from those on pages 195–208, but you should include all this information; every category is designed to help you define your life's work and to compel that recruiter to call you!

Book to Web

You can write your resume directly into Monster's resume builder (**my. monster.com/resume.asp**). You can also create a resume on a computer (with the advice below), then copy and paste it into the resume database.

Do you already have a resume? Challenge yourself to make it better—take the "Resume Quick-Check Quiz" at **monstercareers.com**.

Contact Information

Give everyone a way to contact you—more than one, if possible. Include:

- Your full name
- Home mailing address (including ZIP Code)

- E-mail address
- Phone number
- Other relevant information such as cell phone number or personal URL

Privacy

Privacy is a serious issue in a job search. What information is more personal than a resume? Do you want everyone to know your phone number? While you have to give potential employers an easy way to reach you, here are some options for guarding such information:

- Set up a free e-mail account service such as AOL, MSN, or Yahoo!, and use it only for your job search. This prevents people at your current employer from accidentally finding out you are searching for a job. These services are increasingly protecting users' privacy.
- You may provide a cell phone number or home-office phone number instead of a home phone number.
- You may establish a post office box as your address if you do not want to share your address.
- Never put your Social Security or other important numbers (such as bank account or credit card numbers) on a resume.
- Do not provide the phone number or e-mail of your current job, unless you're certain it would be okay for other employers to reach you there.
- Online, take advantage of the confidentiality features on Monster and other sites.

It's also legitimate to establish contact information that projects a certain image. For example, if you live in an apartment building, you're representing the fact that you don't own a home. If you don't want to do that, you may want to set up a post office box. If you live in Atlanta but plan to relocate to Washington, D.C., you may want to set up a post office box in Washington (and do your business online). This is not deceptive, it's strategic. It's addressing a potential screening issue.

Headline

Technology has made your resume's headline more important than ever. It may be the first thing an employer sees when your resume comes up in a resume search. Often, the person receiving your resume is actually only scanning the titles of resumes in a database or e-mail Inbox. They see a list like this:

They may be compelled to open the third and fourth resumes, because those candidates have put their resumes' promising headlines as subjects of the e-mail. Will those other e-mails be opened? Maybe—if the first don't seem right. But resumes come in so quickly, there might be ten or fifty more e-mails to scan the next time the recruiters check their mail.

Monster senior creative director Sue Duro suggests you make your resume stand out by stating one unique benefit for the customer as your headline. For example:

- Your retail sales will soar! (salesperson)
- On budget. On time. Every time. (project manager)
- Am I a great nurse? Here's what my patients say: (nurse)
- 15 years' leadership in Airport Security (security officer)

You can even be humorous or provocative:

- Your competition's worst nightmare
- The best damn driver in Nashville

My personal advice here is, don't be too "sales-y." Test different head-lines over time; some will draw more responses than others. Customize the headline of your resume before you send it to an employer (just save it on your computer with a new title or create multiple resumes online). The salesperson's headline above, for example, might read, "ABC Juice Company's sales of natural apple will soar!"

One important note about working with resume titles: As resumes themselves get passed around offices, your name can get lost. You may want to add your name in the title of the resume document itself, and use your resume title in the subject line of your e-mail, like this:

Summary or Objective

The summary or objective statement is the most important single item on your resume. A summary is different from an objective, so you'll have to choose which to use. The summary is more focused on the customer (the employer) and what benefits he or she will receive. The objective is more focused on the candidate. A summary is the stronger choice for most.

How to Write a Career Summary

The summary statement features your skills, accomplishments, and career level, and can include your objective as well. It's the right choice if you:

- Have more than five years' experience in the workforce.
- Have strong achievement stories on your resume.
- Are changing careers, job positions, or industries.
- Are trying to move up in your chosen career.
- Are a high-level executive or manager.

Summaries can be a little longer than objectives. Third-party recruiters are especially glad to see a strong summary, because it provides them with the points they need to sell a candidate.

The goal of a summary is to highlight your most sought-after skills, abilities, accomplishments, and attributes. Start with the summary statement on your pitch from chapter 9. To make it really sharp, use the following three customizing tips from Monster's resume expert Kim Isaacs, director of Advanced Career Systems:

- *Relay your value:* Briefly weave your top selling point into your summary. For example: "Finance manager with staff of 6" might start a summary for someone promoting not just his or her finance skills but also his or her management abilities.

- *Light it up with keywords:* Fill your summary with keywords related to your career field. You may highlight items from the list of skills you made in your Job Search Portfolio.

- *Promote your certifications:* Mention certifications, licenses, or advanced degrees you hold—a CPA, a law degree, a computer certification. You worked hard to get those certifications, so show them off!

Here is a career summary for Jean, a real estate executive. Jean highlights numbers to stress her high-level experience and her standout skill in real estate financial management:

SUMMARY: *Accomplished executive with a proven ability to develop and implement real estate strategies that support business and financial objectives.*

- *Negotiated and structured multimillion-dollar real estate and service transactions.*

- *Key initiatives reduced operating budget by $32 million, turned around company's overall performance, and contributed to 550% stock increase.*
- *Recognized as an expert in applying financial concepts to asset management decisions.*

Here's the summary for Barry, who has just received a degree in Human Resources Management and is looking for his first job in HR. Without much experience, Barry chooses to stress his commitment, his skills, and the fact that his training is up-to-date.

SUMMARY: *Entry-level human resources professional with a bachelor's degree in HR Management and a unique perspective on the latest HR techniques. Seeking to provide top-quality HR support to ensure a competitive advantage in the global marketplace. Offering excellent communication skills and computer skills (Microsoft Office, Excel, PowerPoint, and database programs), and an understanding of organizational strategies to help meet corporate objectives.*

Wherever you can, list actual names of tools like Microsoft Excel.

Should you use the past or present tense in a resume? Either is acceptable as long as the resume reads well. Accomplishments in the distant past are best described in past tense. Also, the convention of dropping pronouns ("Seeking to provide . . ." vs. "I am now seeking to provide . . .") is acceptable in resumes.

How to Write a Job Objective

Kim Isaacs cautions, "The objective statement is gradually becoming obsolete," and she recommends summary statements for most resumes. There are, however, four times an objective statement is the right choice:

- You are just entering the workforce.
- You are returning to work after a long time away.

- You are obviously changing careers.
- You are applying for a job with highly specialized requirements.

If you choose to use an objective statement, use one of three strategies.

Be specific. Make your objective as specific as possible concerning what you want to do and where. Here are two examples:

OBJECTIVE: *Selling advanced medical devices to hospitals in the Midwest or Southeast.*

OBJECTIVE: *A senior administrative support position at a university, government agency, or nonprofit organization.*

State your goal clearly. If you don't have a specific position in mind, state a specific goal:

OBJECTIVE: *Advancing to the next level in network management in an Internet-based service, leading to CCNA certification.*

Note that this candidate, who is not a Cisco Certified Network Associate, has nevertheless included it in his objective. This tells a technical recruiter the candidate's level of experience as well as his or her ambition to grow (and not incidentally, the CCNA keyword means the resume may come up in a database search).

Target your objective to the job description. The more closely you can target your objective to the employer's needs, the better your results will be. If you are applying for an advertised job, write your objective using the job's responsibilities. For example, an Executive Assistant candidate seeing the following job advertisement:

A senior executive at ABC Company requires an experienced Administrative Assistant to handle all scheduling, staff communications, and management of staff priorities. Must be capable with Microsoft Office and have at least 4 years' experience.

. . . might write a job objective like this:

OBJECTIVE: *To make a senior executive more effective with my skills gained over 6 years as an Executive Assistant: professional communications, superb scheduling and priority-making, and office software proficiency.*

167

This technique requires that you customize your resume for each job application, but the effort is a good investment. Just be honest. And remember, don't mix up your customized resumes!

Targets

This section is optional. If you have specific jobs, companies, and/or work locations you want to target, you can list them briefly at the top of your resume. Targets tell recruiters where you want to work. Target jobs, companies, and locations are not required on all resumes, but they are good to feature in electronic versions because recruiters use targets to filter their searches. For example, if a recruiter is trying to fill a position in Chicago, he or she might search for the target location Chicago and find candidates who do not live in Chicago but are willing to move there.

It's okay to list targets on a resume you place in a resume database and leave the targets off your paper resume.

Target Job

If you are applying for an advertised job, you may customize your resume by including that job title, or even the company. For example, "TARGET: Regional sales manager at ABC Co." You may add more as your research uncovers jobs you might not have considered.

Here are other, typical examples of target job listings: "TARGET: Help desk manager at technology-intensive business." You can customize this statement by basing it on the requirements for a particular job, for example, "TARGET: Help desk manager for a staff of 8 or more."

Target Company

Placing a target company on your resume is another way to customize. When applying for a position, you may name the company itself, the company and its industry ("JCI or another leading supplier to the auto industry"), or even several competing companies ("Comcast, RCN, Verizon, Cablevision"). Expect your list of target companies to grow as you research the job market in chapter 12.

Target Location

Where do you want to work? If you have roots in one local area, you may want to limit yourself to that area on your resume. In that case, simply list a state or metro area.

Be direct about your ability—or inability—to relocate. If the job is in Boise and you have to stay in St. Louis, employers don't want you to apply. If you can relocate, that willingness may give you an "inside track" consideration.

Work Status

The issue of non-U.S. citizens working in the United States is an ongoing legal, political, and economic question. A U.S. employer doesn't need to know your national origin or even citizenship, but does need to know if you are authorized to work for an employer in the United States. If you require sponsorship, say so. If not, don't include this on your printed resume (although some career Web sites require this information, in which case you should indicate your work status).

Employment History

After the summary, your work experience is the most meaningful part of your resume. If you've completed the exercises in chapter 8, you're well on your way to adapting a powerful employment history for your resume by combining the employment history and achievement story documents in your Job Search Portfolio. (Incidentally, you'll sometimes see other terms for this category in sample resumes, usually "work experience," "professional experience," or even just "experience.")

Even if you are changing careers, your work experience tells a recruiter what kind of employee you will be, what results you can produce, and the career path you've chosen. It will also be a major focus of your job interviews, so spend time perfecting this part of your resume.

Reverse-Chronological Order

The overwhelming majority of resumes list work experience in reverse-chronological order, with the most recent job listed first. Give more detail to your most recent and, in some cases, your most relevant jobs. As you get more life experience, some of your early experience can drop away or be simplified to one or two lines.

In your first resume, when you don't have much on-the-job experience, you might say that you were on your high school debating team. You might give your high school graduation date and list a summer job. Once you have your first job on your resume, your high school experience can drop away; save the high school debating team story for the job interview. Also, high school graduation is appropriate on your first resume and then should drop away; high achievement in sports is appropriate, but intramural volleyball probably doesn't cut it.

Later in life, you can use a summary of related experiences that happened more than ten years ago. For example, a person who worked in printing shops for ten years in the 1980s, then changed into corporate marketing, might list those first ten years this way: "1982–1991: Progressive experience in the field of printing at ABC and XYZ companies." The three marketing jobs that followed from 1991 to 2003 are more relevant to the present. (Those early printing jobs may still supply great achievement stories for the interview, however.)

Your employment history also indicates your career transitions. When writing this section, you should think about how to answer questions that will come up in the job interview. If you are going backward in your career, getting *less* responsibility as time goes on, it's hard to counter the impression that you haven't done so well. If you used to be a Director, and now you're an Assistant, expect to do some explaining.

Keep the chronological path complete. If you had a 9-month job between two 4-year jobs, don't leave a blank. State the job and its responsibilities and/or achievements briefly and move on. If you took two years off to return to school, simply say so at the appropriate place in the chronology: "1994–1996: Full-time graduate student: acquired MBA in Marketing at Florida State University." A break in the chronology raises questions.

Writing Your Employment History

For each job, you want to showcase (1) what you were expected to do and (2) what you accomplished. You do this by combining what you wrote in your employment history and your achievement stories documents.

One of the most effective formats for summarizing jobs on a resume is to state responsibilities simply, and follow with achievements in a bulleted list. Include numbers whenever you can:

1998–2001

Sales Managing Associate, ABC Wireless, Ft. Worth, TX
Directed team of 12 wireless communications specialists in prime urban location. Trained new specialists in sales and customer service techniques. Communicated store revenue targets and operational goals to team and instructed customers in cellular products and features.

- Drove sales to exceed revenue targets by more than 25% for three years.
- Exceeded personal sales quota by more than 200% in two years, and brought team average to 145% of goal.
- Awarded "Outstanding Team Leader of the Year" 2001 and "Top Producer" 1999 and 2000.

Here's an example of an entry with hard-to-quantify achievements, still listed together:

2000–2003

Paralegal—City Attorney's Office, Fremont, MI
Conduct in-depth research and summarize depositions, medical records, and employment records. Devise profiles based on earnings/losses/medical expenses. Organize documents for trial and assist with jury instructions. Provide litigation support by assisting with case investigations, including gathering of underwriting, claim, and agency information and subpoena responses. In charge of updating database.

Key Accomplishments:
- Promoted to paralegal position after serving as an intern in city attorney's office for just over six months.
- Repeatedly praised by senior attorneys for timeliness, accuracy, and precision handling documents for large cases.
- Formally recognized for superior performance in conducting state surveys relating to insurance laws, regulations, and bulletins.
- Organized and participated in advanced NILS computer class for law offices in the Fremont area that successfully upgraded training for 25 paralegals.

As you translate your Job Search Portfolio documents into a resume, try some of the following tips to write a powerful work history:

Ditch the job description. One of the most common mistakes is to write experience sections that read like job descriptions. Some job seekers go so far as to copy job descriptions word for word. That's boring. Focus instead on stating responsibilities and results.

Quantify results. Remember the ways you used numbers to light up your achievement stories. If presenting this information (such as sales figures) is a breach of confidentiality, find another way to quantify your accomplishments. For example, use percentages rather than actual dollar figures.

Lead with the outcome. Write the result of your work first, before listing the problem and action. This allows you to lead with the most compelling aspect of your accomplishment. For example: "Reversed an annual $2 million decline in market share by streamlining the benchmark process and building a top-flight sales team."

Target your experience to your goal. Remember that your resume is a marketing tool. Your employment history should effectively market you for your current job objective. Focus on accomplishments that relate to your goal, and remove job duties and accomplishments that don't support your objective.

Use power words. Avoid dull or stale phrases such as "team leader" and "duties include." Review our list of Action Phrases and Power Verbs in the sidebar for inspiration.

And by the way . . . tell the truth. Studies indicate that job seekers often lie about their work experiences on their resumes. But with honest and well-written employment histories, even job seekers with less-than-perfect backgrounds will secure interviews. The best strategy for your resume is to always be truthful about your background.

Action Phrases and Power Verbs

This list of action phrases and power verbs, from Monster resume expert Kim Isaacs, will help bring your resume to life. Begin your work history descriptions with a power verb or phrase: enlisted the support, formed a committee, sold, budgeted, improved, increased, maintained the client relationship.

ACTION PHRASES

STANDARD RESUME

- Design, develop, and deliver
- Conduct needs analysis
- Write course design documents
- Manage development
- Consult with clients
- Facilitate problem-solving meetings

- Implement solutions
- Develop and implement formatting
- Developed and delivered
- Revamped product training
- Assessed employee and client training needs

- Analyzed evaluation data
- Designed and implemented
- Reduced manufacturing plant's burden
- Reduced material costs by $[number]

RECENT GRADUATE

- Followed special task force
- Assisted special task force

- Proctored and scored
- Facilitated discussion

- Directed project team

EXECUTIVE RESUME

- Managed an [number]-person team
- Negotiated over $[number] in contracts

- Coordinated strategic [number]-year plan
- Created and implemented innovative approach

- Developed new product
- Designed new processes
- Reduced operational costs by $[number]

POWER VERBS

A–B

accelerated acclimated accompanied accomplished achieved
acquired acted activated actuated adapted added addressed
adhered adjusted administered admitted adopted advanced

advertised advised advocated affected aided aired allocated altered amended amplified analyzed answered anticipated appointed appraised approached approved arbitrated arranged ascertained asked assembled assessed assigned assisted assumed attained attracted audited augmented authored authorized automated avail awarded balanced bargained borrowed bought broadened budgeted built

C

calculated canvassed capitalized captured carried out cast cataloged centralized chaired challenged changed channeled charted checked chose circulated clarified classified cleared closed coauthored cold-called collaborated collected combined commissioned committed communicated compared compiled completed complied composed computed conceived conceptualized concluded condensed conducted conferred consolidated constructed consulted contracted contrasted contributed contrived controlled converted convinced coordinated corrected corresponded counseled counted created critiqued cultivated cut

D

debugged decentralized decided decreased deferred defined delegated delivered demonstrated depreciated described designated designed determined developed devised devoted diagrammed directed disclosed discounted discovered dispatched displayed dissembled distinguished distributed diversified divested documented doubled drafted

E

earned eased edited effected elected eliminated employed enabled encouraged endorsed enforced engaged engineered enhanced enlarged enriched entered entertained established estimated evaluated examined exceeded exchanged executed exempted exercised expanded expedited explained exposed extended extracted extrapolated

F–H

facilitated familiarized fashioned fielded figured financed fit focused forecasted formalized formed formulated fortified found founded framed fulfilled functioned furnished gained gathered gauged gave generated governed graded granted greeted grouped guided handled headed hired hosted

I

identified illuminated illustrated implemented improved improvised inaugurated increased incurred indoctrinated induced influenced informed initiated innovated inquired inspected inspired installed instigated instilled instituted instructed insured interfaced interpreted interviewed introduced invented inventoried invested investigated invited involved isolated issued

J–M

joined judged launched lectured led lightened liquidated litigated lobbied localized located maintained managed mapped marketed maximized measured mediated merchandised merged met minimized modeled moderated modernized modified monitored motivated moved multiplied

N–O

named narrated negotiated noticed nurtured observed obtained offered offset opened operated operationalized orchestrated ordered organized oriented originated overhauled oversaw

P

paid participated passed patterned penalized perceived performed permitted persuaded phased out pinpointed pioneered placed planned polled prepared presented preserved presided prevented priced printed prioritized probed processed procured produced profiled programmed projected promoted prompted proposed proved provided publicized published purchased pursued

Q–R

quantified quoted raised ranked rated reacted read received recommended reconciled recorded recovered recruited rectified redesigned reduced referred refined regained regulated rehabilitated reinforced reinstated rejected related remedied remodeled renegotiated reorganized repaired replaced reported represented requested researched resolved responded restored restructured resulted retained retrieved revamped revealed reversed reviewed revised revitalized rewarded routed

S

safeguarded salvaged saved scheduled screened secured segmented selected sent separated served serviced settled shaped shortened showed shrank signed simplified sold solved spearheaded specified speculated spoke spread stabilized staffed staged standardized steered stimulated strategized streamlined strengthened stressed structured studied submitted substantiated substituted suggested summarized superseded supervised supplied supported surpassed surveyed synchronized synthesized systematized

T–W

tabulated tailored targeted taught terminated tested testified tightened took traced traded trained transacted transferred transformed translated transported traveled treated tripled uncovered undertook unified united updated upgraded used utilized validated valued verified viewed visited weighed welcomed widened witnessed won worked wrote

References

Assuming you've completed the references form in your Job Search Portfolio, you're ready. Protect your references' privacy: do not include their contact information on your resume. Most employers don't want to see them until the interview anyway. Unless they're required (and for a good reason), you should hold them for later in the job search. Unless you're a recent graduate, don't bother to write the traditional "References available upon request" at the bottom of your resume—employers assume this.

Education

Whether you're a PhD from Stanford or recently obtained your GED, you can use your resume's education section to outshine your competition. You do not need a Job Search Portfolio document to complete this on your resume; just follow the instructions below.

Where should your education appear on a resume? The best placement depends on what you are trying to emphasize.

- Place experience before education if you have three or more years of experience related to your goal. Hiring managers will probably be more interested in your job accomplishments than your education.

- Place education before experience if you are a recent graduate or have less than three years of work experience. If you are changing careers and have continued your education to support your new goal, education should come first. Academic and scientific professional resumes typically feature educational degrees before experience.

Fair or not, where you went to school can make a difference. If you went to Duke or Stanford or Harvard or another prestigious school, you might mention that in your summary. If you don't think your school is a show-stopper, place your education information at the bottom.

If you are a student or recent graduate, list your GPA if it is 3.0 or higher. If your school doesn't use the standard 4.0 scale, avoid confusion by listing the scale as well as your score (e.g., GPA: 4.1/4.5). As your career progresses, college GPA becomes less important and can be removed.

Include academic honors to show you excelled in your program. For example:

Ace College—*Springfield, Illinois*
BA in Accounting (cum laude), June 2000
–Delta Gamma Delta Honor Society, Dean's List, GPA: 3.9

Degree Incomplete. If you did not complete your degree, you may still list the number of credits you completed or the type of study you undertook. For example:

College of Staten Island—*Staten Island, New York*
Completed 90 credits toward a BA in political science, 1991 to 1994

Or just write, "Attended University of Massachusetts, 1991–1993." That too is perfectly acceptable.

If you are focusing more on experience than education, or if you're concerned about identifying your age, you can drop the graduation date. List the basic facts regarding your degree, including institution name, location, degree, and major. For example:

New Jersey City University—*Jersey City, New Jersey*
BS in Economics, Minor in Psychology

High School Information. Include your high school or GED information if you don't have any college credits. If you have college credits, remove references to high school.

You may be concerned if your education doesn't measure up to a job's advertised requirements. Additional training can help. If you don't have a degree but have been participating in ongoing training, list your related courses, seminars, conferences, and training under the term "Professional Development." Here's an example of a computer programmer without a degree in computer science:

> **Education:** *Completed one year of study toward a BS in computer science at Northeastern University, 1999–2000.*
> **Professional Development:** *Certificate in Data/Telecommunications from University of Massachusetts online (2002); Principles of Wireless Networking course completed online at Jones International University (2002).*

Your training might be so impressive that your lack of a formal degree isn't a deal-breaker! You must be realistic, of course: you can't be a lawyer without a law degree no matter how many debates you've won or criminology classes you've taken.

Jeff's Story: I Did School My Way!

I started Monster without having finished college. In 1996, with the company doing great, I was speaking a lot, and I would be introduced as having "attended" the University of Massachusetts. Or worse, they would say I graduated from UMass. Then I would have to begin my speech by saying, "Actually, I didn't graduate . . ."

So, looking for both credentials and the credibility that goes along with success in higher education, I decided to go back to school. First, I went to Harvard Business School for a three-year (three weeks full-time each summer) certificate called "Owner/President Management" (OPM). Then, when I completed that in 1999, I decided to go back and finish my undergraduate degree. I graduated from UMass in May 2001 at age forty, and was speaker at my own graduation in front of 20,000 people. I went to school for almost five years while I was running Monster. What I learned I was able to immediately apply to my job; it definitely contributed to Monster's success!

Certifications

List the certifications from your Job Search Portfolio. Create a separate "Certifications" heading when a certification is absolutely required for the job. Otherwise, you may want to include certifications in the "Education" section of your resume.

Affiliations

If you belong to a professional organization, a union, or a group promoting professional development, simply list them. Senior candidates should list directorships, advisory boards, and other affiliations that add credibility. These should be relevant to your work life; list other clubs and service organizations under "Additional Information."

Skills/Keywords

This is a new addition to the resume, and once again, it's driven by the technology of recruiting. In the past, people occasionally listed specific skills like fluency in a foreign language. Today, you need to list many more skills, especially in the electronic versions of your resume. There are two reasons for this:

- First, you list your skills because that's how your resume will be located in a database. Employers use computer software to search through all the resumes that they have saved. Your skills are the "keywords" they use to search. A company looking for a skilled accountant will search using keywords like "CPA," "budgeting," and "accounts payable." April Young, who runs Monster's phone support group for job seekers, puts it plainly: "A good selection of keywords makes a difference for so many job seekers."

- Second, when your resume is found, an employer will look for specific skills to find them with a quick scan of your resume. If they see the skills they want right away, they'll read your resume more carefully. If they don't see those skills, they might move on to the next one.

Take out your list of skills and get ready to select those skills that, in your judgment, offer the best "selling" message to employers. This section of your resume can be easily customized to fit a particular job. For example, if you are applying for a job as an executive assistant, you might put more emphasis in this section on your organizational skills or your communication skills or office software skills, depending on the requirements of the job.

Don't get hung up on formatting—a selection of top skills from the skills list in your Job Search Portfolio is fine. In electronic versions of your resume, where brevity is less of a concern, you may want to add the whole list.

Here's a sample list of skills on a resume for an executive assistant:

SKILLS: *Organization, file systems, phone communication, scheduling, calendar, travel arrangements, expense reports, agendas, minutes, meetings, off-sites, supplies. Microsoft Word, Excel, PowerPoint, Outlook, Publisher, Internet, research, fax, PC and Macintosh. On-time delivery, reports, correspondence, memos, presentations, charts; problem solving, listening, interpersonal communication.*

This list contains a lot of good matches to the search terms a recruiter would use to find candidates for this job! In addition, anyone looking at a printed version of this resume can see that the candidate has a wide range of skills.

One of the trends these days is for people to include their skills in great big print. For example, someone who works for a company that's been getting bad press lately may place a bold list of skills right up top, before the resume's "Experience" section, just to distract recruiters from the name of their scandal-ridden company. That's dangerous; recruiters will see through the trick. Instead, deal with difficult situations in the cover letter or e-mail message (see chapter 11).

For a business or professional resume, you may also list "areas of expertise," "core competencies," or "proficiencies." These terms are used more often in business or in professions where technical knowledge is important, such as technology and health care. They all mean how you apply specific knowledge, which is different from skills—as in this example taken from the sample resume of "John Q. Security" at the end of this chapter:

CORE COMPETENCIES
- Network & Systems Security
- Business Impact Analysis
- Regulatory Adherence
- Data Integrity & Recovery
- Disaster Recovery Planning
- Contingency Planning
- Research & Development
- Risk Assessment
- Cost-Benefits Analysis

Here's a reminder for those of you who are gainfully employed: keep a page in the back of your daily planner to note your accomplishments—what you did and how long it took. List the skills and specific expertise that powered those accomplishments. If you do, you'll have beautiful horsepower the next time you sit down to update your resume. Most people sit down to write their accomplishments and then draw a complete blank.

Additional Information

Don't bury your individual life. You want to be interesting, so by all means mention special interests or experiences that boost your candidacy. It's a judgment call which hobbies or interests to include. They're most valuable if they're easily connected to job performance, or if they say something unusual about you. Be selective, specific, and clear. If you run marathons, say so. That tells employers a lot about your persistence and discipline.

This is also the spot to include, if you choose, membership in volunteer service organizations such as Junior Achievement, the Community Chest, or your local school board. In general, however, I'd stay away from affiliations that are politically charged or overtly religious, such as Planned Parenthood, a Catholic archdiocese, the NRA, and the Sierra Club, unless you know for a fact that the organization is culturally compatible with the employer's values.

Resume Style

The advent of online resume databases has made pretty resume design less important than in the past, but you still want to carry a professional-looking resume to an interview. Fortunately, you don't have to be a designer to produce one.

There are many attractive resume templates available free on the Web (see **monstercareers.com** for updated information). To use these, you simply download them from the site to your computer and fill in the appropriate fields. Also, many books show resume designs (see Resources at the back of this book).

If you trust your sense of design, use your word processing program's advanced formatting features such as bold, italics, line draw, industry icons, and attractive fonts to give your resume a distinctive look. I'm a pretty visual person, and I remember spending a lot of time working on my resume early in my career—trying to get a message across that I do whatever it takes to soar to new heights. I played with the idea of having a silhouette of a high jumper going across my resume—one idea I didn't act on.

You'll hear stories about resume gimmicks: a resume that arrives with a cup of coffee or a resume sent as a singing telegram. At Monster, we knew someone who applied for a marketing position at a jeans company by writing his entire resume on a pair of their jeans. He got attention for the stunt. He got the job because he was a good marketer. You can project your resume on the side of the building if you want to get attention—but you'd better be ready to prove you can do the job, and make sure your face-to-face personality can match the creativity of your idea or stunt. If you can't, you've wasted someone's time, and you're not going to advance.

What's the right length?

How long should your resume be? Bruce Wain, CEO of resume-writing service CareerPerfect, suggests, "You need brevity *and* depth, two contradictory requirements that need to be balanced. Brevity works for the initial screening; depth gets you into the final pool of candidates."

Remember, most people's resumes are best on one page. All of the ideas we've been discussing could create a short book if you're not careful! If you follow your intuition, you'll get most of it right—then check with someone whose opinion you trust. Get suggestions to improve what you've written.

Strive to keep your resume focused on your key messages. Let go of past experiences that don't market you toward your current goal. Every word in the resume should sell your credentials and value to a potential employer. Don't use every one of your achievement stories—save a couple of them for the job interview.

Here's a basic guideline:

CONSIDER A ONE-PAGE RESUME IF:

- You have less than ten years of experience.
- You're pursuing a radical career change and past experience isn't relevant to your new goal.
- You've held several positions with just one employer.

CONSIDER A TWO-PAGE RESUME IF:

- You have ten or more years of experience related to your goal.
- Your field requires technical or engineering skills, and you need space to list and prove your technical knowledge.
- You have a special situation that requires explanation (see chapter 18).

CONSIDER A THREE-PAGE OR LONGER RESUME IF:

- You're a senior-level manager or executive with a long track record of leadership accomplishments.
- You're in an academic or scientific field with an extensive list of publications, speaking engagements, professional courses, licenses, or patents. (Those long publication lists should appear under a heading, on their own page. For the first two pages, use the format we've discussed. On second and subsequent pages, include a page number and your name.)

Should you use a functional resume?

The vast majority of job seekers use the chronological resume described above. It's the tried-and-tested format most preferred by HR professionals and hiring managers. However, the functional resume (also known as a "skills-based resume") could be a better choice for you if:

- You're looking for consulting or contract work, and want to highlight special qualifications like Java programming experience or multiple sales achievements.
- You're entering the workforce for the first time or after a long absence, whether you're a recent graduate without formal work experience,

stay-at-home parent now seeking outside employment, or caregiver who has spent a year or more attending an ill or aging relative.

- Your earlier work experience is more relevant to your next job target than what you're doing presently.

- You've held a number of different or unrelated jobs during a relatively short period of time and are worried about being labeled as a job-hopper.

A functional resume groups key skills and achievements into different categories to demonstrate your qualifications. This skills focus allows you to emphasize your strengths and/or soft-pedal a flawed or nonexistent employment record. For example, if you're applying for an international sales management position, you might choose categories such as "Sales and Marketing Experience," "International Business/Foreign Language Fluency," and "Team Building and Leadership Expertise" for your headings, listing appropriate skills and achievements beneath each one.

The actual "Employment History" section of a functional resume is typically brief, with a simple list of positions held, company names, and employment dates at the bottom of page one or on page two to deemphasize their importance. Occasionally some of this information is even intentionally omitted altogether.

Bruce Wain of CareerPerfect cautions, "A true functional resume without ANY employment history is a screaming red flag that the candidate is trying to hide something—something likely worse than the information that you want to play down. Instead, create a functional profile that creates the right skill emphasis, and an employment history highlighting only specific skills."

Leaving off dates or titles can raise employers' suspicions that you're trying to hide something. The functional format can also frustrate readers who are trying to figure out where you performed a particular accomplishment, since these details are listed under skill categories instead of job titles.

One more caution: functional resumes may not work so well with on-line and software-based electronic recruiting systems. A good list of keyword skills is still the best bet that you'll be found.

But, if the advantages of the functional design outweigh the drawbacks, go ahead and defy tradition! A new skills-based format could be just what your resume needs to present you in the best possible light.

Here's an example of a functional resume for a recently graduated student. Certain points are noted on the example.

Justin Graduate

E-mail: jgraduate@jobseeker.com
2349 N. River Range
Hill Valley, California 00000
(555) 567-2486

Professional Objective

A position in **Chemical Engineering** providing the opportunity to make a strong contribution to organizational goals through continued development of professional skills.

It's fine for a recent graduate to open with an objective.

Qualifications Profile

Experience/Skills:

This is a listing of skills relevant to the job he seeks. In a resume database, he'll be found by the right recruiters.

CHEMICAL ENGINEERING: *Projects, related skills, and practicum include:*
—Water quality management
—Preparing water treatment plans for up to 6 million gallons of water per day
—Developing water cleanup plan for nuclear reservation
—Monitoring and testing air emissions
—Evaluating air pollution control methods
—Developing physical and chemical methods for air pollution control
—Performing gas chromatography

Lots of technical keywords listed here, including the names of software programs.

Process Design:
—Analyzing plant and equipment needs
—Developing most economic and effective methods
—Establishing lab procedures
—Designing digital control systems

Computers:
—Coding in C++, JavaScript, and HTML
—Assisting in Website development
—Utilizing Windows-based PCs with various software: Matlab, Simulink, Equation Solvers, Lotus; Microsoft Office: Word, Excel, Access, Outlook

Administration:
—Ensuring compliance with EPA guidelines, environmental regulations, and emission standards
—Preparing technical reports and documentation
—Ordering lab equipment and supplies

Justin Graduate

Education: **Bachelor of Science Degree in Chemical Engineering, 2001**
Hometown University, Hometown, Indiana
Magna Cum Laude Graduate, Academic All-American

Professional Associations:
Student Member, Society of Chemical Engineers

**Accomplishments/
Strengths:**
• Formally recognized for contributions to environmental improvement plan for the City of Hometown, Indiana
• Excellent troubleshooting and analytical skills
• Well organized and proficient with details
• Excellent interpersonal and team skills

Professional Experience

**June 2001 to
December 2001**
CITY OF HOMETOWN, Hometown, Indiana
Air Quality Technician (Internship)
Conducted studies in air pollution control and designed spreadsheets in Excel. Measured levels of pollution and made recommendations to improve air quality, including written reports and public speaking presentations.
• Commended by City Manager for contributions to environmental improvement plan

**September 1997
to June 2001**
HOMETOWN UNIVERSITY, Hometown, Indiana
Teaching Assistant: September 1999 to June 2001
Assisted professors in chemical and environmental engineering courses. Led small group discussions and answered student questions. Graded tests and assignments. Supervised students in lab. Provided instruction in use of software including Matlab, Simulink, Excel, and Word.
• Selected from 75 students to become a Teaching Assistant

Chemical Engineering Student: 1997–2001
Class projects included: Developed cleanup plan for nuclear reservation; prepared treatment plans for 6 million gallons of water per day; assisted in developing laboratory procedures; conducted lab experiments on bioremediation and water treatment; analyzed federal regulations and required remediation levels; ensured compliance with environmental laws and regulations; developed and evaluated physical and chemical methods of air pollution control; measured pollution using air quality equipment; performed extensive research on EPA

Since Justin was in school 1999-2001, he refers to those dates here and below, with no gaps.

Professional experience is brief, so it follows skills and achievements.

Justin describes student work as professional experience. This works because he's completed tasks he'll do in his next job.

Justin Graduate

guidelines and emission standards; monitored and tested air emissions using various instruments; used computer for dispersion modeling; performed gas chromatography in lab; designed and implemented digital control systems; achieved flow rate goals using computer and digital control instruments. Conducted environmental studies and wrote formal proposals. Utilized software applications including Matlab, Simulink, Equation Solvers, Lotus 1-2-3, and Excel.
• Graduated Magna Cum Laude with a G.P.A. of 3.83
• Recognized as an Academic All-American

Additional experience concurrent with education . . .

**September 1997
to
September 1999**

PC SUPERSTORE, Hometown, Indiana
Sales Associate
Sold computers, peripherals, and software. Answered technical questions from customers. Demonstrated use of systems and applications. Generated a strong referral business through quality service.
• Effectively addressed customer issues and ensured customer satisfaction

– Excellent references are available upon request –

It's okay for a student to add that he has references.

Crimes of the Resume

The mistakes below are instant turnoffs for employers. They say bad things about your work habits and, sometimes, your character. Avoid them, or your resume will take a one-way trip to the trash can.

SPELLING ERRORS, TYPOS, AND POOR GRAMMAR

According to a Monster poll, this is the number-one pet peeve of resume readers. These errors make you look sloppy and unconcerned about results . . . exactly the message you *don't* want to send.

LYING/STRETCHING THE TRUTH

This includes different degrees of deception, such as:

- Listing false employers, false achievements, false degrees or certifications.
- Exaggerating your achievements. "Improved annual sales 300%" doesn't count if you started with $50 in annual sales.
- Exaggerating your role, authority, or size of your staff.
- Misleading language: "Undergraduate degree in Education" is not the same as "Undergraduate degree in Physical Education."
  Also, you'll eventually get caught—guaranteed.

REGURGITATING THE JOB DESCRIPTION

Recruiters already know what the job is; you can take key words and concepts from the job description, but don't copy it word for word. Your resume should highlight *your* individual candidacy.

INACCURATE OR MISSING DATES

Missing dates, especially for long periods of time, are a red flag. Include specific ranges in months and years for every position. Fill gaps as described in this chapter, or in the cover letter.

INACCURATE OR MISSING CONTACT INFORMATION

How can someone contact you if the phone number is missing a digit or your e-mail address is incorrect?

INCORRECT FORMATTING ONLINE

Elaborate formats are tempting but fancy resumes can't be scanned. Send an electronic resume in ASCII.

TOO LONG

Recruiters don't have time to read your autobiography, and they won't!

UNQUALIFIED

You may want a job, but if you don't have the skills and experience needed, you are wasting the recruiter's time. Maybe more important, you're wasting your own time.

PERSONAL INFORMATION UNRELATED TO THE JOB

Don't distract a recruiter with your age, height, weight, hobbies, and interests unless they're directly related to the work you want to do.

PROVING YOU DON'T CARE

Don't do the following, which are insults to the recruiter:

- Blasting anonymously to 1,000 recruiters.
- Sending a poorly photocopied resume.
- Sending a smudged, coffee-stained, re-used resume.
- Sending an outdated resume.

See the following for an example of a resume loaded with mistakes. Poor Bob Candidate wrote this in thirty minutes late at night, and at first glance, it looks like a standard resume. Start reading, though, and his carelessness shows. See the list of Bob's ten worst mistakes on page 191.

Bob Candidate
42 Heaven Road
Westcenter CA 90300
(603) 456-790
friskymonkey@aamail.com

Objective: Seeking a challenging position in marketing or health care with a company that offer excellent benefits, flexible schedules and competitive pay.

EXPERIENCE:

1993–94   Sales associate, Shirts 'n' Stuff, Santa Monica Pier.
Sold merchandise. I was responsible for cashing out the register, selling more merchandise than before, and interfacing with the public. Talents included persuasion and the ability to help people.

1996–2000   **ABC Co., Marketing Department**
As an associate in the Marketing department, Bob's responsibilities included planning, persuading and perusing projects that brought ABC's line of new health care products to market. I had many successes, including
- New product launch
- Information gathering and analysis
- Writing and proposing marketing materials, which included brochures, ad copy, surveys, and proposals and plans.
- Taking classes to increase my education in marketing.
- Single-handedly sent 3,000 e-mail a day to customers.

2000–2004   **Marketing and sales, XYZ Corporation Marketing**
Complete responsibility as Marketing Manage for this technical services business's marketing. A well-rounded and successful person with a track record of success. Example: Complete responsibility for all aspects of marketing, including direct marketing and marketing communications.

EDUCATION:

Westcenter college, AB in business, 1993
Upton Sinclair High School, Westcenter CA, 1989. Graduated with 3.6 grade point average. Drama club, swimming and rock band.

OTHER: Personal interests include reading, playing sports and music, and my pets. Divorced. References available. Skills: Marketing.

PROBLEMS WITH BOB CANDIDATE'S RESUME:

1. Incomplete phone number.
2. Cutesy, unprofessional e-mail address.
3. Bob's bland, clichéd objective only talks about what an employer can offer Bob, not what he has to offer (a summary would have been better). Also, "marketing" is part of a business, "health care" is an industry. Does he mean marketing in health care? Or is he looking at health care because it's a growing business?
4. Experience section should be in reverse-chronological order, with the most recent job at the top.
5. Bob's writing throughout the experience section is unclear. What was the title of his latest job? What does "Complete responsibility for all aspects of marketing" mean? Is "Information gathering and analysis" a success? His 2000–2004 job description was copied from the ad for the job he's applying to. Also, Bob refers to himself in the third person once, which makes him seem a little . . . odd.
6. No numbers to prove accomplishments except one that's unclear: Did Bob really send 3,000 e-mails a day single-handedly? Or did he push a computer key that sent 3,000 e-mails?
7. Bob provides more detail about high school than college.
8. Sloppy formatting and style. Two examples: Inconsistent use of boldface type and inconsistent use of periods at the end of bullet points.
9. Do we really care that Bob is divorced? Are his references about that divorce? Also, "reading, playing sports and music" tells nothing of interest.
10. Bob didn't proofread. There are at least four errors that his computer's spell checker didn't catch. Can you spot them? (They're listed on page 192.)

PERFECT IS JUST GOOD ENOUGH

Proofread, proofread, and proofread your resume. Aloud and backward. There are hiring managers out there who will ding you on one single mistake. Share your resume with trusted friends and colleagues to make sure you haven't inadvertently substituted one word for another. Keep in mind that your computer's spell-check function often will not catch these errors, since the problem is one of incorrect word choice rather than misspelling. (A common example: "manger" instead of "manager." Unless you hold fodder for livestock, change it!)

Dennis F. Judge Jr. of the Judge Group, a large staffing firm, suggests you use proofreading as a networking tool as well. "If you know VPs or presidents of organizations, through mutual affiliations such as family, ask them to critique your resume. It's a small favor to ask, they'll improve your resume from a business perspective, and they may even think of a colleague who should see it."

• Spelling errors Bob Candidate didn't catch:

  • Objective: Bob wrote "offer" instead of "offers."
  • 1996–2000 job, line 3: Bob wrote "perusing" instead of "pursuing."
  • 1996–2000 job, fifth bullet point: Bob wrote "e-mail" instead of "e-mails."
  • 2000–2004 job, line 2: Bob wrote "Manage" instead of "Manager."

Resume-Writing Services

Should someone else write your resume? There are good reasons to consider the investment. You'll have to weigh the cost, which can be considerable, against the benefit of improving your presentation.

Many resume-writing services market themselves as a quick ticket to a job, but remember: even the most polished resume can only gain an employer's interest. You are still responsible for knowing what you want, applying for the right jobs, and standing out in the job interview process.

Bruce Wain of CareerPerfect suggests several situations in which a professional can make a difference:

• When you know your writing isn't that strong.

• When you cannot be objective.

• When English is not your native language.

• When your resume isn't getting results and you know it's because your resume isn't very good. (You have to get feedback to know this, which you can do in a networking or informational interview. See chapters 12 and 14.)

• When you are working with a career counselor or other professional who has advised more help.

Resume writers usually work by having you fill out an extensive form about your work history and objectives. They work with this raw material to create a resume, so the more you give, the better the chance you'll like the result.

How do you choose a resume writer? There are currently no legal certifications required to become a professional resume writer. Monster's resume expert Kim Isaacs suggests you use members of one or both of the two national organizations of professional resume writers: The National Resume Writers Association (**nrwaweb.com/**) and the Professional Association of Resume Writers (**parw.com/home.html**). Listings of local resume writers appear on these sites.

Online, Monster offers an excellent resume-writing service through its site at **resume.monster.com/writingservices/index.asp**. Monster's Kim Isaacs is president of Advanced Career Systems, another service, located on the Web at **resumepower.com/**.

Always in View

If you followed the steps in this chapter, your resume is ready to show to employers. It's time to place it in an online resume database. This is called "posting" your resume, and you can do it at any of the popular job Web sites. The sites differ slightly in their methods of receiving resumes, so find the link on each site's home page and follow the instructions.

Of course you'll want to post your resume when you are looking for a job, but you should keep your updated resume active at all times. If you're employed, that doesn't mean you will leave your job next week! It means that, like an entrepreneur, you are managing your career by placing yourself in front of opportunity. It will connect you to others in your field, and this kind of networking is part of an overall strategy to manage your career. Finally, as your experiences and achievements grow, it's a record of your career—ready 24 hours a day to show you at your most promising.

Your resume is your life document. It's a sign of your own self-respect that you keep it active, updated, and constantly improving . . . just like you!

Sample Resumes

The following sample resumes show several different formats, lengths, and strategies. In each case, the candidate has emphasized key messages to grab the employer's attention, and sprinkled the resume with words and phrases that will be picked up by search engines.

Book to Web

There's an ever-expanding library of resume samples and information at **monstercareers.com**.

Online Resumes

The first two resumes appear online; thus they are reprinted here with minimal formatting, as they might appear when found in a resume database. In each case, the candidates have filled in fields online, which are the categories listed in boldface on the left.

Retail Resume—Edward Cooper. Edward is determined to move up. Although his current job title is sales associate, he is now focused on managerial tasks, and emphasizes them in his resume. Edward shows that he was a keyholder to open/close the store, trained new sales associates, and assisted in the daily running of the store. By including some of the mundane tasks that are unrelated to his goal of a management position and emphasizing the tasks that show management capabilities, his resume effectively markets his potential for a higher position. Edward reinforces his potential by including retail lingo throughout the resume. He uses industry buzzwords to show that he is on the same page as the employer in his desire to satisfy customers and maximize sales.

Edward Cooper
100 Main Road
Princeville NJ 24244
ecooper@somedomain.com

Home (123) 456-7890
Mobile (123) 908-7654

Award-winning retail salesperson

Summary

key words:
- *customer*
- *managing*
- *performance*
- *growing*

Experienced, customer-focused retailer offers superior sales and leadership skills. Skills in managing inventory, merchandise display, and improved store performance recognized with awards and growing responsibility.

Target Job

An assistant manager or management trainee position that would allow me to positively influence sales performance in a retail setting.

Good use of buzzword

Target Company

An expanding, customer-obsessed retail operation that offers a fast-paced work environment and rewards superior performance.

Target Locations

New Jersey, New York metro area

Work Status

I am authorized to work for any employer in the U.S.

Experience

6/1997–Present   Retailer 1   Princeville, NJ
Sales Associate
Implement procedures to maximize sales at the Princeville store location. Available to help customers locate merchandise and answer any questions. Maintain a friendly and helpful demeanor, always ensuring that customers are completely satisfied. Keep store immaculately clean and arrange displays to maximize effectiveness. Key accomplishments:

Recognized achievements

- Awarded "salesperson of the year" in 1999 for sales achievements. Attended banquet to receive award.
- Trained 5 new sales associates, teaching them about merchandise, displays, customer service, and sales strategies.
- Entrusted to assist with daily operations, including opening/closing store, processing transactions, dealing with complaints, monitoring stock and ordering merchandise, and coordinating promotional events.
- Helped turn around store's image by offering excellent customer service and sales support. Store moved from #10 to #2 producer in the region within 2 years.
- Named "Employee of the Month" for outstanding performance in March 1998.

key results prove key message.

7/1995–6/1997   Retailer 1   Princeville, NJ
Cashier

Implies a great attitude even in first jobs.

Managed the cash register and provided customer service to customers at point of sale. Known as one of the fastest and most accurate cashiers in the entire store. Even during busy seasons, I never had a long line.

11/1993–6/1995   Company 1   Newark, NJ
Mailroom Clerk
Processed and delivered mail to entire company, representing 500+ employees.

Education   6/1997   State University of New Jersey   Camden, NJ
Bachelor's Degree
Bachelor of Arts, psychology major

Skills   Retail sales, customer service, creative displays, team leadership, inventory management, ordering, special sales promotions.

Uses words that say, "I'm ready for management":
- *Implement*
- *Trained/teaching*
- *Entrusted*
- *Awards*
- *Superior sales*

Source: ResumePower.com

Executive Assistant Resume—Anne Johnson. Here's the resume of executive assistant Anne Johnson, who most recently worked at a regional bank. Anne wanted her resume to show that she was an integral part of the office operation. As an executive assistant, she doesn't just answer phones and take messages; she helps make decisions that improve the way the office runs. Anne demonstrates her value by focusing on her achievements. She incorporates statements made by supervisors right into the body of the resume; these are powerful indications that her performance made a difference to the company. She also listed many keywords critical to her target job.

Anne Johnson
154 Westerly Drive
Rockford IL 61010
(555) 123-4567
ajohnson@thisdomain.com

All execs want to be effective—good attention grabber!

Executive Assistant

Objective

To make a senior executive more effective with my skills gained over nine years as an Executive Assistant: Professional communications, superb scheduling and priority-making, and office software proficiency.

Target Job

A position that allows me to use creativity, organization, and business acumen to positively benefit my employer.

Target Company

A bank or other financial institution that values teamwork and encourages professional development.

Sets up for a good interview by mentioning culture.

Target Locations

Chicago metro; may relocate to Atlanta, GA, Washington, D.C., or Los Angeles, CA.

Work Status

U.S. Citizen

Experience

7/1995–8/2004   Bank 1   Rockford, IL
Administrative Assistant
Provided administrative support to VP of Investment Lending and Corporate Services Department. Contributed to the department's success in several ways:

—Orchestrated all details of a high-level meeting that attracted 250+ attendees and resulted in $1.45 million in new assets. Formally recognized by supervisor for the meeting's success:

Used sparingly, testimony is great.

"Ms. Johnson played an instrumental role in the meeting's success . . . kudos go to her organizational skills and attention to detail."

—Improved department's compliance with payroll procedures by regularly auditing time and attendance records.

—Prepared monthly PowerPoint presentations for VP that were well received by management team.

Anne doesn't have many hard numbers, so she emphasizes efficiency and large capacity for work.

—Known in the Bank for ability to meet tight deadlines while maintaining an emphasis on quality.

—Trained four new secretarial staff members; two were later promoted.

198

—Entrusted with handling confidential data and proprietary information.

—Consistently maintained a professional image and the integrity of the department. The CEO remarked, "Ms. Johnson is a true asset to the Investment Lending Team. Her initiative, professionalism, and follow-through are unparalleled."

Education	6/1995 University of Georgia Atlanta, Georgia **Associate's degree** Associate's degree in communications

| **Skills** | Organization, file systems, phone communication, scheduling, calendar, travel arrangements, expense reports, agendas, minutes, meetings, off-sites, supplies. Microsoft Word, Excel, PowerPoint, Outlook, Publisher, Internet, research, fax, PC and Macintosh. On-time delivery, reports, correspondence, memos, presentations, charts; problem solving, listening, interpersonal communication. |

These will show up in online resume searches so she'll be found.

References	Available upon request.

| **Additional Information** | Dedicated administrative assistant with special knowledge of the banking industry. Strong interest in working with my employer to enhance operations and foster a sense of teamwork among staff members. Always willing to teach and mentor peers, while remaining open to constructive criticism and advice. Fully computer literate and a quick learner on new programs. |

Subtle but powerful: Anne knows every executive has had assistants who didn't work out — she puts doubts to rest by emphasizing the critical qualities: efficiency, capacity, responsibility, initiative.

Source: ResumePower.com

Presentation Resumes

The three resumes that follow are "presentation" resumes, neatly formatted and printed. They're the resume format you show in a job interview. You will notice that they aren't so stringently formatted as the online resumes, but they accomplish the same goals outlined in this chapter. I've made notes showing especially strong points.

These resumes appear longer in part because they are adjusted to appear in this book. See other examples at **monstercareers.com**.

KIM MILLER

789 Evergreen Terrace • Brattleboro, Vermont 05432 • bmill789@jayol.com

SENIOR SALES MANAGER

Strategic Sales Planning / Market Expansion / Relationship Management

Good keywords

Dynamic, entrepreneurial sales management strategist with a 15+ year record of achievement and demonstrated success driving multimillion-dollar sales growth while providing award-winning sales leadership in highly competitive markets. Adept at driving growth of company revenues and improving sales-team performance. Exceptional mentor and coach. Tenacious in building new business, securing customer loyalty, and forging strong relationships with external business partners.

key achievement

She'll use this when the interview moves to "culture" questions.

Core competencies include:

Okay to list her skills up front.

- Strategic Market Positioning
- Solution Selling Strategies
- Team Building
- Key Client Retention
- Reseller/VAR Networks

- Multimillion-Dollar Negotiations
- Territory Growth/Development
- High-Impact Sales Presentations
- Organizational Leadership

—————— **PROFESSIONAL EXPERIENCE** ——————

DIRECTOR, NORTH AMERICAN SALES, 1999–2002
Cybertech Corporation, Brattleboro, VT

Cybertech is a leading innovator in tape storage and automation with 1500 employees and annual revenues exceeding $100 million.

She describes her employer, in case she seeks a job outside her industry.

Oversee all sales and business development functions, including new product rollouts, key account management, customer relationship development, contract negotiations, and order fulfillment. Hold P&L and budget responsibilities. Provide cross-functional team training, coaching, and mentoring. Direct network of district sales managers and marketing associates located throughout the U.S and eastern Canada. Design, implement, and adjust various sales plans and programs for data storage products, with a focus on building two-tier distribution channel and fostering demand in the Fortune 500 arena.

Selected Achievements:

Achievement stories!

- Instrumental in complete turnaround of under-performing sales team; set higher expectations and instituted individual team-member accountability resulting in **450% revenue increase** over three years.
- Met or exceeded all quotas throughout tenure, averaging more than **$57 million in annual sales** in North America and earning multiple company awards in recognition of performance.

Boldface draws attention to numbers.

- Consistently developed strong, sustainable relationships with VAR partners and executive decision makers of Fortune 500 client companies.

MIDWEST SALES DIRECTOR, 1994–1999
Tetradine, Inc., Schaumburg, IL

Tetradine is a leading computer distributor and franchiser with $110 million in annual sales.

Managed 12-state group comprised of 48 franchisees and independent re-sellers, overseeing total annual purchases exceeding $32 million. Developed and implemented strategic plans to market franchises and persuade resellers/VARs to purchase products from company's distribution centers. Responsible for channel/end-user sales development, new market identification and pene-tration, financial channel management, and large-scale contract negotiations. Monitored operational performance of franchisees to ensure alignment with corporate profit goals.

Selected Achievements:
- Team consistently **ranked #1 in company sales** for seven consecutive years.
- Designed and led Midwest location training and team building seminars later adopted as company-wide standard for franchisees.
- Impacted business partner **revenue by over 200%** through continual communications and liaison efforts with both franchisees and sales team members.

REGIONAL SALES MANAGER, DEALER DISTRIBUTION, 1989–1994

SALES REPRESENTATIVE, 1988–1989
Ricotech Image Corporation, Rockford, IL

Ricotech is one of the world's leading suppliers of office automation equip-ment including copiers, facsimile machines, and data processors.

Built and developed 7-state dealership network for sale of entry-level repro-graphic systems. Facilitated sales training for dealer representatives, devel-oped new sales programs, and acted as liaison between dealer channel and direct sales organization.

Selected Achievements:
- Established company's first-ever Northwest channel sales organization.
- Increased **territory sales by 200%** in 1991.
- Promoted after one year to Regional Sales Manager.

Writes less about older jobs, but keeps format consistent.

————————— **EDUCATION & TRAINING** —————————

Leads with most
recent degree.

Master of Business Administration (MBA), 1988
Northern Illinois University-Rockford, Rockford, IL

Bachelor of Science (BS), 1986
Northern Illinois University-Rockford, Rockford, IL

Professional Development Courses:
Dale Carnegie Sales Training
Leadership Through Quality
Account Management-Selling System

This shows she
never stops
learning.

© Copyright 2003 CareerPerfect.com

BEVERLY M. JONES, RN

200 Hacienda Drive, Helena MT 70000
600-555-4000 • bmjrn@notmail.com

Another term for "Summary" →

QUALIFICATIONS PROFILE

Dedicated and patient-focused **Registered Nurse** with proven strengths in acute patient care, staff development, and family advocacy.

- Exceptional capacity to multi-task: manage numerous, often competing priorities with ease and foster the provision of superior patient care.
- Administrative and referral experience including admissions, assessment, treatment, referral, and education for a wide range of patients.
- Widely recognized as an excellent care provider and patient advocate.
- Demonstrated ability to forge, lead, and motivate outstanding healthcare teams that provide top-quality patient care.
- Outstanding interpersonal and communication skills; superior accuracy in patient history, charting, and other documentation.

These key messages contain lots of strong action words.

Certifications and Proficiencies

Certifications:	*Proficiencies:*	
• Ventilator care	• Med/Surg	• Care plan creation and administration
• Telemetry	• ICU	• NG/Sump & Peg tubes
• Intravenous therapy	• CCU	• Patient/family education
• Phlebotomy	• ER	• Training and inservices
• Basic life support	• Triple lumen CVP	• Meditech documentation
• CCU	• AV fistulas	

Fields like health care stress certifications and proficiencies— that's why so many are listed here.

PROFESSIONAL EXPERIENCE

GOOD SAMARITAN HOSPITAL, Missoula, Montana   2002–Present

Staff Nurse, Intensive Care Unit

Serve as charge nurse caring for patients with acute illnesses, including acute congestive failure, acute myocardial infarction, drug overdose, massive trauma, respiratory failure, and disseminated intravascular coagulopathy. Promote health and support patients and families in coping with illness. Skilled in Hewlett Packard bedside monitoring, 12-lead EKG, and Bennett 7600 ventilator.

Without many quantifiable achievements, she stresses her level of responsibility.

- Provide strong contributions as key member of unit quality assurance program designed to identify and evaluate problems, manage patient census, and allocate staff assignments.
- Exhibit motivation and dedication by providing the highest quality of care to each patient.

PEACOCK MEDICAL CENTER, Missoula, Montana   1999–2002

Emergency Staff Nurse

Provided care for patients suffering from trauma, acute chest pain, respiratory failure/complaints, drug overdoses, acute alcohol ingestion, and gastrointestinal bleeds. Acquired and recorded patient information. Prepared patients for surgical and radiological procedures, initiated and maintained intravenous therapy, and operated 12-lead EKG.

- Implemented and coordinated ongoing staff education program.
- Contributed substantially to successful JCAHO accreditation within the department.

It's okay to use jargon—the recruiter will understand it, and the search engines may be looking for these terms!

ST. JOSEPH'S HOSPITAL, Helena, Montana   1994–1998
Registered Nurse
Delivered a complete range of RN services and expertise. Accurately obtained and documented patient history and medication lists, assessed individual conditions and needs, and selected departmental referrals for acute and chronically ill patients. Prepared equipment and assisted physicians during patient examinations and treatments. Monitored patient reactions to drugs and carefully documented progress of individuals participating in clinical trials.

- Repeatedly commended by patients and supervisors for outstanding quality of care; received consistent mention in care-survey responses.
- Maintained a high degree of accuracy to achieve optimal patient acuity monitoring.
- Significantly improved facility's public image by ensuring exceptional patient satisfaction.

MONTANA STATE PRISON, Deer Lodge, Montana   1992–1994
Registered Nurse
Provided triage, referrals, direct nursing care, and medication administration to incarcerated population. Organized and managed regular clinics involving external physicians, including ophthalmology, ENT, Med/Surg, orthopedics, and podiatry professionals. Scheduled and managed external medical consultations in concert with security and other necessary personnel. Created, managed, and maintained patient medical and health records.

Even if she's not expert in these, the experience may matter, so she includes them.

- Selected to serve as Infection Control Coordinator, maintaining tuberculosis and hepatitis standards and conducting screenings and preventive activities.
- Organized and facilitated meetings with security managers to ensure infection-control policy compliance.

EDUCATIONAL BACKGROUND
Bachelor of Science in Nursing, BSN (1992)
MONTANA STATE UNIVERSITY - Bozeman, Montana

Licensure
Registered Nurse (RN), State of Montana

© Copyright 2003 CareerPerfect.com

JOHN Q. SECURITY

100 Main Street • Plano, Texas 30000 • jqsecurity@iq.net • 400.555.6000 • 300.555.7000

INFORMATION TECHNOLOGY SECURITY SPECIALIST

Specific headline— easy to find

Solutions-oriented IT Security Specialist with notable success directing a broad range of corporate IT initiatives while participating in planning, analysis, and implementation of information-security solutions in direct support of business objectives.

Summary is general— positions the list that follows.

- Track record of increasing responsibility in secure network design, systems analysis/development, and full life-cycle project management.
- Demonstrated capacity to implement innovative security programs that drive awareness, decrease exposure, and strengthen organizations.
- Hands-on experience leading all stages of system development efforts, including requirements definition, design, architecture, testing, and support.
- Outstanding leadership abilities; able to coordinate and direct all phases of project-based efforts while managing, motivating, and leading project teams.
- Adept at developing effective security policies and procedures, project documentation and milestones, and technical/business specifications.

Another term for skills

CORE COMPETENCIES

- Network & Systems Security
- Business Impact Analysis
- Regulatory Adherence
- Data Integrity & Recovery
- Disaster Recovery Planning

- Contingency Planning
- Research & Development
- Risk Assessment
- Cost-Benefits Analysis

TECHNICAL PROFICIENCIES

Keywords are critical for tech resumes.

Platforms:	UNIX (Solaris, HP-UX), Windows 95/98/NT/2000/XP, Linux (Red Hat, Yellow Dog), Sun SPARC, Mac OS, VM/370, OS2 Warp.
Networking:	TCP/IP, Novell, DECnet, Banyan, ISO/OSI, IPX/SPX, SNA, SMS/SQL, Ethernet, Token Ring, FDDI, VPN, SSH, SecureID, PGP, PKI, HIPAA, CFR-11.
Languages:	UNIX Shell Scripting, C, Basic, Troff, Nroff, HTML, Perl, PHP.
Tools:	LAN Manager, ISS RealSecure, Checkpoint Firewall, Norton Firewall and Ghost, McAfee/Norton Virus Protection Utilities, HP OpenView, Network Flight Recorder, IBM Tivoli, Tripwire, Snort, Lotus Notes, Microsoft Office Suite (Word, Excel, PowerPoint, Access, Project, Outlook), FrontPage.

JOHN Q. SECURITY
PAGE TWO

PROFESSIONAL EXPERIENCE

XYZ INTERNATIONAL, Richardson, TX   2000–PRESENT

Information Security Manager

Recruited to establish and manage enterprise-wide information-security program. Oversee companywide efforts to identify and evaluate all critical systems. Design and implement security processes and procedures and perform cost-benefit analysis on all recommended strategies. Collaborate with external auditors to conduct in-depth compliance audits and penetration testing, presenting all results to senior management. Develop curricula and facilitate awareness training for management and employees. Supervise daily activities of Computer Security Assistant and Internet Administrator. Accountable for security budget of $1.5 million.

KEY CONTRIBUTIONS:
- Instrumental in developing and implementing Business Continuity and Disaster Recovery (BCP & DRP) Plans for corporate sites throughout Texas, Ohio, and Canada.
- Spearheaded creation of four new information-security departments, including Risk Assessment, Vulnerability, Penetration Testing, and Security Engineering services.
- Hand-selected employees from Information Technology department to build Risk Assessment Team charged with analyzing all critical systems, developing reports to document system vulnerabilities, and recommending appropriate solutions.
- Created company policies and procedures governing corporate security, email and Internet usage, access control, and incident response.

These achievements are written to emphasize management skills and experience.

123 INFORMATION SYSTEMS, Garland, TX   1993–2000
                                               (1997–2000)
QA Manager

Just listing years is enough.

Promoted to manage system development teams charged with performing new product QA. Supervised release testing for all new applications, providing final approval for bug-free, fully functional commercial solutions. Oversaw all staff recruitment, resource allocation, and employee assessment functions. Built and mentored cohesive, qualified teams committed to meeting schedule and budgetary needs. Created development plans, project documentation, and test cases.

KEY CONTRIBUTIONS:
- Authored numerous ISO 9000 procedures and security policies in support of engineering operations, participating in regular audits to ensure regulatory compliance.

207

JOHN Q. SECURITY
PAGE THREE

- Managed creation of high-profile HATP (High Availability Transaction Processing) solution, supervising development teams working in multiple locations.

Older term, so he translates the acronym.

- Developed highly effective Software Manager application to enable disk-free software upgrades deployed through ATMs and desktop systems worldwide.
- Successfully applied for U.S. Patent on new security software design.

Computer System Engineer/Network Developer   (1993–1997)

Provided remote and on-site support for domestic and international customers, including Tier-III support for LAN/WAN products and sales support for key accounts of all sizes.

KEY CONTRIBUTIONS:

- Designed and implemented customer call-center support procedures and customer network design strategy for sales and marketing teams.
- Recognized for outstanding quality of customer service with numerous customer-support awards and personal commendation from clients.

EDUCATION AND CREDENTIALS
Bachelor of Science in Computer Science
UNIVERSITY OF TEXAS AT DALLAS—Dallas, TX

Professional Training and Certifications

Another keyword that can be found in a resume database search

CISSP—Certified Information Systems Security Professional
Microsoft Certified Systems Engineer

PROFESSIONAL AFFILIATIONS
Member—Information Systems Security Association
Member – International Information
Systems Security Certification Consortium, Inc.

John's affiliations are relevant to his job—they say "professional."

© Copyright 2003 CareerPerfect.com

F.A.M.E. ATTITUDE: TRAIN LIKE AN ATHLETE

Your job search is a competition.

Now that you have written your resume, you have to get employers and recruiters to read it. Unfortunately, as we've seen, any employer who posts a job is flooded with resumes. The competition for even a glance at your resume is fierce. To win that competition, you need to create one more document: a great cover letter.

You're about to complete phase 1 of the *Monster Careers* program. Finish it with energy and enthusiasm! If you really want to give a job opportunity your best shot, invest the time it takes to craft a strong message. Work harder than your competition.

The purpose of a cover letter is to persuade the right person to read your resume. It's that simple. The recruiter or employer decides in a few seconds whether your resume belongs in the "resumes of interest" pile or not (and "not" isn't a good place). That decision is usually based on how you introduce yourself.

These days, the classic cover letter is becoming obsolete before our eyes. In the new world of employment, the carefully printed letter on cream-laid paper is a beautiful relic, a luxury most managers don't have time to receive in the mail, open, and read. Today, the majority of cover "letters" are e-mail messages. It's a new fact of life: most of the time, you'll apply for jobs via e-mail. I have referred to "cover letters" in earlier chapters, but now it's time to get up to date. From now on, I'll call the communication introducing your resume a "cover message." (Once or twice I'll refer to paper cover letters, just in case you have to use one.)

A *Monster Careers* cover message is never generic. It is carefully customized to give your resume added credibility, as well as intrigue. It's your first place to show extra effort. It separates you from your competition at the instant a time-pressed recruiter finds the most important document in the pile: yours!

You will write your customized cover messages from a basic draft. This is where using a word processor really helps. You can even keep several different types of message in draft form on a PC, and when the time comes to apply for a job, simply copy one, then customize it to suit that employer and that opportunity.

Create a file named "Cover Messages," either a standard paper file or a new file on your PC. Place in it drafts of the cover messages as you draft them. You might draft several different versions. A graphic designer, for example, might make separate files for "Marketing cover messages," "Advertising cover messages," and "Publishing cover messages."

How the Cover Message and the Resume Work Together

If the resume is the movie, the cover message is the preview. It's fast-moving, short, and persuasive. It must also be crafted as purposefully as your resume.

Monster senior creative director Sue Duro places the cover message firmly in the realm of marketing. She says, "This is your sales message. Get right to the point. First, you have to describe forcefully how hiring *you* will improve the performance of their organization."

Monster members sometimes ask, "If my resume is so good, and time is so short, why send a cover message at all?" Here's why:

- It can capture the recruiter's imagination, which means your resume will be read with extra interest.

- It allows for a message that is 100 percent customized, targeted to the recruiter.

- It highlights specific details of your attributes, skills, and experience—the selling points that set you apart from others.

"Canned" Cover Messages Get Canned

Erin Barriere, Monster's human resources director, passed along this advice: "Personalized cover messages are important. I quickly file the 'canned' covers that show that the person did not make the effort to customize their application. The cover message should detail the job's required skills, and it should also promise to follow up with a phone call in a week. Then the candidate must follow up."

Cover Messages 1, 2, 3

Draft one or more basic cover messages as you work through this chapter. The format we'll follow can be adapted to apply for jobs online, and to request informational interviews, networking meetings, and job interviews (all of which you will do in phase 2 of your search!).

Powerful cover messages can be organized into three parts, according to Michael Hattersley, author of *Management Communication.* He calls this the ME-YOU-WE approach. Here's how it breaks down.

Part 1—The Opener: "Who I am"

You could tailor your tone to suit the personality of the recipient, but that assumes you know the recipient well—not likely. Instead, open by telling why you're writing. With this in mind, there are many approaches that can be customized to grab the recipient's attention.

- **The value proposition:** Also called the "If/then" opener, this introduces you as a problem-solver. "If you are looking for a professional who has repeatedly increased profits, customer satisfaction, and margins, then my credentials will be of interest." The value proposition says, "You want this, and it's exactly what I offer."

- **The business-conservative approach:** State that you are interested in work and show solid credentials. "For your opening in accounts payable, you'll find I have ten years of increasing responsibility and staff size. . . ." This is best for organizations that value exact and predictable performance. (But be careful about the formal language. You don't want to come off as a stiff.)

211

- **Numbers fireworks:** "$2.8 million in new accounts last year. A 75% same-day close rate. An 80% customer renewal rate. That's what qualifies me for a senior sales position at ABC Company." Bang. Bang. Bang. This approach is perfect for positions that value go-getters. (If you use this, make sure you know your numbers cold. They could call you for a phone interview ten minutes after you send the message!)

- **The testimonial:** "'Karen Smith really turned my product production around with her expertise, insight, and drive,' says Mike Jones, president of ABC Company." Your testimonial should be offered by someone familiar to the recipient, or someone with a weighty job title.

- **The referral:** "Mike Jones suggested I contact you regarding my suitability for an entry-level retail management position at ABC Company." This is a tried-and-true method, and works best if your referral gave you a name of someone they know.

- **The news angle:** "After I saw a Segway Human Transporter on CNN, I got excited about joining your international marketing team. You will see the benefit in my credentials, including multilingual fluency (Spanish, Portuguese, and Italian) . . ."

- **The confident opener:** Pretend you've already got the job: "As your next sales manager, my complete focus will be directed toward achieving the same pacesetting results I delivered for my former employer." This approach can be off-putting to some folks, but it works well for sales and leadership positions that require you to project confidence.

- **The career summary:** Open with a long-standing strength: "In my 15-year career, I have a history of saving costs: Fulfillment budgets at XYZ Company remained unchanged under my leadership during a 40% increase in sales. I decreased equipment downtime by 17% at ABC Company. EFG vice president of production Mike Jones testifies that every project I coordinated hit its budget." These examples could have been drawn from two, eight, or twelve years ago. The timing matters less than the point made that this candidate knows how to handle a budget.

Write an opener that works with the summary statement on your resume. Don't simply repeat the summary, but allow the opener to lead to the resume seamlessly. If you've really done your job here, the recipient might skip the rest of the cover message and go directly to your resume . . . mission accomplished!

Part 2—Make Your Case: "What you need"

The second paragraph of your cover message should describe your achievements and qualifications in the context of the employer's needs.

Michael Hattersley, author of *Management Communication*, suggests this is the place to show off your research. "Demonstrate that you understand the company, will fit into its culture, and can add value," he says. "This emphasis is important to avoid the 'I, I, I, ME, ME, ME' tone of so many cover messages. Cite highlights of your job performance. . . . Give them insights to areas where you can shine."

Focus the second paragraph of your message on the connection between you and the job with one of these methods:

- **Showcase your top selling point.** Spell out how your greatest strength meets their needs. Say, for example, "Based on my research into your company, I see you may have a need for a great alliance-builder in your consumer products group, and that's exactly what I deliver." This is the perfect place to create some buzz in their minds by hinting at a major accomplishment. Keep it short and sweet: "I'd like to tell you about my record-breaking deals with vendors last year." Then be prepared to impress them in the job interview.

- **Play off your resume.** Your cover message can hint at interesting items on your resume without spelling them out: "You'll see on my resume a continuous and growing history of initiatives that increased sales from existing customers and even 'tired' accounts!"

- **. . . or *don't* play off your resume.** If used confidently, this tactic can be effective. Summarize a story that is not on your resume. Select an achievement story that you are reserving for an interview. For example, if an advertised sales position includes managing current sales clients, write about a time you increased purchases from an existing client.

- **Refer to language in the ad.** If you are responding to a job advertisement, the second paragraph is the place to use language drawn from the ad. For example, if an advertisement for a job in the food industry refers to "food safety protocols" and "quality control," you can refer to those exact phrases: "I share your concern for quality control and food safety protocols. I have a long record of exceeding food safety specifications."

213

One uncommon way of working off the ad is to create a side-by-side comparison in your message:

Your ad specifies . . .	and I offer:
Communication Skills	Five years of public-speaking experience and an extensive background in executive-level report writing.
Strong Computer Background	Proficiency in all MS Office applications, with additional expertise in Web site development/design.

- **Be specific.** The first sentence of your second paragraph is a good place to name the job you seek. The person reading your message may be reviewing hundreds of messages for dozens of different jobs.

- **Tell a story.** Stories are powerful. Consider using the second paragraph to tell a brief story, such as "my toughest sale" or "my biggest technical challenge," that illustrates your unique abilities.

- **Show off your research.** The cover message is a great place to show you have broader knowledge of your industry. If you haven't used the news angle as your opener, you might try that here: "Your recent moves into the airport security market confirmed my interest. . . ." This is best done if you have been tracking a company for a while and really can speak knowledgably about their business. One caution: Stay away from controversy and bad news, such as a lawsuit or a labor strike, when using this tactic. Nobody likes to be reminded of bad press.

Part 3—Your Vision: "Imagine us together"

You've talked about yourself; you've talked about them. Now you're ready to propose the next steps. They have to read your resume and invite you for an interview, so the last paragraph of your cover message should make all of the following three points:

- **Propose your vision.** Pull together your story and theirs with a brief statement. It should show how both sides win if you're hired. If you

Dead Letter

Here's a cover letter with many reasons . . . to be thrown away:

John Sinclair
11 Centerboro Road
Centerboro, DE 19900

Didn't bother to find a real name!

Human Resources
Shiftmasters Corporation
Centerboro DE 19900

Your competition gave us a <u>reason</u> to consider them in their cover letter...and we'll read their resume first!

To whom it may concern:

Please consider me for the job you posted for a shift supervisor. I am currently unemployed and looking for work in your area.

I enclose my resume. I have experience in working and you will find I am carful with the jobs' responsibilities.

We assume you're unemployed unless you tell us otherwise.

Sincerely,

[not signed]

Just how <u>careful</u> are you?

215

Here's an e-mail version that will lead to a quick delete:

job - Message - Microsoft Word

Normal + Arial   Arial   12   B I U

File Edit View Insert Format Tools Table Window Help

Send Options... Rich Text

To...   info@anyco.com
Cc...
Bcc...
Subject: job

I am applying for the job you advertised. ◄——————————————— Which one?

Okay, it looks like you
want the shift supervisor
job...I think.

I was a shift supervisor at another company. This was after I graduated from
school with a **2.5** grade average and after I worked my up from several other jobs,
as you will see from my resume which is attached and below.

AS I said, I have experience and you will find I am qualified for the job's responsibilities.

What other jobs have you had?

Don't brag about average grades.

Your resume didn't
paste into your
e-mail correctly.
I don't even know
your name!

haven't used one of the tactics described in part 1, such as the value
proposition or confident opener, this might be the right place. For example, having made the case for your sales skills, you may write: "I'd
like to help ABC Company just as I have helped others, by beating the
industry renewal rate year after year."

- **Make your request.** If your message is not a direct application for an
  advertised job, you need to ask for a meeting. Be candid about your
  situation and honest about your goals. If you're looking for a job at
  that company, say so. If you are requesting an informational interview, say so.

- **Suggest a follow-up.** Politely say you'll follow up via phone call or
  e-mail. Invite them to contact you. Nobody wants to be pestered for a
  job, but recruiters look forward to meeting an interesting, curious,
  and informed candidate. Say, "I will follow up with you in a few days

to answer any preliminary questions you may have. In the meantime, you may reach me at (555) 555-5555."

Then write your follow-up date on your calendar . . . and do it!

Cover Message Style

Your cover message should follow the common rules of courtesy in business communication. Here's a short review of the business basics:

- Use "Mr. Jones" and "Ms. Smith" instead of "Mike" or "Mary" in your first approach to strangers. This is one moment that being a little formal works as a tactic—it usually prompts a "Call me Mike" response from them, which sets a nice tone for the next conversation.

- Don't ever say "To whom it may concern." Find a name. If you absolutely cannot find a person's name to write, address a title, such as "Dear Director of Staffing."

- Say "please" and "thank you." Your mom was right, you know. Even a short cover message is asking for someone's time and attention.

- Sign your work. It is proper business etiquette (and shows attention to detail) to sign a paper letter. If you are sending your cover message and resume via e-mail, use the signature feature (most e-mail programs have it) or simply end your message with "Sincerely, Mary Smith."

- Include your basic contact information (phone number and e-mail address) under your name in the message as well as on your resume. ALWAYS make it easy for an employer to find you.

Beyond the business basics, there's plenty of room for your individual style. Here are some style tips for writing a cover message that stands out from the competition.

Use strong words.

Each paragraph must grab the reader's interest, and you achieve this with focused, specific language. Consider the difference:

Weak: Please consider me for your sales representative opening.

Better: Your need for a top-performing sales rep is an excellent match to my three-year history as a multimillion-dollar performer.

217

Use the active, not passive voice.

Say, "I increased sales." Don't say, "Sales were increased by me." Say, "I developed better inventory controls." Don't say, "Inventory-taking methods were improved by my efforts." Active is strong, passive is weak.

Keep it short and sweet.

Keep it under 300 words. Written letters can be a little longer than e-mail cover messages, but if they exceed one page, you may be putting readers to sleep.

Show some personality.

Monster senior creative director Sue Duro points out that it's easier to reveal your individual personality in a cover message than in a resume. This goes to the passion and personal style (or company culture) portions of the job match. If you LOVE one part of your job, it's okay to say so; if your sense of humor is important to you in a workplace, don't be afraid to be a little funny. If you have done your homework, you know whether that style suits the company culture.

Use jargon carefully.

If you're applying for a highly specialized position, you may use technical terms or industry jargon to show your expertise. This is fine as long as the first reader (often a nontechnical HR staffer) can understand what you say. Take your cue from the job description. If it contains many technical terms, you may refer to them in your cover message; otherwise, avoid jargon.

Be creative.

There are situations in which a very creative tone is appropriate. Advertising copywriters, certain consultants, and other creative types are expected to showcase their talents in their approach. An unorthodox message is sometimes okay for a business position. If the job requires extensive public speaking, for example, a candidate might attach an audio file to the e-mail, just to show off his or her voice.

If you must send a paper cover letter and resume, match your cover letter and resume in general appearance. Use the same type fonts and formatting. Use the same paper. As for design, use the standard business letter layout for your cover letter.

Don't bother with fancy formatting in e-mail. In fact, it's a good insurance policy to include your resume after the cover message in plain text. Bruce Wain of resume writing service CareerPerfect suggests you save your resume as ASCII text (see page 160 for instructions on how to save ASCII text) and paste it at the bottom of an e-mail message. There are a lot of older computers and e-mail systems out there that can make mistakes with e-mail attachments, and if the recipient can't see your resume, he or she will move on to the next one.

Finally, if you're not confident about your writing skills, start by studying examples of good cover letters and messages. There are some at the end of this chapter and more at **monstercareers.com**. (Read a range of messages. You may, for example, find wording that you like in a cover message for a nursing job, even though you're an accountant.)

As with your resume, you may decide you need professional help. Resume writers, discussed in chapter 10, also write cover letters/messages.

Crimes of the Cover Message

Avoid these common mistakes, which are tantamount to slamming the door in your own face.

MESSAGE ADDRESSED TO THE WRONG PERSON/ WRONG COMPANY.

Especially if they're in a different company! Message: "I don't care."

SPELLING AND GRAMMAR ERRORS.

Don't count on your software to make it perfect. Proofread your cover message as carefully as your resume.

CUTE INSTANT-MESSENGER DICTION.

"If U need suml for kigazz Dzine . . ." You have to show that you can speak the language of business, not junior high school.

219

THE PREPOSTEROUS LEAP.

"Although I have no experience or license in radiological technical work, please look at my resume for that position. . . ." Hey, go ahead and title your message "A guaranteed waste of time."

THE OBVIOUS CUT AND PASTE.

Patching a cover message together by cutting and pasting phrases from your resume. This is lazy and repetitious—take a few minutes to put it in your own words.

TOUGH-GUY 'TUDE.

"Dear Jeff: Your product design stinks, but I can help." No, you can't.

THE PATHETIC PLOY.

"I've been out of work for 24 months, so I'm an easy hire because I'm desperate." Hmmm . . . was "desperate" part of the job requirements?

OOPS!

If you want me to read your resume, do remember to include your resume in the message.

Sample Cover Messages

Following are cover messages to go with the resumes in chapter 10.

Kim Miller
789 Evergreen Terrace • Brattleboro, Vermont 05432
kmill789@jayol.com • 234.555.6789

February 10, 20XX

John Smith
Vice President, Sales
InfoTech, Inc.
8855 Main Street
Brattleboro, Vermont, 05433

Dear Mr. Smith:

Language reflects the job "personality."

In today's highly competitive and fast-paced market, organizations need strong and aggressive sales leadership to meet ever-changing business development goals. I am certain I can contribute this level of performance to your team, and I invite you to consider my qualifications and accomplishments:

"Me" section— with numbers!

- **Experience**—15+ years of productive regional sales management, coupled with an MBA and a track record of success in leading diverse teams of value-added resellers;
- **Results**—Acknowledged for driving multimillion-dollar annual revenue growth; recipient of multiple company sales awards;
- **Performance**—Recognized as a top sales producer; recipient of numerous team-building commendations.

Hints at her selling techniques.

I am an accomplished sales strategist and solution-oriented manager who thrives in challenging, fast-paced environments where my performance directly impacts the bottom line. In addition, I have solid organizational leadership and decision-making skills that can make an immediate contribution to your operations and business development.

Currently, I am seeking a position where I can continue to uphold strong sales and performance standards. As a member of your management team, I am confident that my innovative and results-focused approach would make a significant contribution to the continued success of your organization.

My resume is enclosed for your review and consideration. I would welcome the opportunity to speak with you regarding opportunities you have available currently or in the future.

Sincerely,

Kim Miller

Kim Miller
Enclosure

This letter sets up achievement stories for the job interview.

© Copyright 2003 CareerPerfect.com

Beverly M. Jones, RN
200 Hacienda Drive, Helena, MT 70000
600-555-4000 • bmjrn@notmail.com

February 16, 2004

Lee Jones
Human Resource Manager
St. Maries Hospital
1200 Main Street
Helena, Montana 75000

She gets right to the point.

Details from the ad

Dear Mr. Jones:

I was pleased to learn of your need for an ICU Staff Nurse as my career goals and expertise are directly in line with this opportunity. My experience and education have provided me with excellent knowledge of ICU practices, acute patient care, family relations, staff development, and other relevant skills required of an effective team member.

The following are highlights of my qualifications and accomplishments:

She's specific—good use of jargon.

- Extensive patient care experience in ICU, CCU, Emergency, and Medical-Surgical environments.
- In-depth knowledge in administration that includes admissions, assessment, treatment, referral, and education for a wide range of patients.
- Frequent commendations by patients and families for providing exceptional care.
- Employee awards for dedication, excellent performance, leadership, and patient advocacy.

My strong initiative and exceptional organizational skills, combined with my ability to work well under pressure, will enable me to make a substantial contribution to St. Maries Hospital. I believe that a challenging environment such as yours will provide an excellent opportunity to best utilize my skills while contributing to the health-care community, patients, and their families.

"us" section

Enclosed is my resume for your review. I welcome the opportunity to discuss with you personally how my skills and strengths can best serve your hospital.

Sincerely,

Beverly M. Jones

Beverly M. Jones
Enclosure

© Copyright 2003 CareerPerfect.com

JOHN Q. SECURITY

100 Main Street • Plano, Texas 30000 • jqsecurity@iq.net • 400.555.6000 • 300.555.7000

February XX, 2003

Mr. John Smith
Director, Information Technology
ABC Corporation
12345 Main Street
Plano, Texas 90000

Shows he understands the job.

Dear Mr. Smith,

It was with great interest that I read your recent posting in the *Times* for an IT Security Specialist. Managing large-scale security projects requires a unique blend of expertise in strategic planning, process development, and leadership, along with in-depth technical knowledge. I believe that my qualifications are an ideal match for this position, and I am confident I would make a valuable and immediate contribution to your operations.

The following are highlights of my qualifications:

"Distinguished" "Proficiency" "Comprehensive" —good strong language

- A distinguished career directing the development of quality network and security solutions, including the design, configuration, and support of fully functional, reliable, and secure systems;
- Technical proficiency in numerous platforms, network protocols, and administration tools;
- Comprehensive industry training providing a broad understanding of preemptive security measures, intrusion detection, vulnerability isolation, and fault analysis; and
- Exceptional leadership abilities, with the demonstrated capacity to build, train, and mentor highly productive and motivated cross-functional teams.

"Imagine us together."

In addition, I offer outstanding organizational skills, which have proven to be a critical asset in developing, maintaining, and supporting dynamic information-security solutions. These qualities, combined with my dedication and tireless work ethic, should enable me to make a positive impact at ABC Corporation.

Enclosed is a copy of my resume for your review. I would welcome a personal interview at your earliest convenience to discuss your needs and objectives and the possibility of working together to meet them. Thank you for your time and consideration.

Requests a meeting.

Sincerely,

John Q. Security
Enclosure

© Copyright 2003 CareerPerfect.com

223

Phase I Review

At this point in the job search, you have all the documents you need. You have a compelling pitch and well-prepared evidence of your abilities. Your work space and work plan are organized, and you're focusing on the actions that will get you to a job faster. Feeling busy yet?

In the 10-week model job search plan, your calendar for phase 1 might look like this:

WEEK I						
MON	**TUES**	**WED**	**THURS**	**FRI**	**SAT**	**SUN**
Read chapters 7–9. Plan time and budget. Set up work space.	Begin to prepare key messages (chapter 8).	Work on key messages (chapter 8).	List skills. Begin achievement stories (chapter 8).	Prepare achievement stories. Finish job search portfolio (chapter 8).	DAY OFF	DAY OFF

WEEK 2						
MON	**TUES**	**WED**	**THURS**	**FRI**	**SAT**	**SUN**
Prepare sales pitch. Practice phone skills (chapter 9).	Prepare resume (chapter 10). Practice sales pitch.	Prepare resume and cover messages (chapters 10–11).	Prepare resume and cover messages (chapters 10–11). Practice sales pitch.	Read chapters 12–14. Practice sales pitch. Tie up any loose ends from Phase I.	DAY OFF	DAY OFF

This is a professional job search! If you are really putting in forty hours a week, you've completed more productive tasks than most candidates ever achieve . . . and this is just the beginning. With this firm foundation, you are ready for the exciting work to come as you enter the marketplace of jobs.

PART III

>> INTO THE MARKETPLACE <<

Now you are ready to show employers just how good you are. In the ten-week model job search, this is the work of "getting up to speed" during weeks 3 to 5. Phase 2 introduces activities that you will pursue until you land a job:

- Research jobs, companies, and industries. You have to know a lot about what jobs are available in your area, whether you fit their requirements, and what they pay.

- Find opportunity in the form of advertised job openings. Also, *create* opportunity, by which I mean going directly to employers and convincing them you should be hired whether they're advertising jobs or not.

- Networking. This means creating a strong web of personal relationships that connect you to "hidden" job opportunities.

The work begun in this phase of your plan tests your ability to manage a full-time job search, so if you want to, bring some flexibility into your schedule. You might want to work some Saturdays and knock off an occasional weekday. Also, mix up the activities: research jobs one day, and work your personal network the next day. You make your job search more personal by managing your activities on a day-to-day basis according to the best opportunities.

This is your chance to become a student of the job marketplace: to know more than your competition, and to get the word out into the marketplace. Go ahead—be like Monster's mascot, Trumpasaurus, and blow your own horn!

12   >> The Power of Research <<

F.A.M.E. ATTITUDE: TRAIN LIKE AN ATHLETE

Training is the only thing that makes you stronger.

EMPLOYER: *"What are you doing here?"*

CANDIDATE 1: *"I'm responding to your job posting."*

CANDIDATE 2: *"I'm here to discuss international and U.S. retail opportunities for your business. I'm interested in the fact that, of your twelve hundred employees, four hundred are in nine countries overseas. Your revenues are up sixteen percent internationally but you're laying off workers at your manufacturing plants in Asia—is that due to slack U.S. or international sales? Your CEO mentioned in the last analyst call that you're trying to get better exposure for your products in department stores, and I'd like to tell you how I tackled that problem in the past."*

Which candidate made the stronger impression?

Candidate 2 got the information she needed with 30 minutes of Web research using Google and/or the company Web site. She also came armed with comments from the company's clients, and (just for fun) a picture of the company's sales team at their Friday softball game. She's asking interesting questions, and her research demonstrates she's especially interested in this company. A little research has put her miles beyond the competition. Now, Candidate 2 might be just a little over the top . . . but even one-third of this answer would set you apart!

229

Athletes train not only their bodies but their minds to become stronger. To become a stronger candidate, you need to train your mind with good research. You need to know more than your competition.

Job research has three goals:

- To widen your horizon early in the search. Too many people explore only two or three job possibilities, usually jobs they're already familiar with. You may be a good fit for many different jobs.

- To inform your choices, so you know where to focus your energy (by location, company, or industry) throughout the job search. This makes your search more powerful and (by the way) shorter.

- To arm you with almost-real-time information about an employer. This helps you to stand out in the first interview.

When I was first in the job market, people's general advice was "Start at the library and do some research." Young people like me all said okay, even though nobody went. It was onerous work, flipping through huge books with names like "The Standard Directory of *Whatever*." The information was old and lacked any figment of relevance.

A few of us also tried "informational interviewing," a technique made popular by Richard Nelson Bolles's classic *What Color Is Your Parachute?* Most of us just relied on the guidance counselor or classified advertising to learn about jobs.

Now there's no excuse. The Internet has made it easy to learn everything you need to know without leaving your chair. It has raised employer expectations, too. You had better know about their company before you step through the door, or they'll send you right back out.

Research is really just detective work—one clue leads to another—and if you dive in with curiosity, you'll find clues to jobs and employers everywhere. This chapter will teach you how to learn about jobs, employers, and industries so that you can truly customize your approach to a company. With research, you can discover and focus on your target customers, the ones who can't wait to find you!

Create two files—Target Jobs and Target Employers. You are about to gain a wealth of information about jobs and employers, but don't get lost! It's terribly frustrating to lose your notes about a job lead. You need to organize all the information you're about to discover, so create the following files:

- *Target Jobs*—In this file, you will keep notes on the *types of jobs* that interest you.

- *Target Employers*—In this file, you will keep notes on the *specific employers* that interest you.

As your job search progresses, you may want to make individual files for specific employers. When you go after a specific job opportunity at a specific employer, create a brand-new file with the job AND employer name on it. This will keep your "hot" job opportunities separate from your research. Then, when the employer calls to talk, you're not fumbling around in your files, looking for those critical notes!

Learn About Jobs

The U.S. Department of Labor lists more than 800 major vocations! The actual number of job titles grows every day. How will you learn which jobs may be right for you? Start by building on the solid foundation of your Job Search Portfolio and the I-AM exercises you completed at the end of chapter 6. As you find out more about jobs and employers throughout this phase of your search, compare your skills, interests, and values against what you discover. This will help prevent you from heading down the blind alleys of "interesting" but inappropriate choices.

With that foundation in place, you can dive into the details.

Use the Target Job form (page 233) to save information about specific jobs. Create a new sheet for each job as you get information from the Internet, the library, informational interviewing, and other conversations. You do not have to fill in every line at once, but generally, more information is better than less.

In the first section of the form, write specifics about potential jobs:

- job titles that seem right for your skills and experience
- which employers in your area employ these jobs
- what the job is expected to accomplish
- a pay (or other compensation) range for the job
- what education, skills, certifications, and so on are required to get the job

In the second section, write information that will power your search:

- people who can tell you more about a job (see "Informational Interviews" later in this chapter)

- what you like most about the job

- what you like least about the job

- where the job might lead you in five years (promotion? more money? a step closer to fulfilling your life's mission?)

At first you may want to keep these sheets together in your "Target Jobs" file. As you gather more information, make separate folders for promising jobs. Name them by job title. Keep newspaper or Web articles about the specific job there. This simple organizational habit—separate files for each job—can prevent you from becoming overwhelmed by information *and* make you impressive in the job interview later.

Book to Web

Like all forms in this book, the Target Job and Target Employer forms are available in electronic form at **monstercareers.com**.

What's that job all about?

You can start your research at the mother lode of detailed job knowledge: The U.S. Department of Labor has an invaluable service called the Occupational Information Network or O*Net, an online encyclopedia of jobs (**online.onetcenter.org/**). If you only do job research on one Web site, make this the one—you will quickly become familiar with details of virtually any job by looking it up on O*Net.

Get familiar with the service by clicking the link titled "New to O*Net OnLine?" The two critical areas for job research are titled "Find Occupations" and "Skills Search." One note before you dive in: The service was designed to be comprehensive, and the "Detailed Reports" you find can quickly become overwhelming. Stick to the job summaries at first. (Also, most of you can skip the site section labeled "Crosstalk.") You might want to print out job descriptions and keep them in your files.

O*Net can match your top skills to detailed job descriptions, and the results may surprise you (who knew that financial sales agents and fashion designers have quite similar skills?). Go to **online.onetcenter.org/gen_skills_page**. You will see a checklist of skills. Check off skills you wrote in

TARGET JOB

Job information:

Title: _____

Alternative titles: _____

_____

Employers hiring this job: _____

_____

_____

What this job is expected to accomplish: _____

_____

_____

Required education or certification: _____

Required experience: _____

Required skills and/or special knowledge: _____

_____

Typical compensation in my geographic area: _____

Search information:

Who can tell me more about this job: _____

_____

What I like most about this job: _____

_____

_____

What I like least about this job: _____

_____

_____

Where this job may lead me in five years: _____

_____

You can download this form at monstercareers.com.

233

your skills list, click "Go" at the bottom of the page, and you'll get a list of jobs that may be right for you. Each job is linked to a highly detailed description of the job and a list of similar professions. If you want to take your research to an even higher level, click on "Custom" in the job result page and follow the instructions.

Another source you may want to investigate is the U.S. Bureau of Labor Statistics' online version of its *Occupational Outlook Handbook* (called the *OOH*) at **stats.bls.gov/oco/**. Its job descriptions are less detailed than those at O*Net, but the *OOH* contains a wealth of job market information, such as which jobs will be in demand during the next ten years. It also contains basic information about pay (see page 250 for more about that interesting subject).

In addition, the U.S. government's Federal Citizen Information Center offers lots of information you can download for free, or purchase offline for little more than the cost of postage. Start at **pueblo.gsa.gov/** and click on "Employment." Here's one of their reports: "High-Earning Workers Who Don't Have a Bachelor's Degree" (**pueblo.gsa.gov/cic_text/employ/ bachdeg/bach_deg.pdf**). Other reports range from "Matching Yourself with the World of Work," to "Tomorrow's Jobs."

You can find information specific to federal government jobs at the Office of Personnel Management (**opm.gov/**). State governments have their own employment sites and should be contacted individually. One useful online tool to get to their contact information quickly is **FirstGov.gov**. Lists of state administrative offices for all U.S. states can be found by following the links at **nascio.org/stateSearch/displayCategory.cfm?Category= administration**. For state and local government entities, you may also wish to use the following site: **statelocalgov.net/index.cfm**. (Also, see the special section on public service jobs in chapter 18.)

Book to Web

Overwhelmed by O*Net and the *OOH*? Monster gives details of more than 150 jobs, with job descriptions, skills and education required, outlook for the next ten years, and related careers, at **monstercareers.com**.

You can also get thumbnail job descriptions when you search for salary information in Monster's Salary Center. Go to **salary.monster.com/**.

Online job sites are a good research tool as well. Monster is one of hundreds of job sites on the Internet (okay, we're the best ;-), and you can use their job postings as a rich source of knowledge long before you apply. These advertisements describe a job's required skills, knowledge, and experience. The better ones also describe outcomes—what the employee is expected to accomplish. This is research in the real world!

As you study all the sites I've mentioned above, you'll get pretty familiar with the descriptions of jobs you want. Then it's time to use the job descriptions that interest you to create Target Job forms. Don't expect to fill out the entire Target Job form based on one job posting at a Web site, however. Different employers have different job titles, requirements, and cultures, and their job postings vary widely. That's why you want to read twenty or more job postings from a number of sources. You'll get a broader view of what it really takes to do each job.

Here's an example of a job description from Monster. I've highlighted the key points you might write on a Target Job form.

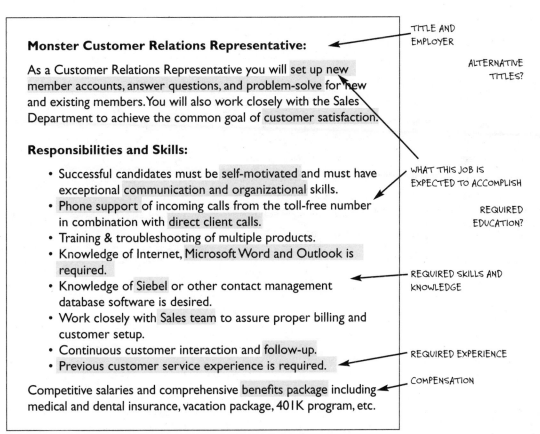

Monster Customer Relations Representative:

As a Customer Relations Representative you will set up new member accounts, answer questions, and problem-solve for new and existing members. You will also work closely with the Sales Department to achieve the common goal of customer satisfaction.

Responsibilities and Skills:

- Successful candidates must be self-motivated and must have exceptional communication and organizational skills.
- Phone support of incoming calls from the toll-free number in combination with direct client calls.
- Training & troubleshooting of multiple products.
- Knowledge of Internet, Microsoft Word and Outlook is required.
- Knowledge of Siebel or other contact management database software is desired.
- Work closely with Sales team to assure proper billing and customer setup.
- Continuous customer interaction and follow-up.
- Previous customer service experience is required.

Competitive salaries and comprehensive benefits package including medical and dental insurance, vacation package, 401K program, etc.

TITLE AND EMPLOYER

ALTERNATIVE TITLES?

WHAT THIS JOB IS EXPECTED TO ACCOMPLISH

REQUIRED EDUCATION?

REQUIRED SKILLS AND KNOWLEDGE

REQUIRED EXPERIENCE

COMPENSATION

235

The highlighted points are connections between you and the job—skills you possess, experiences you've had, and/or items you'd like to research further. In chapter 13, we'll revisit this ad for clues about applying for the job. From this example, you can start building the following Target Job form for the position of Customer Relations Representative. (I've left some lines intentionally blank, because you don't yet have all the information you need. I'll complete the form at the end of this chapter, after showing you additional research techniques.)

The Target Job form isn't complete: only one employer is listed, and there is only one source of compensation, and no information about required certifications—but it's a good view of the job. As you go over several job descriptions and continue your research with the methods below, you will add information to the form.

Try different keywords when you search jobs online, and add new skills, knowledge, and outcomes to your Target Job form. When you run out of new words, you'll have a comprehensive profile of a particular job.

100 Words About Search Engines

Most Internet job searches work like this: You choose a location, industry, and job title that interest you, and hit "Search." On a large job site the search may turn up hundreds of jobs, and that's where keywords come in. Before you hit that search button, type words into a text box to narrow down your result. For example, you may choose south Texas as a location, but if you really want to work in Brownsville, you add the keyword "Brownsville." If you're a pediatric nurse, you add "pediatric" as a keyword. You can add more than one keyword.

For a fast tutorial on searching with keywords, go to **help.monster.com/ jobseeker/jobsearch/keywordtips/.**

TARGET JOB

Job information:

Title: _____ Customer Relations Representative _____

Alternative titles: _____

_____

Employers hiring this job: _____ ABC Co. (others?) _____

_____

_____

What this job is expected to accomplish: _Support customers calling in with questions_

about their products. Support sales staff with billing. Follow up.

Required education or certification: _____

Required experience: _____ Customer service experience. _____

Required skills and/or special knowledge: _Software: Microsoft Word and Outlook._

Seibel or customer relations software. Internet.

Typical compensation in my geographic area: _____ $24,000–31,000 (according to_

Salary.com). Benefits similar to other employers nearby.

Search information:

Who can tell me more about this job: _____

_____

What I like most about this job: _Suits my skills; talking to customers on the phone._

_____

_____

What I like least about this job: _____

_____

_____

Where this job may lead me in five years: _Sales representative, sales engineer_

_____

You can download this form at monstercareers.com.

Some job sites also have message boards where members share information about jobs. On Monster, they're hosted by experts who can tell you more about jobs, as in this exchange between a member and Susan Oldegaard Turner, the health-care advisor:

I want to become a nurse educator
DawnS9962 - 2/18/2003 - 4:01:22 PM

I may be jumping the gun here but I have always loved teaching and really enjoy the health field. How can I combine the two? I am going to have my RN soon and wonder if I will be too old by the time I complete any additional education needed. Can I go on to get a BSN or do I need an MSN? Thanks, Dawn

Re: I want to become a nurse educator
HealthcareAdvisor - 2/18/2003 - 6:22:25 PM

Most nurse educator roles require a master's degree. If you wish to teach in a nursing school, a MSN is mandatory. If you wish to be a nurse educator in a hospital or clinic, you can often do so with a BSN—it just depends on the position. Ultimately you will have more job options and higher salaries—no matter what role you choose—if you get the MSN. Good luck!

Many online sites specialize in an industry, profession, or even type of job (such as part-time or contract jobs). Monster and a few of the large sites also have special sections on the technology, public service, health care, and other fields.

Company Web Sites

Companies post job opportunities on their own Web sites, too. The job descriptions are similar to the Customer Relations Representative example, so print out the ones that interest you and use the same technique described above to fill in your Target Job form. Remember that companies advertise only current job opportunities; often the company Web site won't tell you the jobs that may become available next month, or describe jobs that were open last year.

Bear in mind also that America's 22 million small businesses employ about half the workforce, and provide roughly 70 percent of new jobs. Many of those companies will not have active Web sites; you'll have to use an online job site or offline methods, described below, to find job opportunities in smaller companies.

Expect surprises. Online job postings may show that companies providing health-care services in your area are also hiring accountants. Since health-care services will grow faster than the overall economy over the next ten years, it's a promising industry not only for nurses but also for accountants, programmers, administrators, sales and marketing staff, and others.

Learn About Employers

In the course of learning about jobs, you'll learn a lot about the companies—or other organizations such as government and nonprofit—where those jobs take place. Some of them will interest you enough to become target employers—and you'll research them more thoroughly. Don't limit yourself to employers who are advertising jobs the week you start looking. All employers hire people at some time, and most jobs aren't advertised (see chapter 13 for more on this topic).

David Morgan, manager of college recruiting at Ford Motor Company thinks company and industry research creates two essential benefits. "Your number-one goal is to learn everything that you can about a potential employer before you ever apply for a job there," he says. "And number two is to find out what it's like to work in that company."

When you find an employer that interests you, begin a Target Employer form (page 241). Keep separate forms for separate employers.

In the first section of the form, write down specifics about potential employers. These specifics will give power to your interview preparation:

- the organization's name
- its major business line
- size (annual sales, number of employees, or other significant metrics; for example, a school might be measured by its spending budget, not sales)
- notes about the company culture
- leading products

239

- the employer's customers (they may be consumers, other businesses, the government, or others)

- the employer's competitors

In the second section, add information to help your search:

- people who can tell you more about the employer (see "Informational Interviews," later in this chapter, and chapter 14, Networking)

- what you like most about the employer

- what you like least about the employer

- where the employer might lead you in five years (greater opportunity? a chance to work overseas? helping you pay for further education?)

Again, it's not imperative that you complete the entire form, but the more you know about the business, the better you will look in the job interview. Place each Target Employer form in a separate folder. In this folder, place copies of every communication, every article you clip, every note you scribbled from a conversation about that company.

You might already have some employers in mind, so start Target Employer sheets for them. Then, broaden your possibilities.

You can locate specific companies by searching for the company name at the business or finance sections of any of the large Web services, such as AOL, Google, MSN, or Yahoo! Your search result will give you the company's home Web site as well as news, press releases, and other information. Many of the "news stories" you will find by searching business or finance sections will actually be press releases distributed by two services named BusinessWire and PR Newswire. While these can be informative, bear in mind that press releases are written by the companies themselves and only tell you what the company wants you to know.

To find additional employers, go to the online yellow pages. A good example is the Verizon SmartPages Business Center (**business.superpages. com/business/**). There, you can find all of the listed businesses in an industry within, say, twenty miles of your home ZIP Code. Many provide a Web address. If they don't have a Web site to browse, you can search news sources (see below) for information about them.

TARGET EMPLOYER

Company Information:

Name: _____

Business Line: _____

_____

Size: _____

Company culture: _____

_____

_____

Leading Products/Services: _____

Customers: _____

Competitors: _____

_____

Search Information:

Who can tell me more/connect me to this employer: _____

_____

_____

What I like most about this employer: _____

_____

_____

What I like least about this employer: _____

_____

_____

Where working for this employer may lead me in five years: ____

_____

_____

You can download this form at monstercareers.com.

Libraries and Career Centers

Reference librarians and counselors in career centers (on campus and in state employment centers) are information specialists. Take advantage of them. Your public library can get you started or get you unstuck. Go with twenty blank copies each of your Target Job form and Target Employer form. Your research goals are companies to target *and* people who can tell you more. The resources you can use here are:

- **Computers:** Many libraries offer free access to online resources via personal computer. Some candidates run their entire search from library computers.

- **Directories:** Business directories list all kinds of information about businesses: where they're located, their size, their products, and who's running them. Not every library has access to these expensive directories (business libraries in major cities and business schools are a good bet). Among the most useful directories found online (to which libraries subscribe) are D&B's Million-Dollar Database, InfoUSA, and Hoover's directories (the Hoover's Web site does contain useful free information at **hoovers.com/**).

- **Newspapers and magazines:** *The Wall Street Journal, The New York Times, Fortune,* and *Forbes* are fine places to start, and you can search them online (some searches require payment). Many other business magazines, from *Inc.* to *Working Mother,* can provide in-depth information on companies and jobs.

- **Trade journals:** Specialty journals cover every business, with titles like *Information Week, Air Cargo World,* and *Real Estate Professional.* If you've targeted the industry you want to work in, become a regular reader of its journals. You will find companies, learn about the business, learn job titles, get ideas for questions to ask, and uncover the names of people you will want to approach.

- **Local business journals:** Local business journals also supply you with invaluable news and names. There's a good list of city-specific business journals at **bizjournals.com/journals.html**. One piece of information to look for: the list of upcoming events where you can meet people in the business (see chapter 14, Networking).

- **Major newspaper special sections:** Look for "Top 100 Companies of 2004," for example. The monthly venture capital report is a great way to find emerging companies.

- **Books about careers:** There are many guides dedicated to careers in specific fields, such as law, medicine, social work, banking, and so forth. Browse the ones that seem up-to-date and appeal to you personally.

Keep filling out those Target Job and Target Employer forms. Right now you're still casting your net widely, so create a sheet for any job or employer that interests you and looks like a possibility.

Going Deeper

If one of the companies that interests you has its own Web site, spend some time there. Start with the home page and then go to the "About" or "Media" section. Typically, you'll find information about:

- the company's business lines
- officers and management
- press releases containing news, employee names, recent deals, names of customers (remember those), partners, and vendors
- a mission statement or other clues to the company culture
- employment information, including job opportunities

The Career Guide to Industries is another useful site from the Bureau of Labor Statistics. It organizes information on jobs by industry, describing forty-two different industries and their working conditions, jobs available, earnings, employment outlook, and more. It is located online at **stats. bls.gov/oco/cg/home.htm**. An article titled "How Industries Differ," linked from the home page, is a good place to start.

Publicly traded companies (the kind that issue stock) must file detailed reports with the Securities and Exchange Commission. The reports are available at the SEC's Web service, called EDGAR (**sec.gov/edgar/ searchedgar/webusers.htm**). Go to the EDGAR Web address, and click the "Companies and Other Filers" link. Fill in the name of the company, and you will receive a list of available reports. These reports, largely used by investors, can be very detailed, so this site is perhaps best used for advanced research.

Scott N. Santoro of technology staffing firm Keane suggests that a thorough researcher should understand the real lifeblood of a company: the money and management. Board of director biographies, financial information, and press releases (all usually found on the company's Web site) tell you a lot about the company's financial health and its plans for the future.

Executives should go the extra mile in research, says Scott: "Listen to the 'investment analyst' calls. They're available in audio form at any of the financial Web sites, and when you play them you hear recordings of the Chief Executive Officer and Chief Financial Officer talking about the organization [to the Wall Street investment analysts]. The financials tell you the strengths and weaknesses of the organization."

Scott's advice underscores how research pays off later in your job search. Imagine quoting what the CEO told Wall Street during your job interview! I guarantee you the average candidate doesn't prepare this diligently.

Fortune's annual surveys of companies, including the famous Fortune 500 but also including "Small Business 100," "Best Companies to Work For," and "Most Admired Companies" lists, available online at **fortune. com/fortune/alllists**, can be helpful for finding companies of interest. (Just remember that the better known the company, the greater the competition for jobs.)

Newslink (**newslink.org**) is a good gateway to local newspaper and magazine articles. Use the city and state search fields on the home page to find local publications.

Hoover's (**hoovers.com**) offers free thumbnail profiles and news about public and private companies.

If you are interested in finding start-up companies with venture funding, check out the PriceWaterhouseCoopers Moneytree site (**pwcmoneytree. com/**). Search its quarterly report on venture funding by region, industry, funding stage, and so on. The results will alert you to growing companies that are under the radar of other research.

Vault (**vault.com**), WetFeet (**wetfeet.com**), and About (**about.com**) all host message boards about companies. As with all community sites, the content on these sites is contributed by the sites' users with little or no oversight, so it is difficult to confirm whether what you're reading is fair or accurate.

Remember that a target company's customers, vendors, and competitors may also become target companies. Outplacement firms advise their clients to look to these relationships early in the job search process.

Drowning in Information

The Web is a two-edged sword: it's easy to get lost in too much information. Remember the entrepreneur's F.A.M.E. habit of action, and develop a sense of when you have enough information to act. Then *act*—get networking, approach a company, apply for a job—when you are confident you know enough.

The Amazing Research Method No One Uses

Talk to an employer's customers! Brad Barrell of worldwide transportation firm CHEP offers this simple but powerful research technique. Companies as large as Dell Computer, and as small as your local dry cleaner, talk to their customers all the time. They say it's the secret of their success. And yet, few candidates ever discuss a target employer with the very people that employer serves.

Try to talk to the customers of any target company. Follow the steps outlined in the next section, "Informational Interviews," telling an interviewee that your purpose is to find out more about the products and services of your target company. It is most effective to talk with a customer you may serve in your target job. For example, if you are interested in a regional sales job with an athletic clothing manufacturer, talk to the purchasing manager of a retailer that features the clothing (not just consumers who buy the sweatshirts). You will learn about the manufacturer's quality control, delivery, response to customer suggestions, reliability, and respect for its customers.

Talking to customers is an advanced method of researching a company, the kind of rule-breaking method that separates you from your competition. It reveals hidden information that you can use in a job interview. For example, perhaps that athletic clothing manufacturer has great designers but your research indicates it doesn't always deliver its products on time. If you have inventory or logistics management skills, you have an arresting topic for discussion with the company (like Candidate 2 at the beginning of this chapter).

You may get prejudiced views, and some customers won't want to comment. That's okay. Just practicing this technique is a way of making things happen. It sets you apart from other candidates. It's a low-risk way to practice for a job or informational interview. This depth of research demonstrates

245

that you're the kind of person who goes after answers—going straight to the marketplace. You are, in fact, focused on what matters to the employer.

If you are concerned that talking to customers in advance might be off-putting to an employer, take this attitude: "I'm so interested in your company that I talked to your customers as part of my research. I thought I should know what they were saying about your products."

Recruiter Amy Needelman of MarketSource Sales Services, a leading provider of integrated sales services to Fortune 500 companies, recalls a candidate who made a powerful impression using this technique: "The candidate knew our competitors and our clients, and they'd even figured out the client with whom they'd work [if they got the job]. They had researched the client's newest products and asked me specific questions about those products."

Amy, who interviews many job applicants by phone every day, keeps an eye on candidates like this for jobs now and in the future. Customer knowledge is a key competency of companies today. Demonstrate that you talk to customers before you talk to a company, and doors will open.

Informational Interviews

You are not going to learn everything from the Internet. After you've identified jobs that interest you, it's time to learn more from the people who are doing those jobs.

Let's be clear about the purpose of "informational interviewing," because the term has been abused for a long time. Over and over, people used it with the hidden agenda of showcasing themselves when they couldn't get a job interview. Every manager grew wary that an informational interviewer would hit them up for a job, and some grew to dread the request.

It is relevant *research*, not a job interview in disguise, so let's focus on its purpose. Monster career coach Peter Vogt suggests you think of yourself as a journalist uncovering facts. Your goal is to make informed career decisions, so you're going to ask people about their jobs.

It is also an opportunity to rehearse a short form of your sales pitch. At some point in an informational interview, you will be asked about yourself. You don't have to launch into the full presentation, but the more you practice describing yourself as a professional, the more comfortable you'll be in a job interview.

The first thing you need to figure out, of course, is who you want to talk to. The possibilities here are limited only by your imagination. You might consider approaching:

- family members and friends
- people you have discovered in your research
- people at companies that interest you
- teachers
- graduates of your school
- people who are referred to you by any or all of the above

Don't spend months trying to reach a CEO unless you're sure there's no one else who can give you information. Many times you can gain more information speaking with someone who is doing the job you target than speaking with his or her manager. Get in front of executives as part of networking (see chapter 14), but don't make it a requirement for research.

Start your informational interviews after you've done enough online or library research to ask intelligent questions. What should you ask in an informational interview? You want to know the real-world details of the following:

- **What the job or career entails.** The person you interview can put things in perspective for you because they're actually living their careers each day.

- **How to break into the career.** Some of your subjects will have taken a fairly traditional career path, but many have arrived in their jobs through unusual routes. Most will be in the middle of their careers, and all can talk about where they think their jobs will lead them next.

- **The trends emerging within the career.** How much money are people in a particular job making now, and how do things look for the future? Is this career path growing or shrinking? Where will the opportunities be in this career five, ten, or fifteen years from now?

- **The pluses and minuses of the job.** Print and Internet career resources often focus on the positive aspects of jobs. Don't you want to know about the potential downsides as well? Your sources can tell you about a job's trade-offs.

- **Your list of employers.** You may bring along a typed list of your target employers and ask, "What do you know about these companies? Are

247

there places like them I've missed, or other places that employ my target job?"

- **The people who enjoy and succeed in this career.** If you're wondering whether your own personality would be a good fit for a career, interviewees might be able to give you an idea. They can also help you figure out what education, experiences, and skills you'd need for the career and how you could get them.

- **Other people and resources.** Always ask, "Who else should I talk to?" and "Where can I learn more?" People in jobs know more about hidden sources of information than any librarian.

How to Set Up an Informational Interview

Once you've identified a good prospect for an informational interview, how do you set it up? Executive career counselor Ginny Rehberg, known on TV as The Career Doctor, says keep it simple. Don't propose an informational interview, which still carries baggage: "Instead, just use the term 'meeting,'" says Ginny. "That's it. Let's have a meeting. Not a networking meeting, or an informational meeting. When they ask, For what?, you say, 'To discuss some of the developments in our field and to get your perspective on what's going on.'" You can be upfront about the fact that you're doing research; you can also say the purpose is to learn specifics of their job, or to ask questions about your target employers.

Ask specifically for a brief meeting. You can find out what you need to know in twenty minutes. If the person understands that you're simply trying to learn something, then more often than not your request will be granted. Why? For one thing, most people are naturally helpful. For another, people are genuinely interested in sharing their expertise and insights—in talking about themselves—especially to those who show a sincere interest in them.

Because these people are doing you a favor, you owe them basic professional courtesy:

- If you write or e-mail first, follow up with a call within two days of their receiving your message. It's astonishing how many people write for an interview, then wait ten days to follow up. How can anyone remember an e-mail from a stranger that came unsolicited ten days ago?

- Show up when you say you will, dressed professionally, and meet for exactly as long as you said (no more than thirty minutes; twenty, better).

- Do your homework first! You will make a better impression and get better information if you ask only those questions that can't be answered online or in the library.

- Don't bring out your resume. If your interviewee asks for a resume, smile and say you're very gratified by the request, but you only asked for their insight and you're not there today to hit them up for a job. Then say, "I always carry a copy of my resume, and if you'd like me to leave it here I'll be happy to do that." Don't be coy; just offer to leave your resume at the end of the meeting, and also send it via e-mail later that day (sending an electronic version of your resume with a thank-you e-mail opens the way to a follow-up one week later).

- If the tone of the interview is informal, you might want to show a paper copy of your pitch. (If "pitch" sounds a little too commercial, just call it your personal "summary" or "presentation notes.") This

Sneaky?

Some job seekers believe that the informational interview is really just a sneaky way to get a job interview. I don't buy it—everyone's onto that trick. You must believe that informational interviewing is not a job interview but a workout, training the moves you'll need in the real job interview.

You do need to be just as prepared for the informational interview as for the job interview, however. If you're asked, "Tell me about yourself, and what you are interested in," and you say, "I don't know," you've lost an opportunity in either case.

Take a positive, active attitude: "This is moving me forward, and I can offer something valuable to them." It builds your confidence, gives you more information about an industry, connects you to others, and moves you closer to your goal.

Granting an informational interview is a random act of kindness, and it always leads back around to something else. You don't realize when you touch people what will happen. Somehow the chit comes back to the person who offers help.

Ask yourself, "How can I repay this favor?" And then repay it. Later, when you have landed your dream job, don't forget to keep the good karma going by granting informational interviews yourself!

gives you an opportunity to focus quickly on your key messages, key skills, and achievements in a more low-key manner than a resume would make possible.

- Offer your business card at the close of the meeting, and request one of theirs.

Learning About Compensation

"How much can I earn in that job?"

Compensation in all its forms—wages, benefits, stock options, and so on—has historically been a difficult subject to nail down. Naturally, companies don't want to broadcast their pay scales. In some situations the money is dictated by contract or union agreements. In others, everything is negotiable. The goal of your research at this stage is to find out more about compensation in your local area (pay scales for the same job swing in a wide range around the United States, as does the cost of living).

The Bureau of Labor Statistics publishes its national compensation survey at **bls.gov/ncs/ocs/**. The survey is usually a couple of years old, but it's a good starting point.

A popular compensation research site on the Web is Salary.com, which allows you to search by job title, location, and seniority. Salary uses compensation surveys and experts to keep data current.

SalaryExpert (**salaryexpert.com**) is a similar service, used by *The Wall Street Journal, The New York Times,* and other publications for their salary information.

In the "guide to guides" category, JobStar (**jobstar.org**) is a gateway to industry- and profession-specific salary surveys. It's especially effective for very specific professions like airline pilot or property manager.

Book to Web

You can find Salary.com's Salary Wizard, and much more advice on compensation of all kinds, at the Monster Salary Center (**content.salary. monster.com/**).

Managers, professionals, and executives will find the compensation surveys and articles in magazines like *BusinessWeek*, *Fortune*, and *Forbes* of interest. Trade magazines, with their focused content, are also good sources for this information.

Wageweb (**wageweb.com**) and Realrates (**realrates.com**) are survey-based sites with useful data. Realrates focuses on computer-related positions. Remember that these sites rely on information supplied by visitors to the site—they're only as accurate as the data supplied by people like you.

Three reminders as you study compensation:

- Surveys create a snapshot of pay in a fast-moving economy, and thus the data is always a little out of date. A recession drives down wages; a boom drives wages up. One of the best uses of these surveys is to *compare* different jobs and locations, not establish a benchmark rate for a job.

- The highest pay may not mean the best job. In a Monster survey, only 35 percent of respondents said that higher pay would lure them to a new job. Thirty-one percent said a better, more positive environment would tempt them to move. Don't let a 5 percent higher rate of pay tempt you into a job you'll hate.

- And if you need one more reason to keep learning, here's the bottom line on money and education: Employees holding a two-year associate degree from a vocational or technical school are expected to earn $1.5 million more over a 40-year career than those with a high school education. A bachelor's degree is worth $1.9 million, and a professional degree or doctorate can add $2.8 million in earning power.

Be Careful!

One of the worst things you can do is cut a salary report out of the paper or print it off a Web site and march up to your boss, demanding a raise. Use salary research as a guide, a tool to help you negotiate. Don't throw it in your boss's face!

Many Possibilities

Make research part of your weekly routine. Fill your Target Job and Target Employer files with possibilities. Many people stuck in a traditional job search feel like they've hit a dead end after they've applied to the four employers they already know. Using all the resources in this chapter, from Web sites to magazines to informational interviewing, you can continue to discover jobs and employers that are right for you.

Here's a completed version of the Target Job form you saw on page 237. Even just four or five of these will help you imagine a broader world of job opportunities.

To borrow a term from the military, research is a "force multiplier": it makes every other phase of your job search—from networking to the job interview to negotiating an offer—much more powerful. Your job search is an opportunity to practice the skills that will make you better in any job, and one of those critical skills is getting the right information to make informed choices. Beyond the practical benefits, research can make you a more interesting and curious person. As you step out into the marketplace, that means a lot for your success.

Target job

Job information:

Title: Customer Relations Representative

Alternative Titles: Customer Service Representative

Employers hiring this job: ABC Co., XYZ Co., Spingy International, Flo's

What this job is expected to accomplish: Support customers calling in with questions about company products. Support sales staff with billing. Follow up.

Required education or certification: Associate's degree

Required experience: Customer service experience, except at entry level

Required skills and/or special knowledge: Varies. You have to know the company's products. Some ads mention ability to handle pressure. Most frequently mentioned software: Microsoft Word and Outlook. Seibel or customer relations software. Internet.

Typical compensation in my geographic area: $24,000–31,000 (according to Salary.com). Benefits similar to other employers nearby.

Search information:

Who can tell me more about this job: Ben (Sally's husband—he's a customer representative at XYZ's consumer products division). Maryanne Carter (friend who works at ABC Co.). Learned a lot from informational interview with Mr. Sloan.

What I like most about this job: Suits my skills; like the idea of helping upset customers solve their problems.

What I like least about this job: At some companies, this job exists in a pressure-cooker atmosphere.

Where this job may lead me in five years: Sales representative, sales engineer

You can download this form at monstercareers.com.

F.A.M.E. ATTITUDE: WORK LIKE AN **E**NTREPRENEUR
Entrepreneurs put themselves in the way of
opportunity.

Y ou may think the opportunity to connect with a job looks like
this time line, in which the shaded area is your window of opportunity.

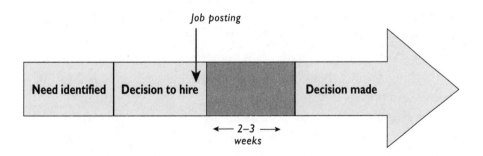

Actually, your window of opportunity looks more like this:

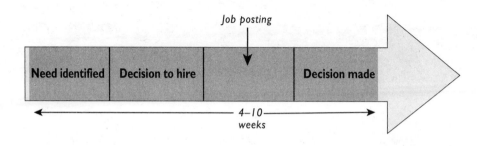

In fact, company management thinks about staff all the time. Are the right people in the right jobs? How should staff size or organization look a year from now? Will they need extra help when that new product line launches next fall?

The public window of opportunity on a particular job may be very short, but the opportunity to be considered for a role in a company is much longer. This is good news! It means you should practice the entrepreneur's F.A.M.E. habit of putting yourself in the way of opportunity whether or not an employer is advertising jobs at the moment. It means you should stay alert for opportunity, too, because it can appear at any time.

Learning to approach an employer in the right way may be the most significant skill you develop in phase 2 of the *Monster Careers* program, because if you get a target company's attention before a job is posted, you will have the advantage. You will stand apart from the stampede of ordinary candidates. Approaching a select series of employers with a finely honed resume, cover message, and pitch is tantamount to creating your own opportunity.

Here's another way of looking at it: Over time, your personal job market looks like an iceberg—85 percent of the potential opportunities lie out of sight. Those are the jobs that aren't advertised, *yet*. They may never be advertised, because good candidates have approached the company before the opportunities become public.

Why aren't all jobs advertised? There are many reasons:

- Business uncertainty. Sales are down, for example.
- Budget restraints. "We'll advertise that job next month, when we have the money."

- Too many candidates. "We have enough resumes in our files. Find candidates from those."

- A department isn't ready to hire yet. "Let's wait until after the reorganization."

- The company uses alternative techniques, such as employee referrals, before posting a job.

- A potential job opening may be confidential.

- The hiring may be continuous. For example, a call center may add new people throughout the year, but only need to advertise once or twice a year to get enough resumes.

In every case above, the employer *may* be hiring next month. They may even be ready to hire now but not ready to advertise. Employers *do* advertise job openings in various circumstances:

- They need to fill positions quickly—when ramping up a new product line, for example.

- They need to fill many positions—when a new plant is opening, or a new wing is being added to a hospital, for example.

- No known candidate is a good fit.

- There is a long-term shortage of candidates to fill this kind of job. Since the 1990s, for example, nurses have been in chronically short supply.

- Recruiters post jobs on behalf of clients and themselves (recruiters collect promising resumes).

The bottom line: An employer that interests you may be ready to hire now, or a month from now. It's up to you to come to that employer's attention, and the rest of this chapter details how to be at the head of the line when the hiring happens.

First, let's work with the most obvious, public opportunities: advertised jobs.

Advertised Jobs

Is this you?

- "I don't get it. I've sent out more than 600 resumes since last summer, but I haven't had one call."

257

- "I read every single want ad on Sunday, highlight the ones that have my job title in them, and on Monday I send a resume to every one."

- "There are a lot of people looking for work now, so I don't have much choice. I apply for any job in my field."

People love to apply for jobs online because it's easy, and job advertisements get your imagination going.

People do find jobs online every day, and you should apply for advertised jobs when you find ones that are right for you. That doesn't mean glancing at job descriptions and shooting off blind resumes, however. If you use a job search site like a giant slot machine, you're gambling with your future. So stop doing what doesn't work. Instead, think of advertised job postings as part of a long-term dialogue with potential employers.

Where Jobs Are Advertised

Millions of jobs are advertised every year, both online and offline. Here's where you will find them:

- The large job Web sites, where you can search for advertised jobs in your local area, in other locations, and even overseas.

- Company Web sites, which also advertise current openings. Some company Web sites also invite you to place your electronic resume in their database, so that they can find you when they have an appropriate opening.

- Traditional newspaper help-wanted sections, which are moving online at the newspapers' Web sites. Of course, some people prefer scanning the printed newspaper help-wanted sections.

- Magazines and trade journals (see chapter 12) also carry classified job advertisements.

- Job fairs, which gather many employers under one roof for a day or two, are a popular way for companies to market themselves. Job fairs are aimed at entry- to mid-level candidates. You'll find them in the classifieds and at state job centers, where you will also find various jobs advertised. (For more about job fairs, see page 365.)

Don't forget bulletin boards in public areas like stores and churches. If you're looking for a private job (like housekeeping or pet grooming), you may find one there. Small local businesses use them, too.

Searching for Jobs Online

Online job hunting on sites like Monster is booming, so have confidence in it as *one* of your critical tools.

At the big job sites, you find open job positions by using the "Search Jobs" functions. The sites differ a little in the way you search, but in general, you are offered a selection of geographic locations and job categories. You select a location and a job category and click on the "Search" or "Get Results" button. To narrow down your search, you add keywords (just like on your resume, keywords are words, phrases, and terms that you can enter to narrow down your search).

Remember the keywords that gave you good results, and use them regularly. If one term doesn't yield the right jobs, try similar terms. Experiment! Keywords can include a job title or skill, the name of an industry or company, or a location. Examples include "programmer," "SAP," "telecommunications," "manager," "human resources," "marketing," and "Cincinnati." Be specific—instead of "Customer," write "Customer Service Representative." Take advantage of the "saved search" or "job search agents" at the larger sites.

Here's an example of the Monster job search. A candidate is looking for hospital-based nursing jobs in Los Angeles, so they've selected "hospital" as a keyword, "California–Los Angeles" as a location, and the job category "Healthcare–Registered Nurses (RNs)."

When the selections are made, and the keywords typed in, the job search page looks like this:

![Monster Job Search screen capture showing a browser window titled "Monster – Search Jobs" at http://jobsearch.monster.com/ with navigation bar (Home, Search Jobs, My Monster Login, Career Advice, Help, For Employers), the Monster Job Search logo, an "Enter Key Words" field containing "hospital", "Choose Location" list, "Choose Job Category" list, Sort Results and View Description options, a "Get Results" button, and a Specialized Search sidebar.]

When you click "Get Results," the Web site's software searches through all listed jobs to find the ones that match your keywords, location, and job category. The result is a list of active (open) jobs, as illustrated on page 261.

Clicking on the job title takes you to the specific job details. From there, you can save the advertisement for later, or apply for the job online right away. The major job sites differ in their methods for doing this, but all have clear instructions.

Book to Web

If you learn to use the job search engines better, you'll get results that match your dream job more closely. For tips on how to search, go to **help. monster.com/jobseeker/jobsearch/**.

A screenshot showing a Monster Job Search Results page with the following content:

Monster - Search Jobs

Back | Forward | Stop | Refresh | Home | AutoFill | Print | Mail

Address: http://jobsearch.monster.com/jobsearch.asp?q=hospital&lid=348&fn=3975&sort=rv&vw=b&cy=US&re=14&brd=1%2C1862%2C1863

Penguin Putnam Inc. Intranet - Home Page | Google | Pearson Global Directory | Pearson to Pearson | Questia - The Online Library of Books and Jou...

Home | Search Jobs | My Monster Login | Career Advice | Help | For Employers

monster® Job Search Results

Refine Search With Additional Key Words:
hospital [Refine]
[New Search] [Tips on Searching] [Previous Keyword Searches]

Search Related Job Titles:
Hospital Administrator, Director of Health Services, Medical Administrator, Health Care Administrator, Clinic Administrator, more...

Save this search and email me jobs (GO)

TRY NOW! Search for degree programs on MonsterLearning. click here.

Jobs 1 to 50 of 137   Show Jobs Posted: [All Jobs ▼]   Page 1 of 3
Sort: Date | Relevance   View: Brief | Detailed

Date	Job Title	Company	Location
Jan 29	Charge RN/Hospital	Kaiser Permanente Southern Cal	US-CA-Los Angeles
Jan 29	Charge RN/Hospital	Kaiser Permanente Southern Cal	US-CA-Los Angeles
Feb 2	Employee Health Services Manager	Childrens Hospital of Los Ang	US-CA-Los Angeles
Jan 24	REGISTERED NURSE	California Hospital Medical	US-CA-LOS ANGELES
Jan 22	Registered Nurse	Antelope Valley Hospital	US-CA-Lancaster

Internet zone

"Speed to the Best"

A popular job posting on Monster may attract thirty to forty resumes per hour, so if you don't answer the job posting quickly, there's a reasonable chance your resume will be buried under a pile of others. Major job boards can alert you via e-mail the moment a promising job is posted. See the sites for details.

Jobs are added 24 hours a day, 365 days a year. The process on large sites is completely automated, and if a recruiter wants to post a job at 3 A.M., it's no problem.

Jobs you see listed online today may be gone tomorrow. Employers deactivate jobs for several reasons. The job could be filled, or the employer may have received enough promising resumes. The job may have expired (they're posted for a set period). Regardless, if you saw a job that looked right for you at a promising company, you should consider networking into that company (see chapter 14) or setting up a "job search agent" to search for jobs there automatically.

Wherever you find them, read job descriptions carefully before you apply. When we asked employers about responses to their ads, 93 percent said fewer than half of all applicants read their postings thoroughly. If it's clear you didn't study the ad, why should they think you want the job?

Keeping Safe Online

Some common-sense rules for protecting your privacy when searching for jobs online:

Do not give your Social Security number, even if they suggest that it is for a "routine background check."

Do not provide credit card or bank numbers, or engage in any monetary transactions related to applying for a job.

Do not provide any non-work-related personal information (such as driver's license number, eye color, marital status, and so on) over the phone or online.

Be cautious when dealing with contacts outside of your own country.

Don't pay money to get a job. If a company asks you to send $495.00 to get the "starter kit," think long and hard about the validity of this offer.

For more, see **resume.monster.com/articles/personalinfo/**.

Employer Web Sites

Employers' Web sites are getting better at advertising available positions. You probably saw open job postings while doing company research (chapter 12). If you see a great job advertised on a company site, use the same application strategies as you would for jobs on large career sites, which I'll describe later in "How to Apply for an Advertised Job" on page 265.

Some leading companies have developed sophisticated job application Web sites, where you can create detailed job applications customized to their needs. Dave Morgan, director of college recruitment at Ford Motor Company, describes its full-service site: "Our Web site gives detailed information about our company culture. [Candidates] look at our products, at our company. There's a job seeker profile on the application: individuals enter information about their life experiences, skills, desires, etc. We compare that to what we're looking for in a specific job. It is a custom application—Ford may have criteria that are different from IBM or Intel."

Get the Most from a Job Ad

Let's take another look at that job advertisement we highlighted in chapter 12:

Monster Customer Relations Representative:

As a Customer Relations Representative you will set up new member accounts, answer questions, and problem-solve for new and existing members. You will also work closely with the Sales Department to achieve the common goal of customer satisfaction.

Responsibilities and Skills:

- Successful candidates must be self-motivated and must have exceptional communication and organizational skills.
- Phone support of incoming calls from the toll-free number in combination with direct client calls.
- Training & troubleshooting of multiple products.
- Knowledge of Internet, Microsoft Word, and Outlook is required.
- Knowledge of Siebel or other contact management database software is desired.
- Work closely with Sales team to assure proper billing and customer setup.
- Continuous customer interaction and follow-up.
- Previous customer service experience is required.

Competitive salaries and comprehensive benefits package including medical and dental insurance, vacation package, 401K program, etc.

This is not just a description of a job. The ad really represents the employer's opportunities and problems. What do they hope the employee will accomplish? What problems do they fear a bad hire, or no hire, will cause?

If you decide to apply for this job, the advertisement provides all the material you need to customize your application. Include some of the highlighted words in your cover message. See that the skills or technical knowledge are listed as keywords in the resume you send. (I'll list these and other application strategies in the next section.)

As you study a job advertisement, you will naturally imagine yourself in the job. It's another moment of truth: Would you like this job? Can you do it? Does it fit with your vision of your career? There are clues throughout the job description that you can use in your application. The clues also help you generate great questions for your research or job interview.

Looking at the highlighted phrases above, you can see that the employer has hopes beyond just "doing the job." Questions you might ask appear below:

Sales and customer service are both focused on customer satisfaction.

- **Application strategy:** In your application, tell a specific achievement story in which a customer was more than satisfied. Better yet—quote a satisfied customer!

- **Research or interview questions:** How do they measure customer satisfaction? How important is it to the company's overall strategy? Is this position just support staff, or does it have real status with the sales team (sales is mentioned twice in the ad)?

The successful candidate must be self-motivated.

- **Application strategy:** Stress that you know how to take the initiative—you don't need close supervision to be on the ball.

- **Research or interview questions:** Is this a job that rewards initiative? Are they open to new ideas? Are they having trouble with employee turnover?

The CSR will both answer the phone and make direct client calls.

- **Application strategy:** Practice your phone technique (page 153) and offer to give a telephone interview before coming in, "to demonstrate my great communication skills."

- **Interview or research questions:** Is the purpose of direct calls to make sure customers are satisfied with a purchase, or to sell them more? The answer might indicate a growth path for this position (into sales, for example).

You can build an entire application strategy in this way, using the job advertisement as a focus for both your application and your job interview.

As you'll see in chapter 15, this kind of focus changes the interview into a conversation about the job, not an interrogation about you.

Remember: if you're not qualified, don't apply. Pat O'Brien, author of *Making College Count,* describes the futility of that tactic: "A proper hiring process is all about a good match," says Pat. "I was a brand manager at Procter & Gamble, handled a $500-million-dollar business, left that and started my own company, wrote three books . . . but if I apply for a job at Schneider Trucking tomorrow, I won't get the job. I'm not qualified. Should I take that personally? NO. I'm not a match. What I have Schneider Trucking does not need!"

How to Apply for an Advertised Job

You're right for the job. You think the job is right for you. You're finally ready to swing into action! You can't control how many other candidates are applying for a job, however. The employer who posted the job may receive hundreds of applications in e-mail, regular mail, or from a Web site. Whatever method you choose, you'll achieve the maximum impact if you customize your approach to that job and employer, and keep detailed records for follow-up.

Here's a quick review (from chapters 8 to 12) of ways to customize your application:

- Include your key messages in both your resume and cover message (chapter 8).

- Customize your resume by inserting key words from the ad and by saving your resume electronically with a custom name relevant to that job (chapter 10).

- Customize your cover message for the job. Use words from the ad when describing your experience (chapter 11).

- Add your most relevant achievement story (or two) to your cover message (chapters 8 and 11).

- Demonstrate you have researched the company; cite a recent news story mentioning the company, for example (chapter 12).

- Finally, always mention the job's name and where you saw the advertisement in your cover message. While you're applying the tactics I've listed, don't forget to say plainly that you want the job! Here's an example of an e-mail application for the Customer Relations Representative position listed earlier.

To: 'recruiter@abcco.com'
Subject: Customer satisfaction guaranteed!

Please consider my application for the Customer Relations Representative position you advertised on Monster today.

In my last position, I was a Customer Relationship Representative at ABC Co. As you will see from the attached resume, I am an experienced, reliable Customer Service professional. I can provide happy testimonials from customers whom I have helped—customers like yours whose satisfaction leads to stronger relationships and higher sales! In particular, I'd like to tell you about my achievements in direct client follow-up, which prevented problems before they appeared AND offered our sales staff opportunities for additional sales from existing customers.

Like your company, ABC has many products, and I gained expertise in all of them to build a quick response record to customer inquiries. Your recent press release mentioned "significant national expansion" of your new product lines, and I'd be very interested in knowing if this is the reason you are growing your Customer Relations staff.

I think you will find my experience, reliability, and self-motivated attitude a great addition to your team. I attach my resume in MS Word format, and I'll look forward to hearing from you.

Sincerely,

Here's an example of an e-mail application for a sales job that was posted on an employer's Web site.

To: 'recruiter@xyzco.com'
Subject: Customer satisfaction guaranteed!

Dear Ms. Sterling:

Your Web site's advertisement for a sales manager fits my experience and qualifications perfectly, and I am writing to express my interest in and enthusiasm for the position. As an accomplished sales leader, my career achievements have included seven-figure revenue growth, international market penetration, and successful product launches for leading global corporations.

In addition to my desire to join your team, you will find I am a dedicated and driven professional whose recent accomplishments include:

- **An increase of international sales from 1 percent of the company's total revenue to 75 percent,** capturing more than half of the entire European market and one-third of the Latin American market within two years.

- **Dramatic expansion of customer base,** leading to seven-figure revenue growth rates that far exceed the pace of larger, more established competitors.

- **Development of a 75-member dealer network** across thirty countries on six continents.

- **Attainment of 100 percent customer retention rate** through expert relationship-building skills and a commitment to a solution-focused, service-first sales approach.

- **Launch of a new London office,** expected to double sales revenue in the next twelve months.

- **Introduction of three innovative product lines,** following comprehensive market research and competitive intelligence gathering.

You offer cutting-edge products that change the way a company conducts business on the Internet. I am excited by this technology and would be able to translate this excitement into revenue for you and satisfaction for your clients. If you agree that my qualifications are a close fit to your needs, I would be delighted to meet with you personally to discuss strategies for expanding [name of company's] market presence.

I will follow up with you in a few days to answer any questions you may have. In the meantime, you may reach me at the phone number or e-mail address below. I look forward to our conversation.

Sincerely,

Leslie Smith
Leslie@1email.com
(978) 123-4567
Attachment: Resume in MS Word format

As discussed, you may wish to copy and paste your resume in ASCII format directly into the body of an e-mail message. Place it below your name and contact information.

Here's an example of a job response sent in the U.S. mail.

Alan E. Walpole
100 Elm Street
Hartwell, GA 30045

David Miller
Director of Personnel
Peachtree Jeweler's Exchange
175 Southborough Street
Atlanta, GA 30303

Dear Mr. Miller:

Please consider my application for the position of security officer you advertised in the June 20 Atlanta *Journal-Constitution*. My resume is enclosed.

I learned security methods from the best trainer in the world: the U.S. Army. My five years' civilian experience in security shows I create a detail-oriented, predictable, and above all, safe work environment.

I am currently managing security in another institution requiring the highest standards (a payroll office for a large retailer), where my track record of reliable performance has earned me regular approval from my manager.

I would like to arrange a meeting to discuss my experience and to share several innovations I have recently brought to my current workplace. I will call you on the morning of Wednesday, June 25, to see if we can schedule a meeting.

Sincerely yours,

Alan E. Walpole
Enc: Resume

If the advertisement requests a resume be sent to the HR department or an anonymous e-mail address, by all means send it. However, if you can find a real name—the head of the department that is hiring—drop a note to that person as well. This is the direct approach, and I'll describe it more fully beginning on page 271. Get right up front with both the hiring manager and the HR manager simultaneously, and they'll get the message that you're motivated.

Should you include salary information?

Salary is a touchy topic. Some employers won't consider an application without salary requirements, but as Monster's Karen Hofferber puts it, "Telling your salary at the outset is like spilling your popcorn while you're still in the lobby." If you're a little too expensive, you won't be considered; if your current salary is much lower than they expect to pay, they may think you're not experienced enough.

"Frankly, it gets down to the level of the job and the competition," says Karen. "Executives, exceptionally qualified candidates, and free agents have more sway. Research has shown that employers will generally consider candidates who don't submit salary requirements, but who DO show professional courtesy. Acknowledge that you'd be happy to discuss requirements if your candidacy is of interest, and provide a range of compensation that you are comfortable with."

Remember that you're trying to get to the next stage—an interview—while setting the scene for the best possible deal when it comes to the job offer. You don't want to waste your time or theirs applying for a job paying less than you can afford. The key is to show respect for their concerns while quietly insisting on respect for your privacy. For more on salary discussions, including five ways to postpone salary discussions, see chapters 15 and 16.

Final Checklist

Before you hit that "send" button to e-mail your cover message and resume (or put the paper letter and resume in the mail), check off the items in this list. Make sure you do this for every job application.

- ❑ Customize your resume and attach it in appropriate format.
- ❑ Customize your cover message.
- ❑ Proofread everything.
- ❑ Create a file (electronic or paper) for this job with copies of the ad, your cover message, and resume.

❑ Mark a follow-up date on your calendar, no more than one week from the time you send your application.

You're done. Send that resume and cover message now! Click the "send" button . . . *once*. Novice Internet users aren't sure the resume went through, so they click the button six or seven times, sending a new copy each time they click. This looks sloppy and unprofessional.

Five Innocent Ways to Say "I'm Unprofessional"

1. Using a cutesy e-mail address for business ("hunkyguy@xyz.com")
2. Forgetting to replace the silly message on your answering machine or voice mail
3. Sending your resume and cover message without proofreading them beforehand
4. Failing to follow up
5. Being unprepared when the phone call comes two days later

Follow Up!

Career coach Ginny Rehberg says the biggest complaint she hears from hiring managers is this: people ask for a meeting, or apply for a job, then don't follow up.

The job application process isn't complete without a follow-up. Recruiters and employers are busy. It's up to you, not them, to press your candidacy forward. A good follow-up is also a good indication to a manager of your overall work habits.

In your final checklist, you're asked to mark a follow-up date on your calendar. When that day comes, pick up the phone and call the employer. You have two simple goals: to send a message that you're a serious candidate, and to arrange an interview.

Make the call early in the workday. Keep it simple, especially if you are calling the HR department: "Hi, my name is Leslie Smith, and I'm calling, as promised, to follow up on an e-mail I sent to Ms. Sterling on Friday. May I speak to her?"

If you reach an assistant or another gatekeeper, remember that one of their jobs is to prevent frivolous calls from getting to the manager. Your professional response can follow these guidelines:

GATEKEEPER: May I ask what this is about?

RESPONSE: I am following up on a commitment I made to contact Ms. Sterling to arrange a meeting.

GATEKEEPER: What is the meeting about?

RESPONSE: (choosing one point from your letter) I'd like to discuss some ideas I have for improving retention rates in existing sales.

GATEKEEPER: If this is about a job, we will contact appropriate candidates when the time is right.

RESPONSE: That's great, and before I follow up on the issues raised in my letter, I wonder if you can tell me when that first group of candidates will be selected?

GATEKEEPER: Ms. Sterling cannot take calls from candidates.

RESPONSE: I respect your time, which is why I sent an e-mail. I think I'm a good fit for this job; how would you suggest I follow up?

Make this a short call. You don't want to discuss your qualifications on the phone with a gatekeeper.

Always Treat the Gatekeeper with Courtesy and Respect

Managers often ask their assistants and other gatekeepers what they think of a candidate. Help the gatekeeper do his or her job: provide relevant information quickly, give your contact information, and promise to follow up later. Remember, the goal is to get the right person to talk with you, not to antagonize the assistant. This is true all the way through the interview process.

The Direct Approach: Create Opportunity

Now let's consider the rest of the iceberg: all those potential jobs that aren't advertised. Having located target employers through your research (chapter 12), you're going to take the initiative and contact them directly.

The reason to go directly to the companies and hiring managers your research has identified, whether they're advertising a job at the moment or not, is that you raise your profile by doing so. Sound difficult? It's not, really.

When you approach an employer who has not advertised a position, but needs to hire, you have created your own opportunity. Most importantly, you have entered that actual window of opportunity illustrated on page 256. Since a potential position hasn't been advertised, you aren't competing with a flood of job applicants. The employer has more time to consider you individually a few days or weeks before they were about to advertise a position. It's one of the best ways to find a job.

Who should you approach directly? Ideally, your research or networking has uncovered the lead HR person and sometimes the hiring manager. If you don't have a name, call the front desk and ask who's running that department! And if the front desk won't give you a name, call someone who has surfaced in your research—a colleague or someone else at the company. You don't have to be deceptive; just say you are interested in talking to the person who runs the area in which your potential job takes place.

If you've written to HR, you might not want to approach someone else in the company with a formal job application. Instead, give that manager a shorthand performance-based statement. Here's an example of that approach from POWERHiring's Lou Adler: "In case you have needs in the marketing department in the future, I'd like to tell you something I did at ABC Marketing Corp. that I think shows the kind of results you're trying to get. I've sent my resume to the HR department but before going through a screening process I'd appreciate the opportunity to share my best ideas with you briefly."

Are you ready to make a direct approach? Pull out the "Target Employer" files you created in chapter 12. Look over your research notes and decide which company you want to target. Keep your Job Search Portfolio and pitch handy as well.

Focus the direct approach on your key messages, and relate them to some tangible challenge faced by the company. Write down the challenges facing this company and the reasons they would hire you. Consider the "five business reasons to hire" discussed in chapter 8:

- How can you improve product or service quality?
- Does the employer need to improve customer service?
- Can you help cut the cost of doing business?

- Can you create new products or services?
- Can you market the company's products or brand?

Then craft a cover message linking your key messages to their needs. Here are some examples of direct approaches:

- Heather read about the company's expansion goals in a trade magazine and sent a letter that outlined how she had helped her previous company manage a similar expansion. The company was impressed by Heather's enthusiasm, knowledge of the company's mission, and ideas for managing the expanded business.

- Stuart compiled a list of his dream companies and contacted them directly, promoting his technical skills. His letter arrived at the right time at one of the companies—a network engineer had just given her notice and a position became available.

- Mark is a salesperson with a passion for sporting goods. His favorite retailer did not have a presence in his local market, so Mark sent a cover letter and resume to the head of retail operations outlining how he would establish a local presence. After reading the letter, the company flew Mark in for an interview and hired him on the spot.

- Gloria asked a manager at a local media company, whom she knew through her church, to consider her as a source of knowledge for electronic publishing. They talked informally from time to time, and Gloria sent the manager news articles regularly. A year after their first conversation, the company decided to explore electronic publishing—and Gloria was the first person the manager called. No other candidates were considered.

Each of these candidates discovered a fact about the target company through research, and built a case around their best selling points. None of them waited for a job advertisement. They followed the F.A.M.E. attitude of the entrepreneur, and put themselves in the way of opportunity. By making a direct approach, and following up, they kept a high profile. When the time was right, they were among the first considered.

Let's examine the direct approaches of Heather and Stuart, the first two examples above.

Heather sent this letter by regular mail to the company's head of marketing.

Ms. Laura Chester
Chief of Operations
Big Footprint, Inc.
15004 30th Street
St. Louis, MO 63100

Dear Ms. Chester:

The news of Big Footprint's expansion goals, as reported in the August 21 issue of the *St. Louis Business Journal,* inspired me to write. I would like to share a few thoughts with you about how my consumer marketing experience might help you meet the particular challenges of your company's expansion into a consumer market.

At ABC Stationery, Inc., I expanded the market of a business-to-business stationery product line into the consumer market. I directed a small team in re-shaping the brand's marketing from a "save money" message to its current consumer theme, "you look so good on paper." With a tight deadline looming, my team and I developed advertising, direct mail, and in-store marketing materials. I stayed in the trenches with every detail (and yes, I licked envelopes, too—ours, of course!).

I've long known the value of Big Footprint's gift products—I have used them myself in the past! As your mission statement implies, they work well to "recognize, reward and retain" a business's best customers.

I also know that you face significant marketing work as you move your gift products into retail outlets and sell directly to consumers. I have several ideas that may be tested on a small scale around the St. Louis area, and I would appreciate an opportunity to share them with you.

I will call by next week to see if we may arrange a 20-minute meeting at your office. Thanks very much!

Sincerely,

Heather Sinclair

Heather did not include a resume, but when she followed up with the call, she did say that she was interested in Big Footprint as a potential employer, and offered to send her resume if they requested it.

Stuart sent this e-mail to the head of Information Technology at one of his target companies, a technical services consultant. He sent a similar letter to the head of HR. Because he is writing directly to another technical professional, he includes appropriate technical terms. He also gets right to the point: he wants to join the company.

To: Paul Soci (paul.soci@xymetrics.com)
From: Stuart Peters (stuartP@ISP.com)

Mr. Soci:

I am writing to ask whether you are in need of a first-rate network engineer who also offers great client-management skills.

My technical skills are a good match with the platforms you service:

- MSCE/CNE certifications
- Five years of field experience with MS Server 2000, NT and Novel NOS platforms
- Three years of in-company experience with various Cisco products
- WAN, VPN as well as extensive wireless network knowledge
- Up-to-the-minute work with security issues

Beyond technical knowledge, I have exceptional communication skills, which your Web site stresses as a strong point of your consultants. It's a pleasure to make difficult technical issues clear to nontechnical customers!

I would like to meet at your convenience and tell you about my particular achievements in the past. I have contacted your human resources department as well with this message. A resume is attached, and I'll call soon to arrange a meeting. Thank you.

Sincerely,
Stuart Peters

Stuart happened to be in the right place at the right time, since he did not know that another network engineer was about to leave the company. They called him right away. Lucky timing, however, was only part of the story. Stuart also made the best possible impression with the right people at that target company, and when a position became available, they thought of him first. If he had not heard from them in a few days, he planned to follow up.

Put a printed copy of your letter or e-mail into your "Target Employer" file, and set a follow-up date. Whether you or they call first, the customized approach you sent will be at your fingertips. You're ready to open the file, stand up, and start talking about the job the moment you make contact.

Your approach can be that spectacular! Do what Kate's candidate did: go to your target employer with a very specific proposal for adding value to that company from day one.

Follow-up Makes the Difference

Just as when you apply for advertised jobs, follow-up is critical. Personalize your follow-up with individual notes. Always say why you are interested in that company in particular (as opposed to its competition, for example). Never follow up with one e-mail blast copied to six recipients at the same company. Instead, send a personal e-mail or letter to every individual you approached.

Follow up in the same way you would for an advertised job, but this time, don't ask for a specific job—just ask for a meeting. When asked what the meeting is about, tailor your answer to the approach you've chosen.

Here is Heather's follow-up call:

"I'd like to arrange a meeting to discuss some ideas I have for marketing Big Footprint's expansion into the consumer market. I am hoping to arrange a twenty-minute meeting sometime next week. Which day is good?"

Here's how Stuart begins his follow-up call:

"I am following up an e-mail I sent to Mr. Soci last week. I'm a network engineer, familiar with all the platforms you service, and I would like to ask some questions about Xymetrics and its customers. I intend to move into client-based consulting, and Xymetrics is a company where I believe I'd like to work, even if there are no positions open at this moment. It shouldn't take longer than 15 minutes."

These quick calls reinforce your professional image. If you are rejected, simply ask when you can follow up. If they say do not follow up, politely say you understand the phone can be an interruption and suggest that you will follow up via e-mail.

Yes, you have to be persistent. And in your persistence, nothing reinforces your case like bringing in another relationship. A hiring manager is much more likely to say "yes" if you have been introduced or referred by someone they know. The most successful direct approach is through a trusted colleague or friend of your target. And that brings us to a very big subject—networking—which we'll explore next.

Direct Approach for Introverts

Monster career coach Peter Vogt has special advice for those of you who, like him, are basically introverts: "You know who you are—you wouldn't make a cold call in a million years. It's completely against your personality, and mine, and it's not a crime. For us, the Internet—especially e-mail—is a godsend, because introverts are more comfortable with the written word. So go after your direct approaches this way:

- Always write a letter first, promising a follow-up on a particular day.
- Send a follow-up e-mail on that day.
- Play to your writing strength—send a business proposal, written information of interest, or an article or report you wrote.
- Offer to ask questions via e-mail: "Knowing that you are often too busy to arrange a phone call, may I send you two or three questions via e-mail?" Never send more than three.
- Send the e-mail very early in the morning or after six at night. Sometimes you'll catch a person who will answer on impulse."

And if you want to ask Peter more about this—don't call! Write to him at: *peter@careerplanningresources.com*

14   >> Networking <<

F.A.M.E. ATTITUDE: THINK LIKE A FREE AGENT
Relationships count: A strong personal network is good for you and good for business.

Does the word "networking" make you think of men and women in power suits passing out business cards? Actually, networking is nothing more than sharing information and building relationships. You do it every day with family, friends, and other acquaintances. All your existing relationships are a personal network, and a strong, ever-expanding personal network is a great way to find a job. After you start a new job, that network will help you do the job better.

Employers will tell you that networking produces many of their best hires. Monster senior vice president Michael Schutzler, a networking expert who helped build Classmates.com, says that 60 percent of jobs are found through some form of networking. Bottom line: if you learn to network effectively, you'll be much closer to your goal.

Career transition firm Lee Hecht Harrison's analysis indicates that it takes an average of twenty to thirty meetings with different hiring managers to successfully find a job. In a soft labor market, that number goes up. Networking gives you the opportunity to get a referral from a manager's colleague, employee, or friend, resulting in your being better able to get those meetings. A personal connection to a hiring manager is the best way to move your resume to the top of the pile.

Nonetheless, according to outplacement executive Colin Moor, many candidates resist networking: "People think, 'I've got the right credentials;

279

you've got the job; what else is there to talk about?' They believe the job interview is the only conversation. It's a costly flaw, resulting in longer job searches and poor outcomes."

Networking requires you to get out of your chair and into face-to-face discussions. That can bring up a lot of fear and self-doubt. After all, who likes to ask for a job? Remember, though, that networking isn't about asking for a job. Networking is about establishing relationships that generate job leads.

For example, I spoke at Syracuse University two years ago, and the young man who was assigned to show me around campus stayed in touch afterward. He's in California now, and he calls me occasionally to keep in touch. Once, when he mentioned his enthusiasm for music, I referred him to one of my college friends who is very senior in a music business. So, what started out as an ordinary student chore turned into a hot job lead two years later—because he saw it as an opportunity to expand his network.

Good Networking Karma

If you find a sincere way to be helpful through networking, you'll be more comfortable. There's a karmic payoff to helping people. Everyone likes a helpful person, and somehow, good things flow toward a job seeker who sees the whole job search program as an opportunity to help others as well as themselves.

Networking is *not* a job interview in disguise. (Fantasy: You network with hiring managers who are so impressed by your story that they offer you a job on the spot. Surprise! It has happened.) Networking, however, does lead you to jobs you didn't know about and managers who are in "hiring mode" during that long, hidden window of opportunity we discussed in chapter 13. It's another type of research, because it fuels your job search with ideas, names, and possibilities.

How Networking Works

Career consultant Chuck Campbell relates a typical networking success story: "A client of mine was a senior HR professional, and he refused to tell people he was unemployed. I took him to a restaurant and made him hand out his business card at every table. After that, he realized he could tell everyone—in the grocery line, at the gas station, at the cash machine—that he was looking for a job. . . . One day he pulled into his regular gas station, and a mechanic asked, 'Aren't you the HR guy? A truck driver for the company down the street said they were looking for an HR director—he told us because they offer employees a referral bonus. Here's his card.' My client is working there now, as head of HR."

I have a story to add to Chuck's: A friend from high school called me out of the blue because he heard I collect Shelby Mustang sports cars. His uncle had one and he arranged a visit. While we were viewing the car, he told me he was out of work (he's an IT network manager). I needed some computer/server work at my car restoration shop so I hired him for a couple of weeks.

Switch gears: I play tennis on Monday nights, and one day a tennis partner mentioned that he was finally going to post a job on Monster. He needed an IT network manager. I smiled. Three weeks later my high school friend got the job.

The amazing part of this story is the way my friend went about this "networking" task. He took advantage of an ordinary conversation about cars. Was it luck that got him the job? I don't think so. . . .

And another: Recently my son needed a sport coat for a holiday function. I went to a clothing store in Newton, Massachusetts, where the salesman recognized me. He told me he was an out-of-work Web designer doing retail to stay busy. We had a good chat.

The following Wednesday I was interviewed by a *Boston Globe* reporter on the subject of high-tech workers who are working in retail for the holidays. I mentioned the guy in the clothing store, and the reporter asked to interview him. I called and got his permission. That Sunday his picture was on the front page of the *Boston Globe* business section. Two weeks later I went in to pick up my son's blazer and I asked about the sales guy. . . . He had received two job offers and was already gone.

It was the retail guy's gumption to "speak up" that got the ball rolling. Starting today, I'm challenging you to speak up!

That's how it works: You tell many people about yourself, and they connect you to other people, who connect you with jobs. It's simple, but you have to work at it. There are four magic ingredients to effective networking, and you've already prepared them in your search:

- communication skills, which you express in your resume and other documents
- information, which you gained from research
- sales skills, which you acquired by developing your pitch
- . . . and a positive, confident attitude

The fourth ingredient, attitude, is critical. Networking allows you to advertise your enthusiasm, curiosity, ability to listen, and willingness to work hard—and that broadcasts a positive impression. People who might not even know you that well may just get enough of a positive feeling to recommend you to a hiring manager they know because you have established a relationship with them.

A good attitude helps you project good "people skills"—like listening, understanding, and persuading—and those skills make a huge difference throughout your search. China Miner Gorman, president of Lee Hecht Harrison, says, "I can't overemphasize the critical need for people skills in the job search process. Those who entered the workforce in the 1990s aren't used to applying solid relationship skills to solving business problems, but the world has changed. Being able to work side-by-side, communicate one-on-one, and work in teams is critical!"

Building a Network

Go back and look at the networking grid you created at the end of chapter 5. Write your name halfway down a sheet of paper. To the right of your name, place the names of some of the people you listed on the networking grid and a note about your connection to them. These are your first contacts. Now draw lines from your name to each, as shown on page 283.

You know these folks. You feel comfortable talking to them, so these are the people with whom you'll start your job network.

Ask each if you can rehearse your pitch with them. Set a time and place (outside your home, if possible), just as if these acquaintances were hiring managers. Bring your pitch document and your resume, and start the dis-

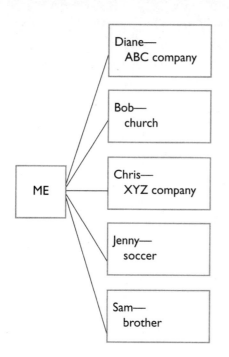

cussion by going through your pitch. Toward the end of the meeting, ask them if they know anyone else you should meet—someone at a target employer, someone doing one of your target jobs, someone who knows someone else. The names they give you will begin your second layer of contacts.

Each of these discussions must be a *face-to-face* meeting. They will help you sharpen your pitch, explore new possibilities, and expand your network by referring you to others. Executive coach Ginny Rehberg puts it bluntly. "Let's face it," she says, "if we're going to help someone, we have to know them first. Nobody will help you until they get close enough to smell you."

In a networking meeting, a printed copy of your pitch can be useful, sometimes more useful than a resume. When you say, "Let me show you an informal summary of what I want employers to know," it's a lot less intimidating than a resume. It's a conversation-starter: Right away, you can discuss an achievement story or a key skill without the "official" formality of a job application. It helps people think of other people you should talk to. It makes your key messages, skills, and achievements easy to understand.

So, you talk to Diane, an old colleague from ABC Co., and it turns out she knows at least three people who might be interested in talking to you: Kaycee, Rick, and Elaine. Kaycee works at a company you've targeted, so you will get in touch with Kaycee (I'll show you how to make that call on page 288). With three new contacts, your network looks like this:

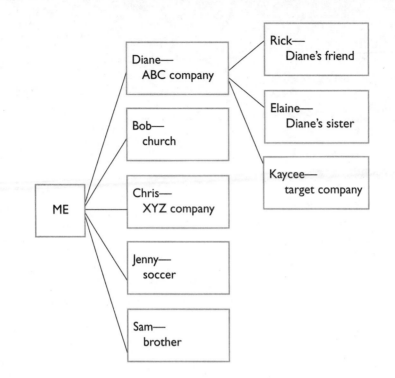

When you talk to Kaycee, she offers to connect you to her manager Susan, and to send your resume to Shelly, an HR manager. When you rehearse your pitch in front of your brother Sam, he thinks of a college friend named David, who works at one of your target employers. When you talk to David, he sends your resume with a recommendation to Jane, the manager of the department in which you would work.

If each person in your initial group refers you to three new contacts, you'll give your pitch to twenty people—and this is just a beginning. If you get just two names from each of the new people, your network totals fifty. And so on and so forth.

That's how a network looks—a growing, interconnected web of relationships. Your first group of relationships grows because you actively pursue new names and new possibilities. The great thing about networking is that it keeps the possibilities coming: every referral brings you one step closer to a job.

A personal network requires brief but continuous maintenance to be effective (nobody but you is going to remind people you're looking for work). Record the vital details of each meeting on a copy of the Networking Log on page 286 (or if you prefer, in your PDA's contact list).

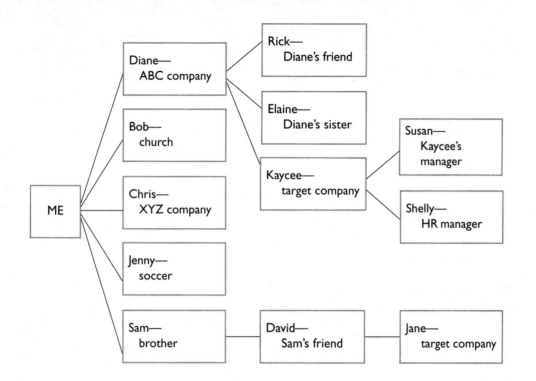

After every meeting, enter the following on the log:

- **Contact information:** Name, organization, address, phone number, and e-mail address of the person.

- **Referred by/Found by:** The person or resource (such as a magazine article) that connected you to this name.

- **Discussion notes:** Summarize your networking conversation, especially new information about companies, jobs, and people.

- **Follow-up:** *This is the most important action in networking.* Note at least one follow-up action you will take, even if it is a simple thank-you note, and put it on the calendar. Then do it!

- **Referrals:** Whatever else you discuss in a networking meeting, you must always ask for more names to contact. Create a new sheet for each one and approach them with one of the techniques below.

Keep completed networking logs in a file labeled "Networking." As you meet people in your target companies, move their networking logs into the appropriate target company files.

Networking Log

Name: _____

Company/Organization: _____

Address: _____

_____

Phone Number: _____

E-Mail: _____

Referred by/Found by: _____

Discussion Notes: _____

_____

_____

_____

_____

_____

_____

_____

Follow-up: _____

_____

Referrals: _____

_____

_____

_____

_____

_____

_____

You can download this form at monstercareers.com.

Book to Web

The Networking Log is available for download at **monstercareers.com**.

If You Have a Referral

The best request for a networking meeting mentions a referral: "I'm calling because Jeff Taylor thought we should meet." Use this whenever possible.

The most convenient approach for most managers is e-mail. Simply state that you're expanding your research, and you hope to set up a meeting. You can say that at this point you are not asking for a job interview. This simple statement opens doors. Not everybody wants to give a job interview, but most people can spare twenty minutes to help a "friend of a friend."

That referral name should open your message, like this:

> Dear Mr. McDermott:
>
> Sharon Hotchkiss suggested I contact you. I am currently researching opportunities to use my civil engineering experience in the Chicago area, and Sharon said you might have valuable comments for my research.
>
> My purpose for this meeting is to expand my list of target employers, and to learn more about different roles I might play at those organizations. In addition, I'd be grateful to know your thoughts about trends in the field over the next few years.
>
> I will follow up in two days to find out if we can arrange a brief meeting. Thank you very much.
>
> Sincerely,
> Peter Brown

If you know the person you are writing to, such as an old school friend, you can use a warmer tone:

Dear Elizabeth,

I am in the process of a job change following my former employer's Chapter 11 filing. I am contacting several old college friends, and your interview in the Alumni Review reminded me of our common interest in international trade.

Attached is an outline I'm using to guide my job search. I wonder if you would meet with me to share your sense of my background. I'm especially interested in knowing which companies you might think could use someone with my experience.

Thanks. I'll call in two days, or you can reach me at the e-mail address above.

Best,
Tracey Swain

Do not send a resume during this initial contact: it throws the cold water of formality on the process. You might as well write: *I'M REALLY LOOKING FOR A JOB BUT I HAVE TO PRETEND I'M NOT SO YOU'LL TALK TO ME!*

If you're making your approach by phone, more often than not you will get an assistant or voice mail. You should not expect to talk to the manager unless the company is quite small. When leaving a voice-mail message, speak slowly. Give your name at the beginning of the message and again at the end, after promising to follow up again the next day. Give your phone number twice. If you feel more comfortable writing a script first, do that—and practice it a few times before you leave a message. Say, for example:

> *"Hello, my name is Peter Brown, and my friend Sharon Hotchkiss suggested I contact you. I am currently researching opportunities to use my civil engineering experience in the Chicago area. Sharon suggested you might be able to suggest potential employers, and perhaps to discuss your firm, whether you have openings or not. You can reach me at (312) 123-4567. I will follow up in two days to find out if we can arrange a brief meeting. Again, that's Peter Brown, (312) 123-4567. Thank you very much."*

No matter what your approach is, when you do get the contact on the phone, the call should be quick: just long enough to get an appointment for a face-to-face meeting. Ginny Rehberg cautions that if your follow-up call is longer than a few minutes, you've just had your meeting on the phone. Say, "I know you're very busy so I don't want to take your time now. Could we set up a twenty-minute meeting for next week or the week after?"

Send your sales pitch in advance, and ask for comments. Chances are they haven't seen a document quite like it, and that makes it more interesting than just another resume. (Of course, you should bring your resume along to the meeting—just in case they ask for it!)

If You Don't Have a Referral

If you want to network with someone for whom you don't have a referral (for example, someone you've found through Internet research), adapt the direct approach described beginning on page 271. For example:

Ms. Laura Chester
chester@bigfootprint.com

Dear Ms. Chester:

I noticed your name in the August 21 issue of the St. Louis Business Journal, describing Big Footprint's expansion plans, and I wonder if I might have 20 minutes of your time to discuss Big Footprint's business. In particular, I am looking to know more about the people who are running successful consumer products companies in the St. Louis area, their business plans, and challenges.

Although my long-term goal is to move into a new position, at this time I am conducting research, expanding my knowledge and network of contacts in the business. For your information, I attach an outline of my research, including my key skills and achievements, as well as companies, positions, and industries I am exploring.

I will call by next week to see if we may arrange a 20-minute meeting at your office. Thanks very much!

Sincerely,

Heather Sinclair

If you are contacting an old acquaintance, you might also use a simple update:

Hi, Tom,

I'm updating my contacts list, and I have the following as your address and number. Are they both still correct?

[address]

And by the way, let me tell you that I'm planning a career change in the next few months. At this point I'm expanding my contacts in health-care firms in the area. I wonder if you would be willing to set up a quick meeting, so that I may show you a list of the companies I'm targeting, and perhaps suggest other people I should contact.

Thanks!

Phil

Agenda for a Networking Meeting

The quality of your networking discussions is up to you. The person you're talking to may want to help, but he or she doesn't know what you need to get out of the conversation. Your goal is to get more names, both people who may hire you and further networking contacts. Bring printed copies of your pitch and your resume. Use the following informal agenda for a 20- to 30-minute discussion and you'll be in good shape.

Establish the tone. Take five minutes to establish the tone of the discussion. Introduce yourself, thank the person for meeting, and establish some rapport. A great opener is to recount the conversation (or research) that led someone to connect you to them. My personal style is to always ask people about themselves first. If they keep going, I ask and ask and ask . . . at some point the person realizes it's your turn, and your good listening skills will pay off.

State your objective. Recall the objective you stated in your approach, whether it's to get feedback on your job search outline, information about potential employers, or another goal. Always mention early on that you will ask for more names at the end of the meeting.

Use your pitch. This is the moment your pitch document can be incredibly effective. You have to tell them quickly about yourself. Give a paper copy of your pitch to the other person and use it as a basis for discussion. You might say, "This is how I'm presenting myself." Start with your 90-second summary. Relate a work achievement. Then ask questions based on the summary, highlights, key skills, and accomplishments. Here are examples of questions you might ask:

- Does my summary give you a clear idea of the value I'd bring to an employer? Does it tell you where I want to work?

- Please comment on the highlights I've written on my pitch. Are they easy to understand? Do they describe attributes that are valuable to employers?

- My pitch lists quantified achievements. What numbers matter most in this field? (Sales figures? Productivity? New products launched?)

- Am I missing critical skills, work experience, or certifications?

Remember, if you think the term "pitch" will seem a little too slick in public, just call the document your outline. Keep asking questions. Give the other person time to answer. You will be impressed at how much information you'll get in a short time.

Ask objective-based questions. Your overall objective is to get more information and more contacts, and now that they have a clear idea of what you offer, to share some of your research and ask them to help broaden it. Show your lists of target employers and target jobs, and ask:

- Are these the right companies for someone like me? Do you know others?

- Am I looking at the right jobs? Are there similar jobs missing from my list? Where are these jobs advertised?

- Do I have a clear understanding of my target job(s)?

- What gaps or objections might prevent me from moving into a new field?

- Can you describe the "company culture" of this particular target employer? Are they numbers-driven? Are they a "work hard, play hard" culture? Are they more interested in teamwork or individual achievement?

- What news sources do you use to keep current in this field?

- Do you know other industries or jobs where my combination of skills and experience would be most useful?

Always have two or three extra questions. It's okay if they don't get answered, but a discussion that ends early because you've run out of questions is *not* okay.

Ask for referrals. At least five minutes before your meeting ends, ask directly if your contact would be comfortable referring you to others for a similar conversation. Remind your subject that your goal is to talk to as many people as possible. Ask, "Who else should I talk to? Do you know anyone at my target employers, or other appropriate employers? Would you be willing to provide a referral to them?" Give them time to think of people. Ask politely if they have contact information. And always say (no more than twice): "Thanks, anyone else?"

Close the discussion. Close the discussion at the arranged time. Leave behind your pitch document and a resume, if they request it. Ask how you might be helpful to them.

Occasionally, your subject will ask for the meeting to continue, and that's fine, as long as you remind them that you want to respect their time and you're happy to close the meeting at their convenience. You should have extra questions to ask in case this happens.

All of these questions are about learning more, not asking for a job. If nothing else, the conversation avoids that tense "job interview" formality. You are more relaxed, and so is the person across the table.

Is networking always useful? According to outplacement executive Colin Moor, "There's no such thing as a wasted meeting. If you are well prepared and curious, you're going to learn something."

Networking Long-Distance

If you're searching for a job long-distance, a face-to-face meeting is not always possible. Set up the meeting as described above, and propose a telephone meeting. Make sure the person has received your sales pitch document. Be prepared to e-mail your resume if they request it. You can hold a networking call using the same techniques as a phone interview (see chapter 15). Your networking agenda doesn't change.

Network into a Target Employer

Employers tell us that the highest-quality source for candidates is employee referrals, that is, current employees suggesting candidates from their personal networks. This makes perfect sense: Employees know better than anyone else the challenges, culture, and rewards of their workplace. They recommend the right people. For you, this means that networking into a company is a great way to bypass that tidal wave of resumes that plagues HR directors.

After your research or networking puts you in touch with an employee at a target company, approach that employee with a conversation around his or her company: What's the company culture from the inside? What are the challenges and the opportunities? What kind of person succeeds in that company? How did they get their job? Handle this network contact well and you will get your internal champion. Get five or ten internal champions at target employers and you'll be inches away from a big breakthrough in your search.

After your discussion, stay in touch. Send a monthly communication to everyone in your network during your search. Don't make it one big e-mail blast—write up your news and then add a personal note. Tell them you're still looking, and still very interested in their suggestions (or their company). This minor investment of time will pay off by keeping warm the contacts you've already made. If you stay in touch, you're likely to hear of opportunities before they become public. Then you can apply the "direct approach" techniques described in chapter 13 to throw your hat in the ring.

Expand Your Network

To be truly effective, your network needs to expand beyond your circle of close acquaintances. The number-one networking mistake is to limit your list only to contacts you have today. Instead, move outward from your current contacts toward your target employers using the following methods.

Use everyday life.

See opportunity to expand your network with everyone you meet. Everyone includes:

- people standing in line with you at a store
- people in a waiting room
- the person next to you on a bus, train, or airplane
- the person waiting to check out a book at the library
- parents at the soccer field

Use informational interviewing.

Review the section on informational interviewing in chapter 12. Simply add that you're building a personal network of contacts while you are researching jobs. Close with the question "Do you know anyone else I should speak to?"

Network on the Web.

Monster and other online services are introducing networking to their mix of products. As of this book's writing, several are live. Go to **monstercareers. com** to learn more.

Network with the well-connected.

Certain professions are just plain well-connected. Seek out the following people to take advantage of their built-in networks:

- clergy
- local business owners
- local government officials
- professional organization leaders
- consultants in your field
- teachers
- health and recreation professionals
- career counselors and coaches
- volunteer leaders of school boards and service organizations

Don't forget to keep them informed of your progress.

Network with alumni.

Universities and other schools keep rich records of alumni, and you can connect with them via your old school's career center—even if it's been twenty-five years since you graduated! It's best to begin at an early age to build professional relationships, so if you graduated recently, get your alumni network going. If you went to college or trade school, ask that your alumni office identify people who work for your target employers.

Network within your company.

Have you just been laid off? Monster member Greg got his layoff notice from a large telecommunications company. Rather than sulk his way to the termination date, he decided to network far and wide within the company:

"I went to a company picnic hoping to meet some managers," says Greg. "I made several impressive plays in volleyball and the director who I knew was hiring for an open position called across the court, 'Who is that guy?' I replied, loud enough for everyone else to hear, 'My name is Greg, and my off-payroll date is in two weeks. Anyone want to offer me a job?' Everyone laughed, but before I left the picnic I told the director, 'You know, I wasn't kidding about going off payroll in two weeks. Here's my full name.' . . . I interviewed for the open position and got the word that he had signed off on my transfer to his department only three hours before [my termination] deadline."

Even if you haven't been laid off, you should be networking informally. Learn more about other departments and other jobs. Talk to managers you don't know. Your next position may come from them.

Use online discussion groups and mailing lists.

Online discussion groups and mailing lists can be sources of connections. You can find these with the older "Usenet" news readers or Google Groups. For example, a professional truck driver can meet others online by typing "trucking" into Google Groups (**google.com/grphp**) or using AOL keyword "newsgroups." Focus on people posting messages in your profession rather than job offerings. One note of caution, however: these groups can get off topic quickly and draw you in for some long, rambling conversations. If it feels unproductive, leave.

Network with an old boss.

Monster member Tom, a sales manager from Arizona, told us this story: "I called our former VP and we met for an hour or so. He told me about a company looking for an eastern regional sales manager. They had offered it to him but he turned the job down, wanting to look for something bigger. He gave them a call, recommended me, and I went over to interview. During the interview I couldn't help but notice a two-inch-thick stack of resumes on my interviewer's desk. I got the job and started about two weeks later."

Get involved with local networking groups.

Professional job networking groups offer practice and training in networking techniques *and* a huge pool of contacts. Every member shares his or her contacts in group and individual meetings. In addition to expanding your network quickly, you'll test new ideas with others who are out there in the market. You can find these groups by searching online, or through your library or career center. Several national groups are listed in the Resources appendix at the back of this book.

Schmooze or Lose!

Networking leads to people who know about job opportunities. Networking with *those* people leads to job interviews. As you tend your personal network, something almost magical happens: all these connections start to become a living, growing part of your career landscape. Opportunity won't just appear once—you will begin to detect it everywhere.

Networking is also a key way for you to take your own job performance to the next level. You can use the relationships you created to learn more, and that makes you better at whatever work you do. That's why all the networking you do in your job search is good for your employer's business as well.

Don't let your network fall apart after you get a job! Keep your networking folder active. Call just one new person a week, just for a conversation about what he or she does. Put the names of network contacts into your Rolodex, PDA, or personal computer, and follow up once or twice a year with a social "update" call: "Hi, I've been at ABC for six months and I was calling to tell you about the great stuff we're doing. . . ."

If you're about to start networking for the first time, congratulations! Your job search is about to teach you a habit that will stay with you for the rest of your career . . . no, make that the rest of your life!

Phase 2 Review

Your first steps into the job marketplace are under way. You are more familiar with the job landscape, and you are probably personalizing your schedule. Flexibility is one of the small benefits of making your own schedule, so take off a weekday if you want—as long as you put in your forty or more hours. Now that you're in the marketplace, you also have appointments for informational interviews, networking, and maybe even some job interviews! (If you get a job interview early in your plan, read chapter 15 before you go.) For some people, the routine of "desk work in the morning, appointments in the afternoon" for weeks 3 to 5 helps them stay productive.

In the 10-week model job search plan, your calendar might look like the one on page 298.

Stepping into the job marketplace is exciting. You are getting more feedback. You are beginning to expand your horizon. There will be days when nothing seems to be happening, and on those days, you will have to kickstart your search by returning to the basics of research, networking, and applying for appropriate advertised jobs. Don't worry, good things will happen.

WEEK 3						
MON	**TUES**	**WED**	**THURS**	**FRI**	**SAT**	**SUN**
Research—government Web sites and publications (chapter 12). Post resume online (chapter 13).	Continue research at career Web sites. List first round of networking contacts (chapter 14).	DAY OFF	Research companies, make calls (chapters 12 and 13). Apply for jobs online.	Send customized e-mail to select advertised jobs (chapter 13).	DAY OFF	Send e-mail approaches for informational interviewing, apply for advertised jobs (chapters 13 and 14).

WEEK 4						
MON	**TUES**	**WED**	**THURS**	**FRI**	**SAT**	**SUN**
Network (chapter 14).	Follow-up e-mails and calls; search online sources (chapters 13 and 14).	Post resume, send custom application to best jobs (chapter 13).	DAY OFF	Job interview! (chapter 15)	Informational interviewing (chapter 12).	DAY OFF

WEEK 5						
MON	**TUES**	**WED**	**THURS**	**FRI**	**SAT**	**SUN**
Approach target company (chapter 13).	Follow-up e-mails and calls. Network (chapter 14).	Research. Apply for jobs (chapters 12 and 13).	Job Interview! (chapter 15)	Research companies. (chapter 12).	DAY OFF	DAY OFF

PART IV

>> LANDING THE JOB <<

I f you have completed phases 1 and 2 of the *Monster Careers* plan, you're armed with all the information and tools you need. Now keep up the good work as you move into phase 3. Your "pipeline" of opportunities will keep flowing smoothly as you continue to research, apply for jobs, and give your pitch to an ever-expanding network of contacts. Soon, you'll reach the point at which all your hard work pays off: an employer will ask you in for a job interview. To prepare for that all-important conversation and its aftermath, learn the last steps of a *Monster Careers* job search:

- *The job interview.* Your preparation has made you ready to talk about yourself. If you know the methods interviewers use, you'll walk into that interview with confidence, ready to turn any question into an opportunity to get your key messages across. In chapter 15, you'll set your interview strategy.

- *Negotiation.* It's said that you don't get what you deserve, you get what you negotiate. In chapter 16, you'll find tactics for working out a final deal that will make both you and your new employer winners.

- *Transition.* This final phase of a job search is often neglected. Don't miss the opportunity to move the habits you've worked so hard to acquire into your next job. You'll set up for success in chapter 17.

I'll round out the plan with a chapter on how to customize your job search according to ten special situations you might encounter.

Phase 3 is the part of a job search that you probably imagined most clearly at the beginning. If you've had the self-discipline to work a professional job search program up to this point, you'll find the process of interviewing, negotiation, and making a transition into a new job incredibly exciting, and filled with opportunities to take your work to the next level.

Let's go get a job!

15 >> The Job Interview <<

F.A.M.E. ATTITUDE: WORK LIKE AN **E**NTREPRENEUR
Entrepreneurs lead and get others to follow.

This is the show, when all your hard work comes together: the job interview. All the exercises in this book, from the F.A.M.E. attitudes to your pitch, culminate in a successful job interview. You are playing the lead role in your job search, so *lead:* Sell your vision like an entrepreneur. Get them excited. Show them what a phenomenal candidate you really are.

Now ask yourself: Are you confident or nervous—or both? It's okay to have that nervous excitement as you prepare to sell your vision to an employer. There's a toxic kind of nervousness, however. Michael Neece, founder of training company Interview Mastery, says most candidates think of a job interview as a hostile interrogation, with the employer performing a cross-examination on the hopelessly outclassed candidate. At an interrogation, just one person is asking all the questions. That's not the way to think of a job interview. A job interview should be a **conversation** in which you and the employer build a common vision. Both ask questions; both give answers; both decide if the job and the candidate are a good fit.

Scott N. Santoro, director of recruiting at IT consulting firm Keane, says, "A candidate's ability to have a conversation is going to differentiate them from someone who just gives one-sentence answers. We don't talk about a job . . . we have a conversation about joining a team."

It's up to you to make the interview a conversation. In your mind, you have to raise your own status to know that you and the employer share a common question—"Is this a fit?"

Tennis Is Better

You can choose whether the interview is more like a game of hockey or tennis:

- If it's hockey, you're playing goalie, just trying to hit away the puck that they keep shooting at you. That's an interrogation.
- If it's tennis, you're on an equal footing. You volley back and forth, asking questions, supplying answers, and promoting your key messages as part of your game plan.

For a job interview, tennis is the better game.

Objectives, Theirs and Yours

Most interviewers are asked to predict the future: "Lisa, please talk to this candidate for forty-five minutes and tell me how he will perform over the next two years." This is impossible! Even an exceptional interviewer can only judge a candidate's *potential*.

Interviewing candidates is a quality-control job. The employer has picked the ten best resumes from hundreds. Now they look more closely and ask three questions:

- **Can this candidate do the job?** Does this candidate possess the right skills, experiences, knowledge, and judgment to meet the job's objectives?

- **Do I like this person?** Will this candidate fit into our company culture? Will he or she feel as passionate about working here as I do?

- **Can we get this person?** Will the combination of salary, benefits, company culture, and other factors make this candidate want to work for us?

Michael Neece, president of Interview Mastery, suggests you have four objectives in a job interview:

- **Prove you meet the job's requirements.** You must make a case that you have the skills to do the job, including softer or "hidden" requirements such as an ability to learn new information quickly. You must do this for each individual interviewer, finding out what's important to him or her.

- **Communicate clearly.** Get your key messages across. Confirm you're understood accurately.

- **Build rapport.** Get your interviewer to recognize you as an "ABC Company type of person." It's as simple as getting him or her to like you, and as complex as expressing your values in the context of the company culture. Rapport arises from those subtle clues, as well as from your demeanor.

- **Gather feedback.** Get specific feedback from each interviewer at the close of each meeting with questions like, "What strengths do you feel I bring to this position?" or, "What concerns do you have about my background?" You won't get feedback unless you ask in a professional manner.

There are three "golden rules" you should follow in order to achieve your objectives for the interview:

- **Listen and clarify.** Remember that free-agent habit of becoming an incredible listener? You have to treat the conversation as an opportunity to learn. Clarify important points by feeding them back: "Just to make sure I have this right, you've told me that you require three years of technical experience. How else, besides length of experience, do you judge technical proficiency?"

- **Prove your case with achievement stories.** One candidate can swear he's qualified to do the job, in effect saying, "trust me." Another candidate can relate quantified achievement stories proving she can do the job. Which would you hire?

- **Get your key messages across.** Answer questions in a way that keeps supporting the key messages of your pitch. Bring them into the conversation. For example, if one of a salesperson's key messages is "I open new accounts," she will want to mention "opening new accounts" several times in a job interview.

Book to Web

For more on listening skills, see Monster's featured report on listening at: **featuredreports.monster.com/listen/overview/**.

Preparation

Good news: if you've followed the steps I've outlined, most of your preparation is already done, and the fact is that *just preparing for the interview will put you ahead of most of your competition.* Most candidates don't prepare more than a few minutes for an interview. Don't be like most people—be better!

Review your Job Search Portfolio and your sales pitch. Choose achievement stories most relevant to the job. You already know how to make your case. Really, all you need now is a pre-interview checklist:

- Which key messages will you spend the most time discussing? (chapter 8)

- Have you dismantled the job description carefully, applying specific achievement stories to the job requirements? (chapters 12 and 13)

- Are you convinced the opportunity is right for you? (chapters 6 and 12)

- Have you thoroughly researched the company, especially by talking to people who work there? Do you have company-specific questions? (chapters 12 and 13)

Appearance

The fact is, appearance is a critical component of that first impression. If your appearance makes a poor impression, the interviewer will (often subconsciously) begin to think of reasons why you shouldn't be hired. The whole mood of the interview starts to spiral downward, as their questions become more negative and you become more defensive. A really great interviewer may be able to overlook a poor first impression, but why would you want to create that mental roadblock?

A good-looking outfit puts a positive focus on your candidacy. How dressy you get may depend on company culture. You might want to stop by a company a few days before your interview, and observe how current employees dress (before 9 A.M. and after 5 P.M. are the best times). Ask the person at the front desk about the dress code. He or she may tell you it's different for the sales, engineering, and creative staffs.

In any event, go to the interview dressed a little better than required. It's perfectly fine to ask the HR people in advance how to dress. Dress appropriately for the most formal setting: If you're going to talk to the CEO and the Creative Director, dress for the CEO. If you have multiple interviews over several days, you may be asked to come in for second or third interviews more casually dressed.

Suit Up

For managers and executives, a suit or business dress is the only way to go. Leave the outrageous tie or scarf at home for your first couple of interviews. If T-shirt and jeans is the company attire, wear a new T-shirt. (Peter Frampton's feelings will not be hurt.) If you're wearing a suit and tie for the first time, ask a friend to make sure all the price tags are off!

Little things matter. When I was just starting out, I had a boss who always looked sharp, right down to his perfectly ironed shirts. I would iron my shirt for longer periods each night, trying to duplicate his "look," only to fail. I finally asked him and heard the magic words, "Dry cleaners; one dollar each. Light starch on hangers!"

Tone down the makeup, ease up a little on the perfume or cologne, and invest in a good haircut. Leave the body metal at home (okay, if you have multiple piercings, you might as well wear one so they get a sense of your "true personality").

Looking sharp sets you up with a positive outlook internally. Your look is the backdrop for your attitude and behavior, which are the critical impression-makers. So make sure the outfit is clean, doesn't have any stains, and is well pressed.

Finally, I don't really have to remind you about personal hygiene, right? Recruiters tell us that dirty hair, bad breath or body odor, and tobacco or alcohol smells are instant turnoffs. Maybe, in the go-go '90s, showing up with cigar breath and a hangover meant you were really self-assured. Now it will eliminate you from the short list of final candidates.

307

Should you bring props?

Bring at least one neatly printed copy of your resume for everyone you'll meet, plus three extras. Bring several copies of your pitch as well, in case the discussion moves into networking-style informality.

Bring a notepad and pens. A professional folder sends the right signal. It's okay to take notes, as long as it doesn't distract you or your interviewer. Taking notes into a laptop or handheld computer is distracting in the interview process, so do it the old-fashioned way. If you carry a briefcase, put your company research notes into it; at the right moment, a magazine article that mentions the company is a good conversation piece. (Occasionally someone opens a briefcase and I realize it's completely empty, which somehow implies this person doesn't have anything going on. Carry relevant materials like your research.)

Other, appropriate props can make you memorable. One of my best television interviews came during the 2002 Winter Olympics, when I brought the torch that I'd carried in the Olympic relay. I felt proud and pumped holding that torch, and because I was there to talk about our Olympic partnership, the torch was an appropriate prop. It created relevant, interesting conversation. You can do the same with something you've produced—a business presentation; a sample part that you machined; a recorded conversation showing your customer service style. If you've won an award, show it off!

If they are relevant to the job, nonwork props can make you interesting at the right moment. If you're a runner, a triathlete, you might bring in your book of your last four race maps. You don't have to show it to everyone, but it's there if the interviewer sees "triathlete" on your resume and asks about it. At that point, you can pull out the book and say, "I feel passionate about this." Then show how that kind of dedication makes you right for the job.

Only bring relevant props, however. Gimmicks are a distraction: don't bring your well-trained dog to show what a good trainer of sales representatives you are. Mind the right proportions, too: if you're a taxidermist, don't cart a moose head into the job interview. (Unless of course you're going for that dream job in taxidermy, in which case that nice brook trout display is totally appropriate!)

Bring to the Interview:

- copies of your presentation resume
- copies of your pitch
- copies of your references (separate from the resume)
- business cards
- notepad and pens
- relevant props (optional)

A Map of the Typical Interview

You may meet with one interviewer or several. Typically, you'll encounter three or four people. They are:

- **Preliminary contacts:** This includes a receptionist, assistant, or employees you meet in the minutes before your interview. They will ask themselves, "Do I like this person?"

- **The first interviewer:** Sometimes this will be your future boss, sometimes an HR screener, sometimes an outside recruiter or headhunter. Their chief concern is "Can they do the job?" To some extent, they're also wondering if you will fit their company culture.

- **Your future boss and colleagues:** Eventually, you have to interview with the person for whom you'll be working. Often you will also meet other employees, peers, or even your future staff. This meeting will be another skills check, with additional emphasis on culture and passion. They're balancing "Do I like this person?" and "Can he or she do the job?"

- **Closing contact:** The person who closes the interview process may be new, or you may return to HR. If you are on the short list, they'll make a general review of matters like benefits, and ask questions about your salary requirements.

Each company has its own interviewing style, but most interviews follow the three-stage progression we saw in chapter 4:

309

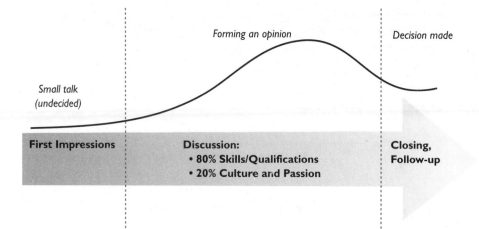

The Natural Progression of the Interview

Forming an opinion

Decision made

Small talk
(undecided)

First Impressions

Discussion:
• 80% Skills/Qualifications
• 20% Culture and Passion

Closing,
Follow-up

Let's go through the phases of the job interview one by one.

Part I: First Impressions

Your interview starts the moment you get up that morning. Give yourself plenty of time to get to the appointment. Be prepared for delays like heavy traffic. If you're late, you'll be flustered and appear unprofessional. If you're early, you have a chance to relax and review your interview strategy, and you will be 100 percent more confident than if you're flustered and worried about appearing unprofessional.

It's also important to be cordial to *everyone.* I learn a lot about candidates from my executive assistant, Kaycee Langford. If they behave differently toward her than me, that's a warning sign. The lesson is, treat everyone with respect, from the cafeteria worker to the CEO.

Monster member Holly T. sent us this cautionary tale about treating the gatekeeper right:

"I was a receptionist in my first job. One day an applicant arrived thirty minutes early. I called the VP she was to meet and invited her to have a seat. The minutes ticked by. There was no sign of the VP. The applicant grew visibly edgy and uncomfortable, shifting her position in her chair, pointedly checking her watch, shooting me aggressive looks. Finally she could take it no more; she fairly shot up out of her chair, strode over to my desk, and demanded, 'Could

you please CALL Ms. Smith and let her know that I am HERE for my INTER-VIEW!!!' . . . She didn't get the job."

Ideally, you should arrive ten minutes early and introduce yourself to the person at the front desk (or announce yourself to the interviewer). Before you walk into that interview, remember to repeat your four key words (from chapter 8) to yourself.

Interviewers form an impression of you in the first three minutes of the interview, so start by making even the small talk interesting. Why is it so important to get the interview off on a congenial note? Rapport is an emotional element of the hiring decision, even if it's unconscious.

"When you get down to the final three candidates, it's an emotional decision," says John Challenger of outplacement firm Challenger, Gray & Christmas. "You're all qualified; you all have positives and negatives. The hiring manager is making a calculated guess. They don't know what you'll be like when you're not at your most upbeat (as you should be during the interview process). But most often the person who is picked is the one who seems to connect best on a personal level with the boss."

To that I'll add, creating rapport with your interviewer kicks off an upbeat interview cycle—they start to think of reasons to hire you and dwell on positives. They ask questions that set up your key messages. They spend less time probing negatives.

So now you've just been introduced to the interviewer, you're making strong eye contact, and you're giving your interviewer that firm handshake. How can you establish rapport quickly? During those first three minutes of small talk, even the most experienced recruiter is likely to be a little nervous, wondering if you're going to be an excellent hire or a waste of time.

The weather is typical fare, so they say, "Wow, big snow last night!" And if you're not thinking, you reply, "Yeah, can you believe it took me two hours to shovel my driveway this morning?" Big mistake. Twenty seconds into the meeting and you're already complaining! A sharp recruiter will then say, "So, you don't like shoveling?" They're not talking about the weather; they're talking about your attitude and your work ethic. You just gave a clue about how you might handle a long, stressful project.

Stick with a simple, positive answer: "Yeah, but you know, I really enjoy four seasons. . . ."

You can turn this moment of small talk right away to a positive message. For example: "I saw the article on your company in the paper. The reporter said a couple of things I want to ask you about later." You just pointed out that you're on top of news about the company. A good interviewer picks up on cues like this.

Also, an easy icebreaker is to thank the interviewer for seeing you, and recount your path to this interview: "It was good of Mary Anne to introduce me," or, "I've been researching this job. It seems like an exciting opportunity." Right away, you've established a gracious, friendly tone AND focused specifically on how you got there.

Part II: Qualifications, Culture, and Passion

The next fifteen to twenty minutes of an interview belong to the interviewer. He or she is going to focus on your qualifications and the job requirements. After that, a good interviewer may actually shift control of the conversation over to you, giving you a chance to make your pitch.

Listening is critical at this point. Remember that you memorized your pitch because that frees you to listen. You're not frantically trying to *remember* your skills and qualifications, but you are *applying* them to what the interviewer says. Since you want the interview to be a conversation, not an interrogation, you must understand the questions and respond thoughtfully.

Relate questions back to your key messages. Craft those messages back into your answers. For example, here's a marketing manager candidate whose key messages are "Creative," "Revenue-minded," and "Strong work ethic."

INTERVIEWER: *"Tell me about your presentation skills."*

CANDIDATE: *"You're asking about a live presentation in front of people, correct?"*

INTERVIEWER: *"Yes."*

CANDIDATE: *"Great! I do about ten presentations a year to other departments. Let me tell you about a time I presented the fall marketing program to our sales staff. Their sales pitches were getting a little dull, so we made sure the marketing program was really creative, and designed to give the sales message more 'sizzle.' I knew that would result in higher revenue and I'm always revenue-minded when talking to sales. I also knew I would have only one chance, so I came into the office for a couple of weekends. I have a strong work ethic and my presentations have to be polished and complete. . . ."*

The candidate goes on to tell this achievement story with details describing the creative solution, the actual revenue numbers he expected the marketing program to generate, and a detail or two about working on the weekend that illustrates his strong work ethic. Of course, the candidate had rehearsed and polished his achievement story, so it was ready at the moment he needed it. One of the benefits of preparation before this moment is the ability to drop these details into a story that takes only a couple of minutes to tell.

Note also that the candidate has already applied the three golden rules: He listened and clarified a point, started to relate a specific achievement (which he'll go on to describe in detail, if asked), and used the words "creative," "revenue-minded" and "strong work ethic."

Close your answers by relating them back to the job opening. A question often works best. For example, the candidate above closes his story with: "Can you tell me when the ability to stand up in front of an audience is important to this specific position?"

Candidates who are prepared to weave accomplishments, research about the job and company, and questions about the job into a conversation demonstrate both confidence and knowledge—a winning combination. They also demonstrate leadership.

Keep these other thoughts in mind during the middle part of the interview:

- **Don't assume your interviewer has memorized your resume.** Be prepared to reiterate points on your resume where relevant. *"That sales program I mentioned in my resume is a good example of a time I got more revenue from existing customers . . ."*; *"In my senior child development project at Tufts, I uncovered some lost research. . . ."*

- **Tolerate silence.** Often, an interviewer simply falls silent. Many candidates are unnerved by this, and try to fill the silence with chatter. Beware this moment—your discomfort can throw you off (which is sometimes the interviewer's intention!). Take a breath and wait. If you encounter a long silence, break it with a cordial follow-up such as, *"Does that tell you enough?"* or, *"Can you tell me more about the type of teamwork that goes on in this hospital?"* Don't change the subject (that also makes you look nervous) unless you can tie the new subject into the flow of the conversation: *"Speaking of teamwork, can you tell me how you organize work among different departments?"*

313

A truly great silence-breaking question poses a choice between your achievement stories: *"Would you like to know more about my process innovations for the hospital lab or my day-to-day supervisory duties?"* The interviewer then must choose one of your alternatives, and either will put you back "on message."

- **Tell stories.** People remember stories. Monster's interview coach Carole Martin has interviewed thousands of candidates, and while she may not remember all the faces or names, she does remember their stories. Use your achievement stories the way good public speakers use stories: to make a point come alive.

- **Open up the conversation.** Use your research to discuss industry trends, changes in technology, and ways in which the job you're discussing might evolve over the next few years. Prove that the time spent in your job search has made you more, not less, valuable.

Part III: Closing

"Once the interviewer has signaled closure, finish the interview quickly and gracefully," says business communications expert Michael Hattersley. "This says volumes about a future employee's capacity to manage time and respond to social signals. If the interviewer signals you to stay a little longer, so much the better."

Often an interview will end with, "Is there anything else?" or, "Do you have any other questions?" Near the end, you actually have the chance to say one last thing. If you don't have that final question or statement, you'll look like a bump on a log. A good question is a great interview closer because it shows you're intrigued. This is the time to ask a question about the culture in a positive way, for example, *"You've said the work-hard-play-hard ethic here is infectious. Would you say that a lot of creative business thinking happens informally, or is it concentrated in those brainstorming meetings?"* You're showing you've listened and picked up on cultural cues, company jargon, and methods.

You can also close with a direct statement about your qualifications: *"I enjoyed this interview. It's made me believe I'm a good fit for this company for at least two reasons . . ."*

Don't forget to ask for the job. A polite message of confidence is a strong close: *"After an hour together, I feel the fit's right and I want to review a couple of points: I have the background to do the job; I've done the job else-where. But most importantly, the achievements I described tell you I can do the job. I'm available next week if we need to continue this discussion. What's the next step?"*

John Challenger tells his executive clients to send that message only if you really *do* want the job. "The person who's a little ambivalent isn't right," he says. Closing an interview is not the time to set up a disappointment. If you're not certain a job is right for you, say, "This has been a really insightful conversation, and I'm sure I'll have other questions as I go over my notes. May I call you with further questions?"

These closing questions allow you to ask for quick feedback, and signal that you want to know where you stand.

Salary Discussions

If they're interested in you, matters of compensation (salary and benefits) will probably come up late in the interview process. In chapter 16, I'll talk about negotiation after you have a job offer. During the interview process, however, you don't want to nail down a price before they're really convinced you're the one and only candidate for the job.

Revealing your price too early puts you in a box. If you expect a lot more than their budget allows, they'll write you off. If you ask for much less than the position pays, the employer assumes they can lowball an offer, which affects not only your salary but how they perceive your value. You may be offered less responsibility, authority, and resources if they think you can be had on the cheap.

Ginny Rehberg, president of Rehberg Management Group, suggests five ways to avoid talking about the salary early:

- **Delay.** *"I'm not really comfortable discussing salary this early in the process. I'd really like to hear a little more about the position and what you have in mind for it, and I'm sure you'd like to know more about me and what I've done."*

- **Turn the tables.** *"Since you have this position open, I'm sure you have a range in mind, and what would that be?"* (Note: do not ask, *"Could you tell me your range?"* because the easy answer to that is, *"No, I can't tell you that."*)

- **Quote the market.** *"My research shows that the market for these kinds of positions is in the range of $45,000 to $65,000."* Give a spread of at least $20,000 for jobs paying between $60,000 and $120,000, making sure the minimum is acceptable to you. For highly paid positions, give a range of 20 percent or more. Do not quote a general salary survey as your only source; find out the range through your networking, trade journals, and so on. Also, make sure you know what the job pays in your local area, because pay varies a lot between different locations for the same job.

- **Cite other job discussions.** *"Positions I'm currently interviewing for are in the range of $60,000 to $80,000. I assume this job falls in that range."* This short sentence packs a punch. It means you're actively interviewing and other employers have revealed their salary ranges.

- **Include ALL compensation.** *"My total compensation package is in the range of $50,000 to $75,000, counting salary, bonus, benefits, and the like. I assume this position has a similar range."* When you include all the elements of your compensation, the range should be fairly large, as much as 50 percent (as in the example above). Mention variable compensation like commission and bonuses, and place a dollar value on benefits. This requires strong research but is highly effective.

For more on salary negotiations, see chapter 16.

References

You may be asked to supply your references. Don't let this opportunity to know where you stand slip away! Say, *"Yes, I have them right here and you're welcome to them. Since you're asking for references, may I assume that you're feeling positive about my candidacy?"* Then confirm you'd like to follow up, just so you can notify your references that they may receive a call.

As you leave, display the same professional behavior as you did coming in. Treat everyone with respect. Say *"Please"* and *"Thank you,"* even if you're just asking the receptionist where the restrooms are. Be a consummate professional; it shows.

Follow-up

Sixty percent of Monster members replied to a poll saying they send a thank-you letter or e-mail after an interview. The other 40 percent are blow-

Be Ready for Surprises

A Monster member offers this reminder that you can't take anything for granted when you are meeting strangers:

"I was on my way to an interview, which I was told was at Highway 10 and Highway 5. It wasn't. I pulled over to call for directions on my cell phone. The lady who was supposed to interview me passed me to someone else, who gave me correct directions. Fifteen minutes late and flustered, I finally arrived to meet the lady, angry that she had given me bad directions in the first place. When I met her, my anger disappeared—she was blind! 'I'm sorry about the directions,' she said. 'I usually take the bus.'"

ing a big opportunity. You've heard it before: the good old thank-you note makes a positive impression. You'd be crazy not to send one.

The thank-you note is the most common follow-up to an interview. As with the cover message, you'll have to decide on a format. Nikki Warren of Giles and Kendall suggests, "A handwritten thank-you is not good today. There's no time for 'snail mail'—shoot them an e-mail as soon as you get home."

HR veteran Chuck Campbell disagrees. He thinks a handwritten note on good stationery sends a stronger message than e-mail. It says the recipient deserves special consideration.

Which format you decide upon depends on your personal style and that of the interviewer. You can always ask toward the end of the interview if they prefer e-mail or letters for follow-up questions, and use their choice for a thank-you.

The format is less important than the fact that you follow up with enthusiasm and a personal touch. Nikki Warren adds that she got her first job not because she was the most qualified but because she followed up immediately. It's another way to show you're highly motivated.

A strong, consistent follow-up can make the crucial difference. China Miner Gorman, president of outplacement firm Lee Hecht Harrison, believes that "People who wow them in the interview but don't follow up are not very successful. People who do okay in the interview, but manage to follow up brilliantly, are very compelling candidates."

A Monster member offers this tip about when to send a follow-up: "If you send your thank-you note at the end of the day, it gets lost in the e-mail. However, if you send it at the beginning of the next business day, it's noticed."

In addition to showing professional courtesy by saying thank you, your follow-up communication can include additional sales points. You can repeat your key messages informally. It's also effective to offer new thoughts based on your conversation. For example:

Dear Mr. Pearson:

Thank you for discussing the fitness instructor position with me today. I hope my enthusiasm for the job came through, because after our interview I'm convinced that I'd be a great member of your team.

Based on our interview, I've given some additional thought to the challenge of motivating your members toward greater participation. I attach a list of small, "customer delighting" touches I employed at my last employer, and I'd be very happy to talk about how those might be used at your club.

Thanks again!

Sincerely,

Louise Gargano

How about a follow-up call? It works if the interviewer is expecting it. You don't necessarily have to ask permission, but it's best to signal at the end of the interview that you will follow up by phone. Often your call will go to an assistant, but that's fine: leave a message that you'll follow up again.

Following up is imperative if you're in a multiple interview situation over several days. Calling to schedule a further interview shows you want the job. If the employer closed with "We'll call you," your response can be, "Great. I wonder when you feel you will have seen enough candidates to decide on who should come back for a second interview?"

If you suggested a follow-up call at the end of your interview, consider it a commitment. Executive coach Ginny Rehberg observes that follow-up is surprisingly spotty, even for executives. Show off your professional habits by following up exactly when you say you will, and schedule that next interview.

What to Do if You Don't Get an Offer

Nobody likes rejection, but it's a fact of life in the job search. How you handle disappointing news can lead you to a more determined search or an emotional dead end.

Make a graceful exit. If you are told that you're not a final candidate, thank your interviewer for their time. Offer to help them; for example, connecting them to other candidates for different jobs (not the one you didn't get). Always express continued enthusiasm for the job! Things happen in the hiring process, and the candidate they've picked may, for various reasons, not take the job. Leave the door open in case you're their number-two choice. You may become number one.

Even if you don't get the job, you may still ask for feedback from your interviewer. Not everyone is comfortable giving feedback to a rejected candidate, but occasionally you'll get valuable insights to your presentation. First, accept that you didn't get the job. Then ask, for example: "Would you mind telling me how I might improve my presentation?" Or, "What concerns might you have had about me that led you to pick another candidate? It would certainly help me in my search to know." In effect, you've transformed the interview into a networking meeting. In fact, there's nothing wrong with a simple request like, "Thanks for your time. Can you think of other employers or people I should meet?"

It's not entirely in your power to get a specific job. But it's in your power to keep an enthusiastic outlook and always conduct yourself like a professional.

A Rejection for the Record Book

Monster member Robert Beringer sent us this rejection he received: "We regret to inform you that the University has decided to hold off hiring for now. But even had we not made this decision, we believe that your background was not an appropriate match for our needs."

Ouch! A simple "no" would have sufficed.

Types of Interviews

As companies devote more attention to hiring practices, several variations on the standard interview have emerged. You can prepare for them in the same manner as above, and be alert to the differences. Here are the different interview types you may encounter.

Phone Interviews

The purpose of a phone interview is to determine whether you should come in for a face-to-face, and since that's your goal, you have to treat the phone interview very seriously. Phone interviewers can be extremely busy; most interviews last less than twenty minutes. Recruiter Amy Needelman of MarketSource Sales Services, a leading provider of integrated sales services to Fortune 500 companies, conducts phone interviews every day, and offers these tips:

- If you've sent a recruiter a resume, be ready for their call. Do your homework on the company and the job. Nothing kills a phone interview like showing you don't really care.

- If the call comes from an employer you don't know (for example, if they've found your resume on a big career Web site), be ready to ask the basics about the job—location, responsibilities, and so on—and apply your experience to what you learn. This is a real test of your ability to listen.

- Conduct the phone interview in a quiet place. It's fine to ask for a minute to turn off the radio. If you cannot break away (for example, if you're at home with an active child), schedule a time to call back as soon as possible (and get a babysitter!).

- Project enthusiasm, confidence, and eagerness to answer and ask questions.

- If you have a scheduled call, don't put an interviewer on hold or respond to "call waiting."

- Have a professional-sounding message on your answering machine.

- If you receive a message from a recruiter, call back within twenty-four hours (even if you're out of town)! This speaks volumes about your professional conduct.

- If you and the recruiter miss each other's calls, it's up to you to follow up until you have a live conversation. Leave them a message with your phone number *and* e-mail address.

- Treat a phone interview just as you would a face-to-face interview. First impressions are the most important.

To Amy's advice, I'll add a few points: Get yourself to a quiet place and a professional state of mind fifteen minutes before a scheduled interview, so when the call comes, you're ready to jump in with your key messages, questions, and answers. Also, close the interview with a request for a face-to-face meeting. Show keen interest by asking how many candidates they're considering and what in particular about your background inspired them to call. If they are calling many candidates, ask if you can follow up in a day or two. Finally, do not discuss salary in a telephone screening if you can possibly avoid it; that can cut you off from getting an interview. Use one of the delaying tactics described above.

Behavior-Based Interviews

This style of interviewing is very effective and growing in popularity. Based on the assumption that your past behavior is the best predictor of your future performance, you are asked to tell stories about accomplishments. This style works beautifully with your Job Search Portfolio and achievement stories.

Behavior-based interviewers request information in open-ended questions like:

- "Tell me about a time you handled a really disappointed customer."

- "Can you discuss a project in which you stepped outside your area of expertise?"

- "When have you felt completely absorbed in a project?"

Your achievement stories are perfect answers to these questions. In fact, if you want to be a really brilliant candidate, you can use behavior-based answers in any kind of interview. To non-behavior-based questions like "Why should we hire you?" you can respond with achievement stories: "You should hire me for my skills in managing scarce resources, as I did two years ago when I managed a big project. . . ."

Here's another example: Your interviewer asks, "Tell me about your Java programming skills." Don't just say, "I'm really strong with Java." Say, "I'm

321

really strong with Java. In fact, let me tell you about this great challenge on the company Web site I overcame with Java." Then tell your story.

Structured Interviews

Christy Peacock of Maxim Health Care Services describes this style, which allows interviewers to compare candidates directly. "In a structured interview, we probe a person's experience in depth. It lasts about ninety to one hundred twenty minutes of face-to-face time. We go over roles and responsibilities of the job, and look for dedication to teamwork, leadership, diversity, customer service, and a strong work ethic. A person's character is important."

A structured interview covers a lot of deep, detailed questions. You should still rely on your achievement stories, but the interviewer controls the agenda. Respect their need to cover a lot of ground.

Case-Based Interviews

This style is used for consultants, high-level finance and other professionals, and executives. It's rare for entry- or mid-level interviews. In brief, the interviewer poses a business problem, and invites the candidate to build the framework for solving the problem. It tests a candidate's technical skills, specific knowledge, and problem-solving and brainstorming abilities.

Aggressive or "Stress" Interviews

This style is meant to uncover how a candidate handles stressful situations. The interviewer tries to put the candidate on the spot with a question that's unexpected ("Why are manhole covers round?") or emotionally charged ("Do you actually think you're qualified for this job?").

Stress interviews can test your cool and uncover hidden attributes such as creativity, organizational skill, and quick analysis. They're becoming more popular for executives and technical professionals.

Attitude is critical in this kind of interview. You may feel threatened, but don't react to that feeling. Think of the question as an invitation to show your best qualities. If you feel angry, smile. If you don't know why manhole covers are round, tell the interviewer how you'd find out. Remember that they wouldn't have invited you to interview unless you had qualifications to discuss. Then name them with your key messages.

A stress interview really tests your F.A.M.E. training, and as Olympian Jimmy Pedro notes, anxiety will kill you, whether it's in sports competition or in a job interview. If you're cool, you rule.

Second and Third Interviews

Treat every subsequent interview as if it were the first. Do not assume the second or third interviewer has been briefed by the initial interviewer. Do not assume you'll be asked the same questions; multiple interviews are intended to gather new information about you. Ask each interviewer what he or she thinks the most important responsibilities and challenges are for the position. Ask each how he or she will interact with the person who's hired.

Off-the-Wall Interviews

Yes, they happen. Sometimes an interview will just defy expectations (or even reality). Monster members sent along some examples of off-the-wall encounters:

- Margaret was invited to interview in her prospective boss's car while he drove twenty-five miles to do some personal banking.
- Maureen, who has an MBA, was first asked about her high school education. The interviewer proceeded to go through her entire life story year by year.
- Toby's interviewer typed on a computer keyboard for five minutes without talking, then dismissed him.
- Marc was asked what he would do if the company's president committed suicide (actually, that was a relevant question—he was applying for a public relations job!).
- Cynthia's interviewer accidentally spilled coffee on her, and then stepped on her shoe until it flipped off. While she was doubled over with laughter, he offered her the job.

323

Have a sense of humor and stick with your key messages, and you'll do all right.

Illegal Questions

You may be asked illegal questions. These tend to be highly personal, and are often asked in small talk, for example, "Are you married?" or, "You have an interesting last name. Is it Indian or something else?" Sometimes the interviewer is reacting to a subtle prejudice, like, "I just don't want one more employee to tell me they're taking parental leave this year." Most of the time, the inexperienced interviewer doesn't know the question is prohibited.

Illegal questions may include (but are not limited to): information regarding your age, marital status, country of origin, religion, sexual preference, parental status, disabilities and/or health status. Some sensitive questions are okay: It may not be legal to ask if you've been arrested, but you may be asked whether you've been convicted of a crime. You may not be asked your citizenship, but it is okay to ask whether you require sponsorship to work in the United States. Security jobs and other sensitive positions may require background checks.

Just to complicate matters, says empowerment advocate Kiki Peppard, state and federal laws prohibiting discrimination in hiring are different.

How do you handle these? You shouldn't divulge personal information, yet you don't want to lecture your interviewer on the law. Cindia Cameron, organizing director of 9 to 5, National Association of Working Women, suggests you redirect the question to focus on the job qualifications. For example, if you are a single parent and an interviewer probes a little too personally into that, you may respond: "If you're concerned about my availability, I'm happy to provide references who can confirm I have an extremely good attendance record."

If the interviewer is persistent on a personal matter, ask questions to uncover the underlying issue, for example: "Is there a requirement in this job that might prevent someone with limited hearing from performing well?" Then address the concern. In other words, help the interviewer do his or her job, which is to discover your true qualifications and no more.

Interview Attitude and Behavior

Your secret weapon for an interview is called BEING THERE. So many candidates get all tangled up in their own thoughts: "How am I doing? Should I have answered that question in more detail? Why are they making me wait out here in the lobby?" They can't bring their key messages forward because they're in a flop sweat over making the wrong impression. You have to get over the fear of failure. *Of course* you'll be nervous, but you can turn that nervousness into enthusiastic energy, and that has a major influence on your success.

Get a positive attitude.

I like the aggressively optimistic outlook that sees *every* interview as a step forward. With this attitude, each conversation seems like a chance to learn, not just a chance to impress someone. This attitude generates qualities like curiosity, confidence, interest, and enthusiasm.

Some candidates prepare for an interview with the athlete's habit of visualizing success, and you can do this, too. The morning of your interview, take ten minutes to imagine yourself succeeding in that job. Write a letter of congratulations to yourself, describing all the great work you're going to do!

Practice a positive attitude in everyday life. If someone says "Good morning" to you, it's just a greeting. You can smile and say, "Morning to you, too, Bob." Or you can say, "What's so good about it? I've got a fever, and I got into a car accident on the way to work, and this job is a pain in the neck. . . ." No one wants at that moment to stop and have a counseling session with you—and an employer isn't going to have a counseling session with you either!

Be a Seller and a Buyer

Here's another point of view that helps: be a seller *and* a buyer. Tell yourself that the purpose of your interview is not only to sell yourself to the company, but to decide whether you're going to like working there. If you were paying to have this job, you'd want to know if it has what you're looking for—challenge, opportunity, and the other qualities we discussed in chapter 3. Remember, you *are* paying for the job with your time and commitment.

Get to the point where you feel like you are interviewing the company, not just the other way around.

Answer briefly and directly.

How long should your answers be? A good rule of thumb is, talk no longer than a minute without checking in. If you are telling an achievement story, tell it simply first and ask if they'd like more detail: "As far as working efficiently, I led my team to cut 20 percent of response time with four or five low-cost improvements. Would you like to hear about the details?"

Factual answers are best stated plainly: "Last year I sold $800,000 of that product, a 12 percent increase over the previous year."

Jeevan DeVore of Monster partner CareerPerfect cautions not to use this technique to dodge questions. "'What do you know about reading financial statements?' should not be answered with, 'How much of this does the job require?'" says Jeevan. "The stronger tactic is to answer succinctly, then use the question as an opener to more in-depth discussion of the job."

Use physical cues.

A good interview also has good body language. Sit comfortably, make eye contact, and keep your mind from wandering. Just keeping your focus for forty-five minutes makes a great impression. While you cannot take command of the interview, you can take command of yourself.

In American business culture, bright eyes, a steady gaze, a firm handshake, and an occasional smile are positive signals. (This is not always true in other cultures, by the way.) Don't cover your mouth or eyes with your hands as you speak. If you're offered a drink (or if you brought one along), use a cup or glass, not a bottle. Don't smoke, don't chew gum, and don't adjust your clothing. Follow the training of television newscasters: Square your clothing as you sit, then incline slightly forward. Sit up straight, just like Mom told you. Don't fiddle with a tie, jewelry, or eyeglasses—when you fidget you look like a witness under cross-examination. A good interviewer picks up on all kinds of clues that most candidates don't notice.

Eric Winegardner, recruitment manager at Great American Insurance, says that candidates may even miss not-so-subtle clues. "I interviewed a candidate who had been in her last position six or seven years," he remembers. "She was very nervous, even during small talk, and she took the gum out of her mouth and held it in her hand for the interview. When I offered her a tissue, she said, 'No, thanks, it's got some life left in it.' It was like a train wreck! I couldn't think of anything else."

Act warm, keep cool.

Two qualities that shine out in stressful situations are the ability to relate to others on a warm level and the ability to remain calm under pressure. Many interviewers use prearranged, tactical questions to keep on the offense and keep you on the defense. For example, they might ask difficult questions ("Why have you been unemployed so long?") to test your self-confidence. Conversely, they may behave in a very friendly, easygoing manner in order to learn information you don't necessarily want to divulge early, such as your salary.

Whatever demeanor they exhibit, you should display both warmth and confidence. They're infectious. If you truly believe that no meeting is wasted, that you're saying the right words, telling the right stories, and asking the right questions, you will radiate confidence.

Interview Questions—with Answers

Most job interview questions don't have a single "best" answer, especially if your interview is a dynamic conversation. The content of your answers matters, but the way in which you answer a question may be just as important as the words you say.

General Questions

"Tell me about yourself." This is one difficult question! It's a scene-setter. A way to establish rapport, it sets one party at ease, because now the recruiter can sit back and gain a first impression of someone's personality. Remember that this first impression will set the tone for the rest of the interview—positive or negative—and your answer really has to state your case. Don't give in to the temptation to repeat your resume.

What are the interviewers trying to discover? Are they wondering about how you work with a team? Are they asking about your hobbies? Are they asking about your family? You don't know, and you mustn't ramble, so you clarify: "I could go several ways with that question. Do you want to know about me personally, or should we go right to my qualifications?"

If the answer is, "I want to know about you personally," you should have your three examples ready: "What I feel passionate about outside of work is raising my family, learning and growing in every part of my life, and running marathons. You may have noticed that at the bottom of my resume."

If they want to dive straight into your qualifications, you should also have your top three ready to go: "Judging from your ad, the top three qualifications for this customer service position are an ability to respond quickly and completely to customer inquiries, an ability to be very familiar with details of your product line as it grows and changes, and a focus on understanding the customers' needs quickly. Is that correct?"

If the answer is yes, you're off and running: "Great! When I tell you about the successes I've had in each of these areas, I think you'll agree that I'm a great match." Then follow with an achievement story for each qualification.

"What do you know about this company?" Your research prepares you to answer this one. You might start with facts about the company that make you want to work there. Christy Peacock of MarketSource suggests you be able to discuss a basic history of the company, its products or services, its annual sales, its competitors (and where it ranks among them), and its mission statement. This is a great chance to close your answer with a broad question about the company culture, for example: "Do you think the 'constant innovation' mentioned in your mission statement is reflected in the pace of work here?"

"Why do you want to work here?" Carole Martin, Monster's interview coach: "The interviewer is listening for an answer that indicates you've given this some thought and are not sending out resumes just because there is an opening. For example, you might say, 'I've selected key companies whose mission statements are in line with my values, where I know I could be excited about what the company does, and this company is very high on my list of desirable choices.'"

"What are your strengths?" This question comes in many different phrasings, such as, "Tell me which qualification in our ad is a real strength of yours." Here, you're being invited to make your best case, and you can take a little time.

Don't regurgitate the entire job description. Instead, focus on your two or three most relevant strengths. Say, "There are three qualifications out of the six in your ad that are my particular strengths—technical skill, management skill, and personal accountability. I have stories to illustrate each. Would you like to hear them?"

Once you get the go-ahead, briefly tell achievement stories confirming that you have each qualification. Check in with your listener as you go, to make sure you're on track and not overwhelming him or her with detail.

Finally, repeat the qualifications as you sum up: "So, technical skill, mentoring my staff, and personal accountability are the three I'd particularly emphasize."

"What are your goals?" They mean your career goals. You need to decide in advance how your goals relate back to the position. Send the message that you see this position as a career-building move. That doesn't mean you'll immediately have your eye on promotion; it means you're motivated. If their reply is, "Well, this position doesn't really grow into a management role," you can ask how management talent is recognized and career growth planned for outstanding employees.

Sometimes it's best to talk about short-term goals at their organization rather than speculating on the distant future, when you might or might not be there. For example, "My immediate goal is to bring my marketing skills to a consumer product company. My long-term goal in marketing is to extend my track record of innovative marketing campaigns."

"What has been your most significant achievement?" A double-sided question: talking about an achievement boosts your candidacy, but the interviewer is really wondering what you value and why. Focus on the importance of your chosen achievement's results to you and the organization.

This is not a time for false modesty. If you ran a newsstand, talk about how your great attitude, ability to remember customers, and organizational skills built customer loyalty. If you ran a corporation, discuss your best achievement in terms of financial performance, customer satisfaction, and the corporation's long-term mission.

Select one achievement. If you really can't decide among several, pick one that relates best to the position you want and offer to tell others.

Position-Specific Questions

"What do you believe are the critical success factors for this position?" This one's a snap if you've done your homework. What makes the difference between hitting the goals and missing them? The success factors may include personal skills and energy, funding, staff skill, creative problem-solving, processes like product development or logistics, and management support. This is an ideal opportunity to ask how the company supports this position in reaching its goals.

"What role did you play on that project?" This refers to a project you've mentioned in your interview or on your resume. The recruiter is doing a fact-check on your level of responsibility, and also to learn what your priorities are. Simply relate your formal role ("I ran the sales end." Or, "I wrote the budget.") and perhaps your informal role ("I spot-checked schedules to insure timely delivery, even though it wasn't my job.") Your answer may be checked later with your references. Don't exaggerate your achievements; this question is sometimes also used to probe your honesty.

"Do you prefer to work in teams or alone?" Michael Neece of Interview Mastery says, "The interviewer is trying to put you in one of two boxes with this one, and it's your opportunity to jump into both. Say, 'Here's an example of each,' and give two examples. Then say, 'The reality of work today is that sometimes people work alone and lots of times they're part of an interdependent team. What's the mix of independent work or teamwork for this position?'"

Another angle from which to attack this question is to combine the team/alone concept over the long term: "I'm focused on effectiveness. Here's an example of when it was most effective for me to work alone, and here's an example of a time I took a problem to a team, because that was the right way to solve it."

"How would you solve this problem?" This is asked with an example (often from a current project). Most candidates think they're only being asked to describe the final resolution of the problem, but that's a trap, because most of the time they don't have enough information. Instead, describe the *steps you would take* to solve the problem. You can state assumptions first: "Assuming you have the financial analysis done in both business plans, I'd choose which product to pursue by analyzing which one is better connected to existing lines. We can then build a marketing strategy around existing customers. Here's how I've put teams together in the past to solve problems like this. . . ."

"How would your last manager [or colleagues] describe you?" Stay position-specific and project a positive professional image: "They would describe me as intelligent, energetic, and an enthusiastic problem-solver. They'd tell you the same stories of my leadership as I've told."

This is a great opportunity to talk about personal culture as well: "They'd also probably tell you I'm really funny." (But if you're not funny, don't claim you are. The next question will be "Tell me a joke," and you don't want to go there.)

"When were you most satisfied in your job?" Again, you want to talk about results, but this is a good time to tell more about your daily satisfaction at a job: "I was very satisfied in my last position, because I worked directly with the customers and their problems every single day. Knowing I made someone's day better is very satisfying to me."

Behavior-Based Questions

Behavior-based questions work perfectly with your achievement stories. Most behavior-based questions have two purposes: to check your past actions and to probe your attitudes. These are revealed not just in what stories you share, but in how you recount them.

To respond effectively, remember the Problem-Action-Result method described on page 127: state the **P**roblem, the **A**ctions you took, and the **R**esults of your actions. If you are asked to tell a story, don't be shy about clarifying what the interviewer would like to know from the story.

Career consultant Julie E. Miller warns against the temptation to respond to behavior-based questions with general answers: "Don't say, 'Flexibility is important to me.' Say, 'When we had a last-minute glitch in the product, I ordered pizza for my whole team and told them we were staying there until the problem was fixed. We hit our deadline.'"

Here are some common behavior-based questions.

"Tell me about a time you handled a really disappointed customer." The interviewer is investigating your ability to handle stress, your attitude toward customers, and perhaps your ability to think on your feet. Explain the problem, your point of view about the customer (positive and supportive, I hope), and the results or resolution of the problem. Did you take responsibility for finding a solution, or spend time blaming another department? Did you follow up to make sure the customer was satisfied? Did you behave as if customer service was paramount?

This is a good time to finish your story with a question such as: "Every company says customers are important, but customer service is so often bad. How does this company focus on serving its customers?"

"Can you discuss a project in which you stepped outside your area of expertise?" What an opportunity! You can show off your initiative and signal how you want to grow in your job. Select a past accomplishment that makes you proud. Focus on the "outside your expertise" part of the question: Did you learn a new skill? Did you handle "turf" issues or defensive feelings from others? Did you volunteer for the work? Did you see the project through to the end, even if that wasn't your job? These are all signs of a self-starter, which every manager values.

"When have you felt completely committed to a project?" This is a critical question about character, but which story to tell? Lou Adler, in his excellent book *Hire with Your Head,* points out that real character is better observed in less-than-ideal circumstances, so telling a story about a time you felt committed *and* beat the odds is a winning strategy. Employers prize perseverance.

"Tell me about a time you solved a really tough problem." This question is about commitment, intelligence, and which problem-solving methods you prefer. For example, are you analytical, preferring to get lots of information in advance? Or are you action-oriented, probing solutions by trial and error? Do you rally a team to solve a problem together? You can speak up front about your preferred style, then tell a story that shows results. (This is a question in which the outcome really does matter as much as the process, so pick a story with a clear win at the end.)

"Give me an example of a time you had a critical project without the time or resources to do it." This is a stressful one, and it's really tempting to talk in generalities. Instead, think for a minute: Why are they asking this question? It's likely that the position you're discussing will have this problem.

Don't criticize former bosses or companies for unrealistic expectations. You can describe a very limited project. For example, "Let me describe a situation I met last year in which a customer's need moved a deadline up. . . ." Stick with the facts. When you have finished your story, politely prod back: "I imagine this is important to you. Is lack of resources or moving deadlines a problem I'm likely to encounter in this position?"

You can prepare for additional behavior-based discussion by reviewing the "five reasons to hire someone" on page 120. In a behavior-based interview, they would appear like this:

- "Tell me about a time you improved product quality."
- "Tell me about a time you improved customer service."
- "How did you/would you cut our cost of doing business?"
- "Tell me a story about creating new products or services."
- "How did you sell or market your last company's products and brand?"

Select achievement stories that answer as many of these questions as you can. Even if you're not asked them directly, your preparation will reward you near the end of the discussion, when they ask, "Is there anything else you'd like to say?" At that point, you can add professional luster to your pitch with a response like, "We haven't discussed another strength of mine, which is cutting the cost of doing business. May I tell you a quick story of a time I did that?"

Stressful Questions

"Why should we hire you?" Don't be flustered. This is actually a huge invitation to state the best parts of your pitch. An answer from a financial professional who wants to stress five years of experience, cost-consciousness, confidence, and teamwork might be: "With five years' experience working in the financial industry and my proven record of saving the company money, I could make a big difference in your company. I'm confident I would be a great addition to your team. I'd like to tell you a few stories that will convince you of that."

A more experienced candidate can put this question in the context of career management. Carl Lopes, head of recruiting at Staples, says, "We're looking for people who have prepared for the interview for twenty years, revealed in the way they've managed their careers." You can leverage that powerful point by describing how your career has led logically to this company and this interviewer.

"Aren't you sick of looking for work?" Wow, this is an in-your-face question! This is 100 percent about keeping cool and positive. Point out that everyone looking for work has to choose their attitude: to get this over with as quickly as possible or to take advantage of a unique time. Say that you're taking the time for a truly careful job search, one that will result in a great career, not just a job to pay the bills. Also, point out that your job search program is sharpening important business skills such as research, communication, and networking—which most candidates don't bother to do.

"What can you do for us that other candidates can't do?" Carole Martin rephrases this question: "'What makes you unique?' It's a great time to get to your key messages, for example, 'I have a unique combination of strong technical skills and the ability to build strong customer relationships. This allows me to use my knowledge and break down information to be more user-friendly.'"

"Tell me about a weakness." Michael Neece: "They don't care about your weakness as much as they care how you handle the question. It's an opportunity to communicate that you have plenty of strengths, and add, 'Here are some areas I'm trying to improve professionally.' Stay away from the job's core requirements. If you've made it to the interview, they've decided you can probably do the job. Finally, add something that differentiates your value from other candidates. For example, in an HR job, say you're improving your knowledge of business finance because that will make you a more valuable business partner to the managers."

"Why shouldn't I hire someone less expensive?" This question can mask a prejudice against older, more experienced candidates. The effective answer is a discussion of value as opposed to price. First, your research should tell you if there's a real discrepancy between their salary range and yours. It may be minor, and if so, simply say they'll get better performance, more quickly (if you can come up to speed faster than other candidates, that's valuable).

Next, go to those key skills and messages reflecting your experience:

Can you perform the job faster, at a higher level, with better quality outcomes? If so, you're worth more than a cheaper, less efficient candidate.

A more dramatic answer, if you can support it with facts, is, "You should hire me because I'm not going to make a $100,000 mistake, because in the past I've seen people in this position make those. I know where the landmines are buried, and less experienced candidates do not."

The message is, they'll get what they pay for, and you're very confident that their return on investment with you will be high.

"Aren't you overqualified?" This is related to the last question, and you should see a red flag: 90 percent of the time, "overqualified" means "overpaid." Again, focus on the value that your experience creates. Mention qualities like judgment, insight, and understanding of the business's big picture. Companies recognize that talent without good judgment can lead to useless work. Effort without understanding the big picture is often a wasted effort.

"Your experience doesn't match our job description." Answer: "I believe you invited me here today because you saw value in my skills and accomplishments. Are there requirements in the job position that make you wonder about my ability to do the job?"

"How would you deal with a high-strung (or otherwise difficult) personality?" If you are asked any question that relates to how you'd deal with a difficult personality, answer with a short story or reassurance about your people skills. Then ask why the interviewer is asking. It's best to find out early if you're interviewing for a job with a lunatic. This is definitely a time when you need to "be the buyer," and probe deeper.

"Why did you leave your job?" (or, "Why are you leaving your job?") This question is asked often, and it's the reason you wrote your personal story in chapter 8. Use it. If you were laid off, state your reason for leaving in a positive context: "I managed to survive two rounds of corporate downsizing, but the third round was a 20 percent reduction in the workforce, which included me."

If you were fired, state the reason plainly and discuss action you have since taken. For example: "I was fired because I did not acquire enough new customers in my first six months on the job. I believe I can perform

335

much better in this job because it focuses on servicing existing customers, and my record shows I'm excellent at that."

If you are employed, focus on what you want in your next job: "After two years, I made the decision to look for a company that is more team-focused, where I think my work style can be more effective."

"What do you like least about your current (last) boss?" Eric Winegardner of Great American Insurance says that this is one of the most effective double-edged questions. The interviewer is only partly interested in your likes and dislikes, but *very* interested in how you answer the question. Do you trash your current or former boss? Do you gossip? Do you whine about how your brilliant talents weren't recognized? If you do, you won't get the job.

"Your answer on why you left your last manager can keep you from getting a job if it's extremely negative," says Eric. "Be prepared to turn your boss's negatives into positives. Say, 'I'm not one to pick people apart; I treat all my colleagues with respect, and my last boss showed a lot of stamina in a very difficult position.'"

"What do you like least about your current (last) job?" You want them to believe that you love your current or last job, which raises your standards (and price) for accepting a new job. This question can be flipped back into a question about how much better the current opportunity might be. For example, if they called you first, you might say, "I'm very happy in my job, but always curious about what else is out there. This position seems to offer a high level of autonomy. Can you tell me more about its decision-making authority?" You have just told them something you want without specifically saying you don't have it now.

If you were laid off, the answer is simple: "What I like least is that the position was eliminated!" Then focus again on your key messages about what you're looking for in a job.

"How do I know you won't want to change jobs in two years?" This is a fair but provocative question. Are they testing your loyalty? Think like a Free Agent: "These days, every job arrangement is really a contract between employer and employee. None of us can say accurately where the business will be in two years. However, I'm sure my track record of increasing value to my employers tells you that I'm someone who can adapt to changes in the business environment. I wouldn't think of leaving a position where I'm challenged, growing, and fairly compensated."

"What salary are you seeking?" Your first or even second interview is not the time to discuss salary. You can say, "I've heard enough about the responsibilities of this position to be comfortable that it will be reasonably paid. I'll be happy to discuss all matters like salary and benefits when we both feel there's a good fit here." You will very often get the reply, "We want to know if we're in the same ballpark, so we don't waste anyone's time." To that you can reply, "That's a reasonable question. Since you must have a salary range budgeted for this position, why don't you tell me what that is?"

Questions to Ask the Interviewer

Finish some of your answers with questions. Factual questions about the job's responsibilities are good. Consider this conversation an extension of your research. For example, an executive assistant candidate may want to ask about the scheduling software and methods used by the company.

Find out more about the job's path to success. The following are examples you can customize to the specific job and company:

- "How is success measured in this position?"
- "Who does a person in this job work with, and how?"
- "What roadblocks does this job commonly face?"
- "What resources (time, money, staff, and technology) does this job employ in reaching its goals?"
- "What are the acceptable and unacceptable methods of reaching those goals?"
- "What's the work atmosphere of the department?"
- "Are there unusual time or money pressures faced by this position?"
- "What, specifically, would I be expected to accomplish in the first thirty days in this job?"

Your questions will vary with the details of the job. You want to know the employer's expectations. Many poor hires are made because expectations weren't clear, and the new boss, without having stated expectations, becomes disappointed. It's an all-too-common sign of weak hiring skills.

337

When asking about the company or the job, repeat a recent news item about the company and ask your interviewer what impact that news might have on the job. For example: "There's a lot of press lately about your CEO retiring. Will that have an impact on my business unit?" What's important here is to find out if the company is right for you and to carry the conversation forward.

Asking the following questions sends the right message about you as well.

"What made you join this organization?" If you are currently in a position at another company, this is an invitation to the interviewer to sell you on the company. For a moment, you can "be a buyer." Now use the interviewer's technique and listen carefully to how they answer as well as their words. Are they all lit up about working there, or are they just putting in their time until retirement?

"What made you call me?" Nikki Warren: "One of the first questions you should ask in an interview is, 'What is it about my resume or phone interview that caused you to invite me here?' From there, you can expand on the qualities that they tell you they think are impressive."

"Did I give you enough information? Would you like me to elaborate?" It's a good idea to check in with questions like these after you've shared an achievement story. Your interviewer has a chance to refocus on his or her agenda, and while you want to get your key messages across, you don't want to hijack the interview.

"May I tell you about a time I accomplished something special?" This is a direct request to tell your favorite achievement story, if you haven't had the opportunity. It's a nice answer to an interviewer's "Do you have any other questions?" near the close.

"What is our next step?" I'm deliberately putting the "our" in there, because both you and the interviewer have decisions to make. If they give a typical answer like, "We'll talk to a number of candidates, then call you back," you can say, "That's great! Is there anything more I can tell you that might give you a clearer idea of how I fit this job?"

Book to Web

Monster's Career Fit Indicator test, located at **monstercareers.com**, includes customized questions to ask interviewers based on your personality type.

Crimes of the Interview

There are some near-fatal mistakes you can make in an interview. Most reflect either poor communication skills or negative indicators of what kind of employee you'll be:

- bad-mouthing your former company or boss
- deception of any kind—lying, exaggerating, taking false credit
- not having done your homework
- not having answers
- not having questions
- talking too much
- not talking at all
- lack of focus
- poor language skills, slang, or vulgar language
- too much perfume or aftershave
- revealing too much personal information

Not the End of the Game

The job interview is a huge milestone in your job search program, but it is not the end of the game. You are likely to have several interviews with several companies before you find a match. Don't be discouraged if your first interviews don't result in a dream job offer. If your job interviews are really conversations, you will see them as opportunities to learn more about what employers want, and to practice your interviewing skills. You will, sooner or later, go through the set of interviews that concludes with a job offer. That feels great! All your hard work has paid off. When an employer says, "We want to offer you the job," the ball goes back into your court.

It's time for the next step in your job search program to kick in. Before you say, "Yes, I'll accept that job," you need to find out a little more. Now, your Free-Agent attitude will guide you to set up the right expectations before you accept the final job offer. That next step in your job search program is negotiating the best deal, and I'll take you through negotiation step-by-step in chapter 16.

16   >> Negotiating the Best Deal <<

F.A.M.E. ATTITUDE: TRAIN LIKE AN **A**THLETE

Your job search is a competition.

A new job offer feels great. This is the "yes" you've been working toward! You're interested in the job, you like the people; you're ready to say "yes!" in return. Before you do say yes, however, consider this: how you manage the job offer sets the tone for the job itself.

No matter how permanent the job seems, the chances are you will be employed in it for three to five years before some shift in the business environment moves you along, either into a new job at the same company or to a new employer altogether. You must think a little about that time now, and set up the right conditions so you'll be ready for the inevitable change. Those conditions—salary as well as working conditions and opportunity—are subject to a certain amount of negotiation. That's why, at this point, I want to remind you of the F.A.M.E. attitude that a job search is a competition. By that, I don't mean you have to make unreasonable demands or try to "beat" your employer in a game of nerves, but I do mean this: you won't get the deal you deserve unless you've trained yourself in the negotiation methods that make a good deal possible.

Now the roles are reversed. When you have a job offer, you really are the buyer, and the employer is selling its offer of salary, benefits, and working conditions to you. You're choosing whether to spend your time and energy with this employer and this group of people. You're deciding your final "price." Close the offer by creating a win-win relationship with your new employer.

341

Job negotiation is not just about money, and it comes in two phases. You have to get all the details of the offer first, and then come to agreement on a deal that leaves both you and the company feeling good about the hire.

How to Know if a Job Is Right for You

They want you. Do you want them? This process actually began when you were asking questions during the interview. Make sure you know the answers to the following:

- Do you have a complete picture of the job's responsibilities, authority, goals, and measures for success?
- Will you and your new boss work well together?
- Are you convinced there's a good match of skills, experience, and culture? Do you really want to be part of this company? Do you want to serve its mission?
- Will you have the resources (people, technology, money, and time) to do the job? Do they want you to succeed?
- Does this job have a clear growth path?
- Does your research convince you that this company is going to be around in five years? How important is that to you?
- Does the job fulfill the criteria you wrote in your "What's Important to Me" document at the end of chapter 3?
- What have your references, networking contacts, and friends told you about the company? The position?
- Is the job located in the right place? What are the expected work hours? How's the commute?
- How does your spouse or significant other feel about this offer?

It's perfectly okay to return to the hiring manager, recruiter, or HR staffer who was your main contact to get more information. Good employers respect a careful decision-making process. Usually these questions can be answered on the phone, but get them all together so you can make just one call; don't keep calling with "just one more thing. . . ."

This is really an opportunity for professional communication. If you need a little time to decide, ask for it and explain why. Since they have an offer on the table, they have a reasonable right to put limits on the time you take. A couple of days or a weekend is generally fine.

Benefits, stock options, and other forms of compensation can be worth another 25 percent to 50 percent of your salary. Get details. Benefits, especially health care and 401(k) retirement plans, are valuable, yet vary widely from employer to employer. It may be worth giving up salary dollars now to invest in your future with stock options. That decision, however, should be thought through before rushing ahead. Many who expected stock option riches in the last decade were disappointed.

How to Negotiate

When your questions are answered, when your significant other says okay, when you know the job is right for you, then it's time to negotiate. Most employers expect a little negotiation, and you're doing yourself a disservice if you don't work out the best deal you can.

The keys to successful negotiation are these: do your homework well in advance, and keep the conversation focused on your best interests, not on dollar figures or inflexible demands. I'll assume you've done your homework, so you know what salary range you need, what benefits you expect, and what people are paid in your local area to do comparable jobs.

Establish Common Expectations

Here's a failure: You've been through four interviews, you and the employer are crazy about each other, and you're privately thinking you're not going to take a penny less than $55,000. Then they say, "We're proud to offer you this job for $40,000."

You say to yourself, "You're kidding me." And then you smile and say, "I need a couple of days to think about it."

If you go back and say, "I really need $55,000," they'll be surprised. They may come back and say, "We can go to $42,000, and that's it." Now you're on the downward spiral. Your chances of a successful closing to this deal drop 25 percent a day; four days after the offer, the deal's dead. Even if you take the job at the low salary, you've signaled that your expectations were off.

Moral of that story: Do your homework and confirm early in the process that your expectations are reasonably close to theirs. By the second interview, before the job offer, your research and discussions should have confirmed that the job's compensation is in your general range.

BUT, here's a different kind of failure: You sit down at the beginning of the interview and say, "How much does the job pay?" In those critical first minutes, you've told them you don't really care about challenge, culture, and opportunity. You're in it for the money.

You need to find the right emotional moment in the process, before the offer is made, to confirm that you and the employer are both in a negotiable range of compensation. If it's clear they like you at the close of the first interview, you can say, "Can you give me a sense of the range of pay you're thinking about for this job?"

If you don't find that moment, you can say as a follow-up question before your second interview, "I feel good about your company, and my sense is you feel good about me. Before I come in for a second interview, could we have a chat about the compensation range?"

Ask the right person at the right time. What you may find is that the HR person will say, "I'm not authorized to negotiate money, but the line manager will talk to you about that." Wait until the end of that interview with the line manager to have some discussion about compensation, and don't make it a hard-core negotiation—just information-gathering to decide if you both will take the next step.

How to Talk About Money

In chapter 15, we discussed ways to postpone talking about specific dollar figures before an offer is made. Once a job offer is on the table, however, you must talk about money. Let's assume you've given them a broad salary range during the interview process, and postponed the detailed salary discussion until now, when they're sold on you.

An employer decides what to offer based on several criteria:

- **Budget.** Management has budgeted money for the position in advance.
- **Contracts.** Union or guild agreements set salaries based on position, seniority, and other factors. Professional service firms, and others, base some salaries on existing contracts with clients.

- **Fairness.** A manager does not want to pay you $50,000 for doing a job someone at the next desk is doing for $35,000.

- **Established value.** You're offered what the person who just left the job was paid.

The salary level is usually presented in one of two ways:

"The job pays $25,000. Welcome to the party." The fact that you want $29,000 is irrelevant if sixty other people doing the same job all make $25,000. Welcome to a negotiation that has a very clear end: $25,000. If you can get them to increase your salary to $25,500, consider that a huge win.

OR . . . "This job's salary is commensurate with your experience." When you see that in a job ad, it probably means there's a pay range. The job may pay $55,000 because the person you're replacing was paid that, but if you have stronger skills and experience, and you establish their value, the job could pay $60,000.

If you're qualified for the $55,000 job and you're now making $36,000, you're not likely to get $55,000. They're likely to offer $43,000. You get about a 20 percent raise and the company gets an experienced employee. Good deal all around.

If your total compensation range and the offer are too far apart for comfort, you may still explore options for changing the job. Could they add responsibility to the job in order to legitimately change the job title? Employers often leave themselves some "wiggle room" between titles like "Customer Service Representative" and "Senior Customer Service Representative" to recognize that people come to jobs with different levels of experience. Be prepared to offer specifics—not only how you might deserve higher pay, but what additional service you can offer that earns it.

Brainstorming can lead to a win-win solution. You can't have this conversation unless there's a cultural fit, and you should expect to raise your performance for a higher salary, but if you've made it to the offer stage, the fit is probably there.

Many companies go straight to a best offer (on salary, at least). Kyle K. Laverents, a recruiting specialist at Paymentech, says that the better companies think hard about the offer before it's made, and don't expect a long counteroffer process. "When I call a candidate up with an offer, it will be the best possible offer we can put together," he says. "We go through all the details with the candidate. I'll explain to them the thought process behind the offer, and ninety-nine percent of the time it's perceived as a good offer."

You can respect this level of openness from an employer. They are not playing games, and your response to a sophisticated offer like this has to be equally mature. Explain your reasoning if you ask for more.

For example, when the offer seems a little low, you might say: "I'm happy for the offer, and it's obvious you've thought this through. I have two questions: one is that I am making $48,000 in my current job, and you've offered $44,000; I think I need to be earning at least what I am earning in my current job." Then don't say anything, because the next person who talks loses. Don't blurt out, "But I'd take $46,000!" while they're thinking, "I guess I should offer $48,000."

You're nervous that they'll say no. But if you're on a career plan, you have to measure your level of risk. If you've been out of a job for nine months, with two kids to support, your dollar threshold might be different than if you're currently working in a job that pays $48,000. If you're without a job, you may be happy with a $46,000 job that offers a chance to get back on the path of growing your value to an employer. You're moving forward again!

Sometimes it's a close call. When you think the job is going to come in at $50,000 and you're making $46,000 in a good job, you may decide that your skills are not for sale for less than $48,000. Your confidence in your skills is in direct correlation with your tolerance for risk as you make that statement.

Tell them you want to talk it over with your spouse or a close friend. "I'm really excited about coming to work for the company. I just need to present this to my spouse. I will call you by ten o'clock Tuesday morning." And then do not miss that deadline.

Higher-level jobs usually command more flexibility in negotiation, and there's more to discuss. Large corporations often have structured pay scales; smaller firms or start-ups may be more flexible (conversely, they may have less cash and want to talk about taking a stake in the company). At times of high demand for your skills, you have more leverage.

If you believe they can pay you more, frame it once again in a positive manner. "That's a very respectable offer, and I'm delighted to have it. I had anticipated something a bit higher, however, based on our discussion and my research." At that point, you will be expected to name a figure.

This is where negotiation definitely becomes more art than science. Many simple negotiations end up splitting the difference between two positions in a process similar to buying a house. If you're okay with the middle point between their figure and yours, you may be fine.

Emotion

ometimes settling on a price for a job is like a classic real-estate negotiation. You walk through a house, and you think "I like this house." Then you go to four others, and go back for a second time to the first house. And you really like it.

The seller wants $200,000. You were only planning on spending $150,000—but already your emotion is taking over. "I gotta have this house." Then you offer $150,000—and the seller comes back and says $195,000.

That is a scary moment for the buyer. You've offered 25 percent less, and they came down 2.5 percent. Now you come back and say, "$170,000, and leave the washer and dryer." The seller replies, "$190,000 and not a penny less." Then you say, "$179,900, you leave the major appliances in the house, you fix the broken brickwork, and that's my final offer."

After some discussion about the brickwork, you meet at $183,000. It was a panicky, emotion-driven negotiation on both sides. You broke through the panic by expanding the discussion.

Let the emotional investment drive you to a win-win solution, not just to splitting the difference between two prices. Explore options like those listed in "Beyond Salary" below.

Beyond Salary

Depending on the position, you should be prepared to discuss other compensation as well as benefits. There is nothing wrong with asking about each of the items below. The employer may not volunteer information on all these, and chances are they don't have all of them. With that in mind, here's a checklist of items on which you may negotiate.

Non-salary compensation. The position may pay additional compensation in various forms:

- commission on sales
- a bonus based on hitting various performance targets (yours, your department's, the company's)
- stock options or stock grants
- starting bonus (a single cash payment when you start work)

347

- early review on salary (for example, 6-month review, with a possible raise)

Start date. You should take a breather between jobs, even if it's just a few days. A two-week notice to your current employer is traditional. Acknowledge your new employer's eagerness to get you on the job, but come to the discussion with an acceptable date in mind. You can say, "I'm sure you'll agree that I should treat my current employer with the same regard I'd treat you, and I'd like to give them ten business days' notice. Also, I need to be available for one or two calls until June 1, because there are a couple of big projects going on. I want to take my family away for a week together—just to get reconnected. So that's two weeks' notice and a week before I start. I hope three weeks from today works for you." If they have a desperate need, you can offer to be available on a limited basis during your transition.

Benefits. Benefits can add 20 percent or more value to your total compensation, but they vary widely among employers. Get a detailed description. Common benefits include:

- Medical, dental, and vision plans, covering health-care costs. Check the plan you'd choose. Compare coverage with the plan at your current employer. What's the deductible? The employee contribution? How about co-payments for doctor's visits and prescription drugs?

- Employee assistance programs, such as family counseling, outplacement services, and counseling for substance abuse. Even if you don't plan to use this, ask about it.

- Retirement plans such as 401(k) plans or pension plans. Find out if the company matches any part of your contribution. These plans can help you save tens of thousands of dollars, or more, for retirement.

- Paid vacation and holidays. For more experienced candidates, an extra week of vacation is significant, and companies that focus on your performance may be more flexible in vacation than salary. You may also negotiate an escalating scale of vacation, such as adding a week after two years' service, for example.

- Insurance (life, disability, long-term care, and so on). With the cost of insurance premiums escalating, company-provided insurance can be a significant addition to your total compensation.

Relocation payments or assistance. If you are relocating for your job, your new employer may foot the bill. Large companies may have discount deals with moving companies, saving you money and hassle. This benefit tends to go with higher-paying jobs.

Tuition reimbursement. Many companies will support new learning by re-imbursing tuition in degree programs or paying for certification training.

Perquisites. These "perks" are more popular in boom times and for executives. They include use of a company car, company-provided mobile phone, trade association membership, and so forth. There are special perks for employees who travel a lot, such as membership in airline clubs.

Working conditions. These are cultural as much as financial. It's good to let a company know your preferences at the outset. (In fact, some of this should be part of your job interview.) What will your title be? How often will you see your boss? Will you have access to executive management? Is your working place private or open? What equipment will the company pay for?

Accelerated salary review. You may be able to get a performance review and raise in pay after six months instead of the traditional one year. This arrangement can bridge a gap in salary expectations by tying greater pay to performance. You propose the following: "I'm willing to start at the salary you are offering if you are willing to move my performance review to six months from my start date, and if I'm outperforming the job's require-ments, I'll receive a raise then."

When you've come to agreement on all terms, you should get the de-tails in writing. At a minimum, you should send an e-mail confirming your acceptance with a summary: "I'm excited about the job—just want to re-view a couple of things: We talked about a six-month review. We agreed that, if my performance was good, I might move into the job I really wanted at the six-month point, and I just want to make sure you're com-fortable having that conversation."

Crimes of the Negotiation

- Pulling out the salary survey you printed from the Web and saying, "This survey shows you're not paying enough." Salary research informs your negotiation, but it's too inflexible to apply pressure to an individual. That paper isn't exact about factors like opportunity for promotion, company culture, your experience, pay equity, or local supply-and-demand factors.
- "This job title pays a lot more at my current company." This is a nonstarter, because titles mean different things to different companies, industries, and geographical areas. A Marketing Director at IBM and a Marketing Director at the Pioneer Valley Land Conservation Trust are different jobs and will most likely carry different salaries.
- "Jimmy makes more." You've been offered $46,000 but you know that Jimmy down the hall makes $52,000. It's negotiation suicide to say, "If Jimmy makes $52,000, I want $52,000." Information about others is valuable in negotiation, but it's not tangible evidence of your value. You need to ask yourself, "Why does Jimmy seem more valuable? How can I use that information to persuade them I'm worth more?"
- Lying. If you make $46,000, say you make in the mid-forties. Don't say you make $52,000.
- Getting caught unprepared. Your research (chapter 12) should give you a good idea of the pay range for comparable positions in your area. Don't get your only information from the job offer.
- Ganging up. Don't join three of your buddies one year into your job and try to negotiate together. The person who's worth more will make less than they deserve, and this arm-twisting tactic is resented by employers. (Of course, this doesn't apply to contracts or collective bargaining, in which negotiating as a group is the point.)

The Power of Multiple Offers

The ultimate marketer's goal is a buyer's frenzy, where everyone is demanding your "product" (you). In an ideal situation, you've prepared and executed a job search that results in multiple offers from companies, not just to get the highest price but to get the best overall deal.

The timing of multiple offers, however, is hard to pull off. You need incredible organizational skills, good timing, and a disciplined approach. In boom times, it's easier to find and time multiple offers.

Here are some tips for handling them:

- **Be direct.** "I have another offer pending, but I am very excited about this offer. I will call them and ask for a decision by Wednesday. May I call you then?"

- **Be discreet.** If you have another offer, do not give the amount. Your interest is deciding between the total opportunity represented by each offer. You can say to both employers, "$1,000 in salary isn't going to make the difference. I'm looking at the total package."

- **Be ethical.** You cannot practice sandbagging, which means raising the price of a job you don't intend to take just to get another employer to raise their price. The scarcity of talent in the 1990s made this practice common and employers deeply resent it. (If you have declined an offer in the past couple of months, that's a legitimate point to give some juice to a current negotiation: "I'm excited about the job, but I must tell you that I had to decline an offer for that salary two months ago.")

- **Don't bluff.** If you say you'll take offer B unless offer A increases its salary by $5,000, be prepared to have offer A withdrawn.

- **Don't drag out the process.** Once you have closed with one employer, you are obligated to notify the other(s). Remember that the employer's second choice for the job is a candidate like you, waiting for an offer.

After a thorough back-and-forth discussion, there finally will come a time when you agree on the total job-offer package. Congratulations!

There's just one more thing. . . .

You're about to go into a transition from one job to the next. Don't shut down your job search program completely. Strange things can happen: the company can have an unexpected problem, or be acquired, or have to withdraw the offer. It doesn't happen that often, but it *does* happen. Don't send your official "I've landed" e-mail until you're actually in the new job. Instead, prepare your transition, in which you'll move your working life to the next level in the days and months following a successful job search. I'll tell you how to do that in chapter 17.

17   >> Your Transition to a New Job <<

F.A.M.E. ATTITUDE: THINK LIKE A **F**REE AGENT

Your ongoing value grows with your relevant skills.

The time you spend in transition to a new job can mark a significant change in your career. You have worked hard to get to this point. You've gained new skills and, I hope, you've made some of the F.A.M.E. attitudes a habit. Now that phase 3 of your job search is coming to a close, the free agent's dedication to growing relevant skills is a reminder to keep in motion. It's not the time to settle back into old habits.

If you have a little time off between jobs, use it to clear your head. Do something to recharge your batteries and realign your perspective. Even if you only have a weekend off, go do something that's meaningful, or else within weeks you'll only remember that you jumped from one job to another.

If work has taken you away from time with your family, reconnect with them. It may be enough just to play more with your kids, or treat your sister to a surprise weekend at the beach, or fly home to visit your parents. The point really is to mark that transition with a new commitment to connect with the people you care about.

Close Your Current Job Well

If you are leaving one position for another, the way you exit your current job says a lot about your character. Sometimes, you are so euphoric about getting a new job, you just think, "I'm outta here," and you get out as fast as possible. That's like getting accepted to college in April and forgetting to finish high school! Instead, start improving your new habits as you exit your old job.

For example, if you're the type who leaves loose ends for people, tie them up this time. Call the appointments you have three months from now, and explain you're going to another job. You don't want your former colleague saying, "Here's another appointment that Jeff never told anyone about." (Remember, too, that those people on your calendar are part of your personal network.)

In addition to covering your appointments, here are some other ways to tie up those loose ends:

- If you manage a staff, meet with them right away to plan a transition.

- Fulfill any responsibilities you cannot pass on to a colleague or your successor.

- Tell important clients, customers, or vendors about your transition (and assure them that they're part of your business network going forward).

- Go through the business processes completely with HR. Roll over your 401(k) money, plan a transition of benefits, and get the paperwork finished before you leave.

- Return anything that belongs to the company—a PDA, a computer, a list of customers, a phone. If your company paid for home Internet access, plan to roll that over to your new company or pay for it yourself. (A new job can be a neat opportunity to upgrade any of those tools.)

- Clean up your files and e-mail. If your personal and business contact lists are all mixed up together (as mine are), ask your current employer for permission to keep the data.

- Follow their lead on storing your business data. Delete or transfer your personal e-mail, delete the cookies on your browser, and delete your personal files.

Get a "360-degree" exit review: Ask for candid comments on your job performance from bosses, peers, and staff (the full circle of your job acquaintance, thus "360-degree"). Talk to your customers if you can. This is a

Throwing Money Away

The most common mistake in transition is forgetting to move your retirement savings. Every year, millions of savings dollars go into limbo just because people forget to move them.

It happens more often than you think. After a successful job search, people become so focused on the next job that they leave behind stock options, 401(k) retirement savings, and other money. Do that a couple of times and you're really throwing money away, because even a few thousand dollars can grow enormously over the length of a career. Roll the money over to the new employer's plan or start a personal retirement plan such as a SEP or IRA.

Resist the temptation to cash out your company-supported savings and spend it because you've saved "only" a few thousand dollars. You could lose up to half of it in taxes and penalties by withdrawing early. If you didn't miss the money as you were saving it, put it away somewhere safe—and let it continue working for you.

relatively new practice, so your company's HR director might offer some guidance. Why should you talk to everyone? Let's start with saying thank you: to your boss for mentoring you, to your colleagues for working with you, to your staff for supporting you, to the CEO for inviting you to be part of the company.

If someone has acted as your mentor, promise to stay close—and follow up. They will be a reference for you long into the future. You may even ask them to write a statement about you (although they'll probably ask you to draft it first). A note that says, "I'm really sorry Jennifer is leaving us . . ." can be a great reference years later.

If your resume is posted at an online career site, you will need to update it in a few months to reflect your new job. You don't have to take it off the site, but for a while you may want to "deactivate" the resume, which means potential employers cannot find it in a database. It's not a bad insurance policy to keep an updated resume online and ready to go—it's one of those lifelong habits that goes with sound career management.

Take an hour or two to review and file the materials you created for your job search. Read your correspondence and tie up any loose ends. Make sure all the people you talked to are in your contacts list or Rolodex. Keep copies of your resume and your pitch where you can find them.

And finally, don't forget to thank everyone who has helped you find your new job! Call or write to them personally—don't send a blanket announcement. People love to hear that you've landed, and sharing good news is a fun way to follow up on contacts. They've participated in something special—your search—and you want to show your appreciation. Remember that your job is your best current reference. Working hard for three years at a company and then leaving without notice blows that reference!

Make a Change

You made a lot of professional changes to build a good job search. Here are a couple of activities that can help you take advantage of the transition time, and move that new attitude into your new job:

- Before you start a new job, write five strengths and weaknesses from your last job. Privately determine that you're going to change one or two of those weak behaviors in your next job. They don't have to be big changes. For example, are you always late to meetings? Decide to change that from day one at your new job. In those first few weeks, always be on time for your meetings.

- A lot of people at mid-career wear the same clothes every day. A new job is a great opportunity to update your wardrobe (or your look) a little. Those shoes you've loved for five years . . . they're *old*. Throw 'em out! You don't have to break the bank to make a statement that the good changes are permanent.

- Develop one new work habit that will make you more productive. Perhaps it's an organizing habit you already practiced in your job search. For example, if you've always put sticky notes all over your computer as reminders, move to an electronic to-do list in the new job. It's not only practical; it's a symbol that you're making progress in your career.

- It's a great time to start working out, start eating better, or learn a new skill. You've just proven to yourself that you can make positive changes happen in your work life, so why stop at that?

- The great management teacher Peter Drucker suggests this powerful habit: Just before beginning a new job, write down what you *expect* will happen. Then check that statement six months or a year later. You'll get a reality check on where you are and are not effective.

- People's expectations of you are open, so think of a change that's fun. Always wanted a nickname but never had one? Introduce yourself with your new name on day one! Within a few months, instead of hearing "Hello, Jeffrey," you'll hear "Hey, JT!"

- Mark a day on your calendar ten days into your new job. On that day, spend one hour reviewing your F.A.M.E. principles. Under each, write a new behavior relevant to your new job that would satisfy that principle. In fact, write them right here:

How I could bring a **F**ree Agent's mindset to my new job: _____

_____

_____

_____

How I could train like an **A**thlete to make my performance better: _____

_____

_____

_____

How I could prepare like a **M**arketer to know my customers better: _____

_____

_____

_____

How I could work like an **E**ntrepreneur to lead, not follow: _____

_____

_____

_____

The First Days

When a U.S. president enters office, the press talks about the administration's first 100 days, which is the best time to get momentum behind major legislation. Okay, you're not the president, so you get about ten business days to make your first impressions at the company and get the momentum going.

Start with an assessment. If you're a replacement, make a list of the things the former occupant of your seat did right and wrong (you'll have to ask around a little). If it's a new job, make a list of all the reasons why the position was created.

Don't fall for that friendly cliché, "It's great if you just find your desk and the bathroom in the first week." You were hired with big expectations! Buckle right down to exceed them.

One great way to start is to conduct your own, informal 360-degree assessment of all the ways you can succeed. Talk one-on-one with your boss, your peers, and your staff. Ask your boss to mark twenty names in the company directory of higher-level people you should meet, and then set about talking to four or five each week. You can ask them about the company, their expectations, and their priorities. Meet "shared service" employees, like the technical services team. Get a meet-and-greet habit as if your success depends on them (because it does).

This doesn't require more skill than you already learned for your job interview. The real key is, don't stop being a curious person. The more you know, and the more you expand your network of relationships in the company, the more effective you will be.

Set up a 10-day check with your boss. Say, "I've been working on the following five things. Do you feel I'm spending my time in the right places?" This gives your boss the opportunity to say, "I'd really like you to be spending more time on this. . . ." This isn't a formal performance review. You're just finding out if you're on track. Do this again after thirty days, and listen very intently to your boss's suggestions. One hundred days into the job, you'll be fulfilling the high expectations they have of you.

Practice Good Habits

It's said that if you practice a behavior for twenty-one days, it's a habit. So your first month in the company is the time to practice good habits and wipe out bad ones.

- Find a mentor. Look for an experienced person who has been with the company for a few years. Have regular conversations about what is going on in the company, and why. Your boss may be a good candidate for this role, or it may be someone in another part of the company.

- Play fairly and openly with others, and leave office politics to the politicians.
- If you cannot avoid office politics, *still* play fairly and openly with others.
- Keep confidences.
- Keep upgrading the work habits you planned to improve.
- Mix it up with colleagues, staff, peers—don't get isolated.
- Send e-mail updates to your personal network every four to eight weeks. These "touch base" notes can be informal; tell people about the progress of a project, or news about your team. The idea is simply to stay in touch and remain in people's memories. Big broadcasts to three hundred people are less effective than custom messages, but if you don't have time for the second, you can at least send two kinds of messages: one to everyone who helped you in your search, and one to a broader network. Don't forget executive recruiters, counselors, and coaches.

Raises and Promotions—A Timetable

You make all your money in a two-minute salary negotiation every year or so. That discussion probably takes place around the time of your performance review. The rest of the time, you should be focused on increasing your value through good work (not on asking for an extra nickel).

Here's how an employer looks at pay: When you first get a raise, you're probably overpaid. In the middle of the year you're at the right compensation level, and as you continue to grow, you become underpaid. A big part of doubling down early in your job is moving toward that third level faster. When there's an imbalance between pay and value in your favor, you're ready to ask for a raise or promotion.

If, when joining the company, you arranged for a performance review after a set period of time (a year or perhaps six months), it's up to you to follow up. Most managers don't retain the details of these conversations six months later. Don't take it personally. It's your responsibility to remind them of your agreement . . . even if it was just a spoken understanding.

359

- Review the items in your job search portfolio every six months. Even if you don't look for another job for years, this is a good check on whether your skills, knowledge, and career path are growing as well as you like.

- Stay curious. Ask questions. Don't be a know-it-all. Ask for recommendations on good books, trade journals, newsletters, and Web sites.

- Be innovative! If you're doing it the same old way, you're probably missing an opportunity to do it better.

And Finally, Check In with Yourself

At 100 days, check in with the big picture. You're the CEO of your own life, so ask yourself the important career questions. How are you doing toward your goals? Ask yourself, "Do I like this company?"

What is invisible in the job interview can be crystal clear after 100 days. If the position looks like a dead-end job, if it's not turning out to be what the promise was in the interview, you need to take that free-agent attitude back to your original understanding with your employer (whether that's a written contract or just your notes from the job interview). Are your expectations being met? Are you meeting their expectations?

If after 100 days you say, "This is a good company, I'm happy I'm here," you can loosen up. Continue the habit of touch-base reviews with your boss three or four times a year. Don't just talk about performance (although that's important); talk about what's changed, what are the outside influences that might move you in exciting new directions. What would make you more effective, and keep your skills growing?

And any time you come to one of those choices—when your integrity, growth, job performance, and self-respect are on the line—choose carefully. Your job and employer may change in the years to come, but the choices you make help define you as an employee and as a person. Pick the path that's right for your career plan, your values, and the rest of your life.

Oh, and don't forget to have fun!

18   >> Special Situations <<

F.A.M.E. ATTITUDE: PREPARE LIKE A MARKETER

Deliver a memorable message.

People frequently ask me how to handle special situations in their work lives, such as changing careers or transitioning from military to civilian work. Students and others ask how to customize their search toward their particular concerns. They usually think they're at a disadvantage when their situation is a little out of the norm. A unique story is actually an advantage in this game—if you control the message. It helps make you memorable. Here are some guidelines for adjusting your job search in ten special situations.

Students and First-Timers

Your key objective when starting out is to spark your resume. So many new graduates or first-time candidates churn out a generic resume, thinking they just have to find someone to give them a chance! But employers aren't in business to give chances; they're in business to accomplish something. Replace "give me a chance" in your outlook with "here's what I have to offer you," and have something unique to offer. Here's how to do just that!

Build work experience into your education through internships.

Interns work temporarily at employers, generally doing entry-level work and learning about the business. "Internships are, for the most part, a prolonged job interview—for you and for the organization that offers you the internship," notes Steve Pemberton of online counseling service Road to College. "You can get an internship just about anywhere, from nonprofit agencies to traditional business organizations, and they can be full-time or part-time and paid or unpaid. They can also be required as part of a classroom course or used to gain a foothold in a chosen profession. And while we typically associate internships with college students, anyone can be considered for this type of employment."

Regardless of type, there are three things you should be looking to get from an internship:

- *Career introduction and development:* The best way to decide if you like a field of work is to spend time there. You'll get a reality check as you ask, "Is this what I want to be doing for a living?"
- *Practical experience:* The real world can be quite different from the classroom. An internship provides the opportunity to move from the theoretical to the practical, to take what you've learned in the classroom and apply it to the real business problems.
- *Personal growth:* Whether honing your decision-making skills or establishing contacts in a particular field, an internship provides the opportunity to develop confidence and form judgments.

Try to find an internship that exposes you to several areas of a business. You will have to compete for the best internships, particularly in lean economic times. Starting early and using career centers, alumni contacts, and faculty members can go a long way toward helping you accomplish your goal.

Combine your education, skills, and abilities into a compelling vision.

Maximize your relevant experiences in your resume and cover message. Students and new graduates with little work experience may use their education as the centerpiece of their resumes, showcasing academic achieve-

362

ments, extracurricular activities, special projects, and related courses. This is similar to the functional resume. Here's an example:

Mary Graduate   **1 Fifth Street**
mgrad@jobseeker.net   **Brooklyn, NY 11231**
                                                                   (718) 123-4567

OBJECTIVE
To bring my proven creative and analytical skills to a media planning or marketing position at a successful advertising agency.

EXPERIENCE/ACHIEVEMENTS
2000–2004
Brooklyn College — Brooklyn, New York
Senior Project: Currently completing mock advertising campaign for Brooklyn Cola (billboard/print/spot TV/radio ads, direct-mail campaign, and press releases).

Related Coursework: Advertising, Advertising Writing, Direct Marketing and Telemarketing, Media Plans in Advertising, Marketing and Advertising, Public Relations, Broadcasting.

Teaching assistant, Department of Communications (Professor Emilie L. Rose), 2003. Assisted teaching introductory courses in Direct Marketing and Online Marketing.

Paper Media, Inc. – Brooklyn, New York
Summer internship (2003) as assistant marketing planner. Wrote and designed brochure for borough-wide chain of auto service centers. Assisted planning for tri-state radio spot campaign, including budgeting, timing, and release schedule.

Cobble Hill Academy – Brooklyn, New York
Editor of weekly school newspaper, The Academy News, 1999-2000. Reporter and copywriter, 1997–1998.

SKILLS
Analysis of online response data, interpretation of demographic data, copy writing, script writing, media planning, trafficking and coordinating production. Radio and television production. Skilled with Microsoft Office, Quark. Familiar with Avid, Adobe Illustrator, Photoshop, After Effects.

EDUCATION
Brooklyn College—Brooklyn, New York
BA in Communications, concentration in advertising, anticipated graduation December 2004.

Online marketing methods—InterLearner online university, 2002.

Copy writing—2-day workshop at Brooklyn Friends Extension, taught by Gordon H. Merritt. April 2004.
References available from professors and employers

Choose the right field and the right location.

Pat O'Brien, author of *Making College Count,* advises students to find out about jobs and industries as early as freshman year: "You need to see how many people are looking for what you'll learn in four years. If there are only a few hundred job openings for anthropologists, you need to understand that reality as a freshman, not a senior." By all means study anthropology, if that's your passion. But also use the tools and resources mentioned in chapter 12 to find out what you can do with that major.

Location matters. Do you love big cities? Do you want to work in your hometown? Do you want to work outdoors? Although the Internet makes long-distance work more possible, opportunities in many industries, from filmmaking to finance, are still concentrated in certain areas. Early in your research, find out if your potential employers are clustered in one or two places, and weigh the trade-offs of living there.

Book to Web

The Monster Major to Career Converter translates your major into potential careers: **content.monstertrak.monster.com/tools/careerconverter/**.

Use your school to network early.

Alumni connect you to jobs. Gerry Crispin of CareerXRoads offers this prescription for networking while you're in school: "As a student, in my sophomore year, I would join a club on campus that relates to my area of interest. I'd go to the alumni association and find people with my degree who have interesting jobs. Then I'd call them up and say, 'Please come to our college and give a talk about your study and your career.'"

Gerry adds that this makes you memorable. "You will show initiative, and you'll learn enough to be good in a job interview," he says. "You'll be remembered by those alumni. I can assure you that anyone who does that a couple of times has a job before they graduate."

Take advantage of job fairs.

A job fair is a large gathering of recruiters and job seekers in one location. Independent recruiter Alison Rosenblum tells you how to arrive prepared: "At a campus job fair, everyone's on the same level," says Alison. "So presentation is the differentiator. The key to being remembered—your most important goal at a job fair—is to put together the whole package: resume, research, communication skills, dress, and attitude. Research the employers you want to meet and get to them. Show a sincere interest by asking intelligent questions. Bring a good resume and turn off your cell phone. Collect business cards and follow up!"

Job fairs can get crowded, so you'll only have a few minutes to make an impression. Review chapter 12 on research, and chapter 15 about job interviews, for more preparation tips.

Understand the economy.

The state of the economy is a serious wild card for candidates just entering the workforce. Your job search program won't change dramatically, but your initial choices of target companies may be fewer in a slow economy. You'll have to work more intensely. You may have to support yourself with the "Plan C" job described in chapter 7, while you search for the position you really want.

Recently, the fields most open to entry-level employees were in sales, health care, and administrative work. You may treat a sales or administrative job as on-the-job training for a specialty you'll grow into later. Fortunately, those jobs open up in every industry, so if your favorite business is really on the skids, you still have places to build up strong experience.

Book to Web

Monster features more information for first-time job seekers at **monstercareers.com**.

No Degree

If you have less than a four-year college degree, you're like the majority of American workers. So what about all those job ads that say "College degree required." Are they all out of your reach?

Not necessarily. College counts (and a two-year associate's degree may be all you need), but that phrase is also a resume filter. To employers, a four-year college degree indicates you have intelligence, perseverance, and drive. You can prove those qualities without a degree, but you must confront the doubts right up front.

For many jobs these days, formal education is taking a secondary role to on-the-job learning. You don't need a degree in computer science from Cal Tech to demonstrate you can write good computer code. If a job requires a college degree, and you are otherwise qualified, you can approach the subject with an emphasis on your achievement stories and a candid statement such as, "Have earned 20 credits toward my associate degree in business." If you are currently in school, or completing a degree part-time, emphasize that in your resume and cover message.

Many jobs that pay above-average wages do not require a bachelor's degree at all. Examples are found in most industries, and include computer programmers, power line workers, air traffic controllers, mechanics, nurses, and jobs in the public sector, from firefighters to administrators. The U.S. Department of Labor's publication "High Earning Workers Who Don't Have a Bachelor's Degree" is highly informative in this situation. Download it at **pueblo.gsa.gov/cic_text/employ/bachdeg/bach_deg.pdf**.

Book to Web

Jobs in the "skilled and hourly" category (such as construction, transportation, retail, and skilled trades) are fully integrated into Monster's job search. Check them out at **jobsearch.monster.com/**.

Relocating

More than 80 percent of Monster members said in a poll that they'd relocate for the right opportunity. In good economic times, people—especially younger people—flock to the country's growth centers. In tough economic times, many people consider relocation to a job in another city as "Plan B," (described in chapter 7).

If you have decided to relocate before you have a new job, your challenge is to manage a long-distance job search. The Internet has made that much easier. Most of your research can be conducted at a home computer or in the library. In 1990 you had to subscribe to the Sunday edition of another city's newspaper to find job opportunities there; now you can just go to local Web sites. The big career Web sites also let you narrow your search to a city or state.

In addition to research, networking and informational interviewing are great for finding those less well-known employers. For long-distance networking and informational interviewing, you absolutely must have your act together. Do your research. Practice your phone skills with friends (see chapter 9). Approach potential contacts using the e-mail techniques described in chapters 13 and 14. If you conduct a networking meeting over the phone, set a time when you can give your full attention to the other person, just as if you were face to face. Send copies of your pitch and resume in advance via e-mail.

Don't conduct a phone meeting in sweatpants and a T-shirt. You actually sound more confident and professional, even over the phone, when you dress up. There's usually less small talk in these phone meetings, so thank them for taking the call, tell how you found their name, and get to the point. Deliver your pitch, explain that you are relocating and looking for contacts in your target companies, and focus the last five minutes of the call on getting more names. Since phone meetings are less personal and lack the face-to-face touch, you may have to make more calls and do more research.

If you are actively looking for work in another area, you may want to schedule a visit for face-to-face meetings. The rule for this kind of visit is to maximize "face time" with people, and minimize time spent doing anything you can do at home. So, set up your visit well ahead of time, after you have established which employers interest you. Schedule three or four meetings a day; with enough advance notice, people who might otherwise delay meeting with you may be open to an approach stating that you will be in town for one week and would appreciate a short face-to-face meeting. Your follow-up on this approach (see chapters 13 and 14) can point out that, even if the employer doesn't have any open positions, a short face-to-face meeting can be beneficial in case the right position comes up.

However you get an employer interested, your first round of long-distance job interviews will usually take place over the phone. Nobody wants you to travel to a face-to-face interview unless there's a reasonable chance you'll be right for the job. In recent years, a few employers have used video-conferencing for interviews; that is, both parties can watch each other on video screens while they converse. It's still more the exception than the rule, but if you are invited to a video interview, dress and act as if you are sitting in the CEO's office.

If an employer in a distant location requests a face-to-face job interview on their initiative, they will typically offer to pay for your transportation. If the visit is your idea, it's usually on your nickel as well. Don't forget that this may be a tax-deductible expense, so save your receipts!

If you get a job that requires you to move, the employer may pay for you to relocate, or they may have a "we don't pay relocation" policy. It's often a matter of negotiation around the job offer: the higher your new job is in the organization, the greater the chance you'll receive some relocation assistance.

Book to Web

For advice on managing a move, go to **monstermoving.com**.

Career Changers

If you've decided to change careers, congratulations—you're thinking like a free agent! The people who receive your resume, however, won't necessarily be up to date on this huge career trend.

Career coach Barbara Reinhold points out that for experienced workers, changing fields is one of the most invigorating things you can do. It's like experiencing youth all over again, except with the wisdom of whatever age you are now. It's also, she notes, risky business, requiring more time and work than a traditional move up in an organization.

Managing a career transition is a two-stage process. It's hard to learn new skills and shift industries simultaneously. If you are moving to a new industry, seek jobs that require your experience first, and then plan a second transition as you acquire new skills and knowledge. For example, a financial manager in insurance who wants to move into marketing may find a financial management position in a marketing firm first, and then work toward a transition into marketing within that firm.

One rule-breaking resume tactic for career changers is to include both a career summary and an objective at the head of their resumes. Start with the summary, emphasizing qualities like leadership, reliability, and results-orientation. Then make the objective short and sweet: "To transition my record of success from sales management to public relations management."

Focus on the skills that powered your work achievements, rather than the specific industry knowledge. Instead of saying "I was a series 6 broker," say, "My focus on customer retention, and my persuasive skills with customers, increased sales by 28%." If you do have specific knowledge that would be useful in a new career, such as knowledge about certain software programs, list it in your resume's skills section.

Don't ask an employer to figure out where you'd fit in the organization; your research should tell you where the organization is going and what skills and competencies it's going to need.

This is one of those times you may be better off using a functional resume, because it offers you the best opportunity to showcase skills rather than job experience. It's forward-looking, which fits well for a career changer (see chapter 10).

Book to Web

There are great resources for career changers at **change.monster.com/**.

Returning to the Workforce

You may have taken some time away from employment—to raise a family, for example, or to pursue your education. When you return to the workforce after an absence of several years, you must prove that your skills and knowledge are up to date.

If you're going right back into your field, you have fewer doubts to overcome than career-changers, but like them, your strongest tactic is to get the issue out of the way quickly. Create a resume with both a summary and an objective (see chapter 10). In your case, the objective is not to change careers but to pick up where you left off. For example, a sales manager's objective might read: "To continue and grow my record of increasing sales in home furnishings."

Some employers may doubt your commitment, so put that issue to bed in the first paragraph of your cover message, and put some passion in it: "After five years as a full-time parent, I am resuming my career as a quota-busting sales manager. . . ."

If your time away from the workforce has enhanced your education or skills, include that message in your pitch. Obviously, earning a college or graduate degree gives you material for this message, but so do other reasons for an absence; for example, temporary military service (see below). Include in your pitch relevant informal education, such as taking courses online or learning a new software program.

You may want to include more time in your job search plan for research. Since research enhances the credibility of the person re-entering the workforce, it helps you make the case that you are still conversant with your field. If you're in a fast-changing field such as medicine or technology, this is critical, but even in slower-to-change fields such as manufacturing or sales, being up to date confirms your commitment to doing a job well.

Over Fifty

Age discrimination in hiring is real; it's also difficult to prove. If you frequently hear "You're overqualified" or "We're looking for a better cultural fit" in a firm that's populated by people thirty years younger than you, you may be bumping up against prejudice based on your age.

The reasons for this are not surprising. For better or worse, the youth culture is real, and employers may be unconsciously affected by the "younger is better" messages. In addition, some employers may feel that younger employees come with fewer responsibilities, lower pay expectations, and more flexibility.

Adapt your key messages to emphasize the advantages of your maturity and experience. Use your resume, pitch, and achievement stories to focus on those strengths that come with experience, like judgment and thoroughness. Also, use achievement stories and resume keywords to prove that your skills are up to date.

"But I don't feel old!" you say. Great! Now send that message past an employer's prejudices. You might consider changing your appearance to more closely match how young you feel. You might update your wardrobe, lose a few pounds, or finally move your card file to a handheld PDA.

Above all, an older candidate needs to project energy and enthusiasm. Smile. Radiate confidence in your skills and your ability to do more for an employer than someone who was born the day you graduated from college.

You need to overcome doubts that your specific job knowledge is out of date. That means learning necessary new skills, and dropping irrelevant or obsolete skills from your resume.

For more on discrimination in employment, go to the Web site of the U.S. Equal Employment Opportunity Commission: **eeoc.gov/**.

Working in Public Service

About one million people are employed by the federal government (excluding the armed services) and about 7.5 million more work for state and local governments. Public service work is a huge market for candidates.

Max Stier, president of the Partnership for Public Service, says, "The federal government is America's 'Fortune One' company—the largest employer in the United States. Effective private sector strategies [in a job search] absolutely work for public service jobs." There are, he adds, three important considerations to add to your strategy:

- The timeline in public service hiring is longer. Few government agencies can respond to a candidate in less than six weeks. This is changing (for example, the Transportation Security Agency hired 30,000 inspectors in one six-month period of 2002), but for now, you have to plan accordingly.

- You really need to shop around. The federal government in particular is not so clearly divided into silos as you may think. Lawyers and managers work in every department of the government. You can do foreign policy work at many federal agencies, not just the State Department. State and local governments hire candidates with all kinds of experience and qualifications.

- As in any large organization, there are going to be good and bad places to work, not just agencies but offices or supervisors.

Probably the most important consideration, says Stier, is *why* you might work in public service. "The best candidates are those who want to make a difference rather than just make a dollar. The problems are different, and often more consequential, than those in the private sector. Likewise, your capacity for significant effect is greater in all sorts of issues, from environment to education to security."

Book to Web

You'll find lots of information on customizing your search to government jobs at **publicservice.monster.com/**. Federal government jobs of all kinds are found at **usajobs.opm.gov**.

Transitioning Out of the Military

Developing a job search program for civilian use after leaving the service can be a daunting task. Even the most decorated and capable veteran needs to help civilian employers imagine him or her in a civilian job. Employers may assume most of your experience isn't relevant to their workplace. More than most candidates, you'll have to clarify what you can do to meet that employer's needs. How do your military skills translate to the skills and qualities employers seek?

Adjust your military resume. It's very common to see military resumes that are too long, too broadly focused, and filled with military jargon. All those acronyms only emphasize that you're coming from a very different culture than most companies.

Like a career-changer, you may want to include both a career summary and an objective. Write your summary with the target job in mind, and state in the objective that you wish to bring your skills into that job. This is most effective if you've chosen a specific career path. If you are examining several, use multiple resumes.

Now, here's the hard part: Information that does not relate to your goal should be eliminated from your resume, and this includes long lists of unrelated military awards, training, and distinctions. That medal you won for rifle marksmanship doesn't belong on a civilian resume. You may bring a list of those distinctions to the interview, ready to discuss them. If you discover that the person across the table also has a military background, a separate sheet listing military achievements can be an influential leave-behind. The key here is to use your own best judgment.

Showcase your accomplishments. Your military career has offered you excellent opportunities for training, practical experience, and advancement. Tout your accomplishments so the average civilian understands the importance of your achievements and the measurable outcomes. Here's an example of a "demilitarized" work achievement statement:

> Increased civilian employee retention rate 16 percent by focusing on training, team building, and recognition programs. Earned reputation as one of the most progressive and innovative IT organizations in the Army's communications and IT community.

For every distinction you note, including awards, ask yourself, "Why might this employer care about this experience?" Here's an example of incorporating a military award so civilian employers understand its value:

> Received Army Achievement Medal for completing 400+ medical evaluations and developing patient database using MS Access. The database improved reporting functions and tracked patient demographics, records, medication, appointments, and status.

A military background can be invaluable proof that you possess qualities like discipline, self-motivation, and learning ability. By running your job search according to civilian rules, you show that in your attitude, professionalism, and readiness to work, you are *already* making the transition to a civilian career.

Book to Web

For more on transitioning from military to civilian work, go to: **monstercareers.com**.

An Uneven Work History

While hiring managers are more understanding of an imperfect work history than they used to be, you still need to present your experience in a positive way. You can't change a spotty history, so the best strategy is to develop a forward-looking resume that shows the value you offer potential employers.

Start by evaluating your situation. If you were unemployed for six months back in 1994, your job search will not be affected. If you have any of these "red-flag" issues, however, you need to have a strong story:

- long employment gaps
- a history of job-hopping
- a history of being fired or laid off
- nonwork red flags such as a criminal record

Long Employment Gaps

Have you been unemployed and looking for work for more than a year? You can overcome negative impressions with three tactics:

- Turn up the preparation so your job search itself demonstrates your abilities. Show that you don't quit when the going gets tough.
- Prepare a clear statement of how economic factors, or other circumstances beyond your control, are causing your search to take longer.

- Make it clear that you are being very selective; you intend to find the right job, even if that takes more time.

If you have obvious gaps in your experience (such as taking years off to raise children), explain them in your cover message or introduction. On your resume, a simple statement does the job:

1997–2003: Primary caregiver for children, at home. Volunteer and educational experiences include the following [describe achievements outside the workplace].

"It always helps to continue your education and training and to list any volunteer work during a slow period," says Kathi Bradley of Bradley Resources. "Listing these under education or volunteer work should explain some of the gaps."

A History of Job-Hopping

Have you switched jobs every eighteen months? That's a red flag to some employers. The best way to handle job-hopping depends on your specific job titles and companies. You may be able to lump two or more similar positions under one heading on your resume (for example, Sales Representative, ABC Company and DEF Company, 2/94–4/96). Independent contractors and temporary workers should consider grouping their experience under one time period (such as: IT Consultant/Network Specialist, 4/95–present) with project highlights.

Use your cover letter to explain your work history and put a positive spin on your circumstances. Also, indicate your interest in a long-term position.

Finally, if you have an extremely poor work background with extended gaps, several firings, or a repeated pattern of job-hopping, consider using a functional resume (see chapter 10).

Criminal Record

Most hiring managers will react negatively to a criminal record, and you must take the lead. The best policy is to address the issue up front, in a cover message, offering to discuss it further. A functional resume may be best if your history includes incarceration. Again, the more you focus on preparing like a professional marketer—using all the tools and information in chapters 7 to 14 of this book—the more you will put the issue behind you.

Been in One Job a Long Time

One dilemma more people are facing in this era of short job tenure is the opposite of the job-hopper's problem: how to handle long-term employment on a resume—jobs lasting ten years or longer with one company. Sometimes employers see this on a resume and wonder, "Is this person a dinosaur?"

Turn this fear on its head by discussing your growth in responsibility and skills. Offer your long-term work history as proof you're in for the long haul. Since employers make a heavy investment in new hires, demonstrate you are a worthwhile investment.

In your resume's summary, use terms like: enduring value, long-term, growth-oriented, longtime results, commitment, retention of staff, and employee investment. In the skills or keyword section, remove obsolete skills, technologies, and credentials, which are definitely dinosaur tracks. If a technology isn't in use at your target company, skip it.

In your achievement stories, present the experience, skills, and training that relate to your current goal. Emphasize the advantage of having seen your accomplishments through from beginning to end.

Finally, play up your promotions by listing different positions in the same company separately. They show your last company realized your worth and offered you more responsibility.

Be Unique

As you work this program, don't run away from the parts of your story that make you unique. Anticipate questions and create forward-looking answers. As you do, you will build an approach customized to your own skills, values, and story. That will make you memorable. And that leads to the right job!

Phase 3 Review

You are in command of your calendar at this point in the 10-week model job-search plan (weeks 6 to 10). With so much action, you'll have to be flexible. A typical week might look like this:

MON	TUES	WED	THURS	FRI	SAT	SUN
Networking, research, prepare for interview.	Job interview	Follow up leads. Networking meeting.	Apply online. Start next round of networking with e-mails.	Follow up on interview. Research compensation at ABC Co.	DAY OFF	One hour of research. Rest of day off.

Once you start going to job interviews, your calendar might focus for a couple of days on one opportunity, and that's fine. Don't let the inevitable waiting time slow you down, however. While you are waiting for that call back to a second interview, keep your calendar filled with research, networking, direct approaches to employers, and online job applications.

It helps throughout phase 3 to keep track of your progress. Put a gold star on your calendar when you complete a job interview, or write a single list of all the people who have heard your pitch. Just seeing that list grow gives you a feeling of progress—and it should, because it *is* progress. A job search, like any big project, is accomplished one step at a time. Soon, you'll be writing "plan transition to new job" on that calendar!

>> AFTERWORD <<

In case you're one of those people who start to read a book by looking at the last page, let me tell you what you've missed. The Monster way to manage your career is about *dealing with change.* Constant change is the fact of life in business today. The old "job security" concept is gone. Today, you make your own job security by studying the job market, updating your skills, and watching for new opportunity.

I encourage you to embrace the new career habits in this book. In these first years of the twenty-first century, a smart candidate manages his or her career actively whether the economy is booming or in a slump. Yes, there are times you may be unemployed and focused full-time on landing a new job. Even after you have landed that dream job, however, you should continue the good habits you have practiced here. Do this because someday your situation will change. That's the new reality.

To be prepared for that change, you should, in a sense, always be looking for a job. Go on informational interviews. Learn more about jobs and employers in your field through research. Continue to expand your skills. Continue putting yourself "out there" in the marketplace by going to conferences, talking to people about their work, and remaining curious about "what's out there." Continue putting yourself in the way of opportunity so that when change comes, you are ready to act.

I don't mean you should become a "job-hopper," who jumps from employer to employer every year or so just to gain a little more money. Someone with a free-agent attitude keeps his or her commitments and takes a longer view than that.

Monster's F.A.M.E. attitudes are the foundation of a professional job search. You have to practice those attitudes, and you have to provide the hard

379

work a modern job search requires. Here's how those attitudes give power and depth not only to your job search, but also to the rest of your career:

Think like a Free Agent. A person with a free agent mindset never stops adding skills—including career management skills. You can and should cultivate a strong series of relationships through networking; doing this will set you on a path to creating a lifelong professional network.

Train like an Athlete. An athlete knows that the way to stay in shape is to train a little every day. Send a couple of networking e-mails every day. When nothing is happening, pick up the phone and call someone. Stay alert to the opportunities you encounter every day.

Prepare like a Marketer. A person with a marketer's preparation walks confidently in the world of work, ready to have a conversation about someone else's job at a whole new level: as a lifelong student of the job market.

Work like an Entrepreneur. An entrepreneur sees opportunity everywhere and never stops striving toward a dream.

Choose!

Psychologist Viktor E. Frankl wrote that the last of human freedoms is to choose one's attitude. When confronted with difficult times in your career, you have a choice: you can be a victim of circumstance or an agent of change. Which path you choose may well define the meaning of your career.

Monster's F.A.M.E. attitudes can carry you through the ups and downs of the economy. They can keep you moving in whatever direction you choose. Make it your habit to revisit these principles from time to time. Since you have to work hard at managing your career, why not engage that work with enthusiasm and a sense of adventure?

Be curious; show up for new experiences. You will discover new ways to use your skills, knowledge, and values at work. Ask questions. Read the news. Listen more than you talk. Develop an insatiable curiosity about how you may use your talents to improve your life and the world around you.

Finally, I'd like to ask for your help. Come visit us at **monstercareers. com**. Tell us your job search story; offer others your best advice and insights. Let us know what you'd like to see in a future edition of this book. Add your voice to the millions of Monster members who are changing their lives, their workplaces, and their world!

>> RESOURCES <<

The resources listed here are either widely used or especially helpful in working your job search. They are not necessarily endorsed by Monster. I've emphasized Web resources, which tend to present the most up-to-date information. Remember, however, that Internet sites may change at any time. If you don't find what you're looking for, visit us at **monstercareers.com** and let us know. We'll update future editions of this book!

BOOKS

These are some of the most popular, and most substantial, books about finding your dream job, and some—like Richard Nelson Bolles's classic *What Color Is Your Parachute?*—are also about finding your dreams. More book recommendations are available at **content.monster.com/bookstore/**.

Boost Your Interview I.Q.
by Carole Martin
McGraw-Hill, 2003

Cool Careers for Dummies
by Marty Nemko
IDG Books Worldwide, 2001

Do What You Are, 3rd edition
by Paul Tieger and Susan Barron-Tieger
Little, Brown, 2001

Free to Succeed: Designing the Life You Want in the New Free Agent Economy
by Barbara Reinhold
Plume, 2001

From Army Green to Corporate Gray
by Carl S. Savino, Major USAE, and Ron Krannich, Ph.D.
Impact Publications, 1999
(Also *From Navy Blue to Corporate Gray; From Air Force Blue to Corporate Gray*)

Getting to Yes: Negotiating Agreement Without Giving In
by Roger Fisher and William Ury
Penguin, 1991

Guide to Internet Job Searching, 2002–2003
by Margeret Riley Dikel, Frances E. Roehm, and Public Library Association
McGraw-Hill/Contemporary, 2002

The Harvard Business School Guide to Finding Your Next Job
by Robert S. Gerdella
Harvard Business School Press, 2000

I Don't Know What I Want, But I Know It's Not This:
A Step-by-Step Guide to Finding Gratifying Work
by Julie Jansen
Penguin USA, 2003

Information Interviewing
by Martha Stoodley
Ferguson Publishing, 1996

Job Hunting for Dummies
by Max Messmer
IDG Books Worldwide, 1999

Job Seeker Secrets: Making the Internet Work for You
by Thomas J. Ferrara
Thompson South-Western, 2003

Knock 'Em Dead!
by Martin Yate
Adams Media, updated annually

Making College Count: A Real World Look at How to Succeed In and After College
by Patrick S. O'Brien
Student Success, Inc., 1999

Negotiating Your Salary: How to Make $1000 a Minute, 4th edition
by Jack Chapman
Ten Speed Press, 2000

The Organized Executive
by Stephanie Winston
Warner Books, 2001

The Pathfinder: How to Choose or Change Your Career
for a Lifetime of Satisfaction and Success
by Nicholas Lore
Fireside, 1998

Rites of Passage at $100,000 to $1 Million
by John Lucht
Viceroy Press, revised 2000

The 7 Habits of Highly Effective People
by Stephen R. Covey
Simon & Schuster, 1990

Transitions: Making Sense of Life's Changes
by William Bridges
Perseus, 1980

Weddle's Directory of Employment-Related Internet Sites for Recruiters and Job Seekers
by Peter Weddle
Weddle's, updated annually

What Color Is Your Parachute?
by Richard Nelson Bolles
Ten Speed Press, updated annually

Win-Win Career Negotiations
by Peter J. Goodman and Roger Fisher
Penguin USA, 2002

Zen and the Art of Making a Living
by Laurence G. Boldt
Penguin USA, 1999

PUBLICATIONS

The following publications all have online companion sites that are great places to conduct research. Not all content published in magazines and journals is available online (there's no single rule for this, so check out print editions of particularly helpful publications). Some charge a fee for access to archived articles, especially older material (check the date on articles; those over three years old may be less useful). Remember that public libraries may have online access to material via their computers.

Newspapers

Business sections of newspapers are rich sources of company information, including news and names of management. Reporters, especially for local papers, can be a good source of information.

The Chicago Tribune   **chicagotribune.com**
The Los Angeles Times   **latimes.com**
The New York Times   **nytimes.com**
The Wall Street Journal   **wsj.com** (requires subscription)

A good listing of local city papers can be found at **newspaperlinks.com**.

News Magazines

Newsweek **newsweek.com**
Time **time.com**
U.S. News and World Report **usnews.com**

Business Magazines

Specialized business trade journals **bizjournals.com/journals.html**
Business 2.0 **business2.com**
BusinessWeek **businessweek.com**
Entrepreneur **entrepreneur.com**
FastCompany **fastcompany.com**
Forbes **forbes.com**
Fortune **fortune.com**
Inc. **inc.com**
Money **money.com**

Forbes magazine also publishes a library of lists including 200 Best Small Companies and Best Places to Live. Go to **forbes.com/lists**.

Fortune's annual surveys of companies—including the Fortune 500, Fortune Small Business 100, Best Companies to Work For, and Most Admired Companies lists—are available online at **fortune.com/fortune/alllists**.

Inc. magazine publishes its annual list of "the fastest-growing privately held companies in America" at **inc.com/inc500/**.

You'll find a helpful list of special-interest magazines and trade journals at **specialissues.com/lol**.

INTERNET RESOURCES

General Job Search Sites

6FigureJobs.com
6figurejobs.com

America's Job Bank
ajb.dni.us

AOL Careers and Work Channel
[part of AOL service]

CareerBuilder
careerbuilder.com

CareerJournal (Wall Street Journal)
careerjournal.com

Craig's List (general classified ads, including jobs)
craigslist.com

Execunet (membership required)
execunet.com

Flipdog
flipdog.com

HotJobs
hotjobs.com

MonsterTRAK
monstertrak.com

MSN Careers
careers.msn.com

Net-Temps
net-temps.com

Government: Federal Job Search Sites

Career OneStop
careeronestop.org/

Google's government search
google.com/unclesam

Job information for federal employees
safetynet.doleta.gov/

USAJobs
usajobs.opm.gov/

Government: State Job Search Sites

Every state has its own job site. There's a convenient index of state job sites at **statejobs.com/gov.html**.

Niche Job Search Sites

Niche job sites advertise jobs in a narrower category, such as industry, profession, geographic location, or type of employment sought (for example, temporary work or contract work). Google's directory lists about fifty subcategories of job search site by industry at the following URL:

directory.google.com/Top/Business/Employment/By_Industry/

Niche sites also concern themselves with workplace issues and special interests, such as the following:

385

Diversity

HireDiversity.com
hirediversity.com

Imdiversity.com
imdiversity.com

latpro.com
latpro.com

Monster's Diversity & Inclusion site
diversity.monster.com

International Job Search

JobPilot.com
jobpilot.com (Europe)

The Monster Network—21 countries around the world; links located at:
about.monster.com/

Not for Profit

Guidestar
guidestar.com

Idealist.org
idealist.org

Internet Nonprofit Center
nonprofits.org

Specialized Search and Advice on Monster

content.monster.com

Includes:

Admin/Support
Campus (MonsterTRAK)
Career Changers
Contract & Temporary
Diversity & Inclusion
Finance
Health Care
Human Resources
Learning
Management
Public Service
Sales
Technology
Work Abroad
Work/Life Balance

Also, a number of special reports on subjects as diverse as "Finding Your First Job" and "Military Transition" are available at **featuredreports.monster.com/**.

JOB AND COMPANY RESEARCH

You can begin job and company research at AOL, Google, MSN, Yahoo!, or another favorite search engine. All are good, with different features that will appeal to different people. (Much of the online research for this book was conducted using Google.)

AlltheWeb
alltheweb.com/

AOL service (non-Web)
search.aol.com

Google
google.com

MSN
search.msn.com

Yahoo!
yahoo.com

If you are looking for help finding keywords to use in searches, this site is very helpful:

inventory.overture.com/d/searchinventory/suggestion/

The Riley Guide is a fine online guide to information on many phases of the job search: **www.rileyguide.com/**

Business Locators

Infospace
infospace.com/info.zip/

Verizon Superpages
business.superpages.com/business/

U.S. Government Information/Research Sites

The U.S. Department of Labor
O*Net service
online.onetcenter.org/

O*Net skills search (matches skills with jobs that use them)
online.onetcenter.org/gen_skills_page

The Career Guide to Industries
stats.bls.gov/oco/cg/home.htm

The Occupational Outlook Handbook (OOH)
stats.bls.gov/oco/

U.S. Government's Federal Citizen Information Center
pueblo.gsa.gov/

The Secruities and Exchange Commission's EDGAR service for researching public companies
sec.gov/edgar/searchedgar/webusers.htm.

Lists of state administrative offices for all U.S. states (follow the links) at
nascio.org/stateSearch/displayCategory.cfm?Category=administration

Information on state and local governments
statelocalgov.net/index.cfm

Company Research Sites

The following sites provide press releases written by companies about themselves (you can also find press releases on most company Web sites):

BusinessWire
businesswire.com/

PR Newswire
prnewswire.com

Business Information

The basic business information for public companies may be found at most financial sites, such as the following (some are free; some require a subscription fee):

Business.com
business.com

CBS MarketWatch
cbs.marketwatch.com

CNN/Money Magazine Online
money.cnn.com

Morningstar
morningstar.com

New York Times Business
nytimes.com/pages/business

Other Company Research

Most financial sites and search engines concentrate on stock market and personal finance issues. The following sites focus on researching companies:

About.com is a Web directory with more than 500 topics, job search and careers among them. Each topic has a page with a number of links, built by an about.com "guide," a person who acts as a host, mentor, and "community leader" for people visiting the topic. **about.com**

Hoover's bills itself as the "Online Business Authority." It has recently reserved its most useful information to subscription customers. **hoovers.com**

The PriceWaterhouseCoopers MoneyTree Report describes current venture capital funding for companies at various stages of development. You can research which companies in your area have just received money . . . and may be hiring. **pwcmoneytree.com/**

Standard & Poor's, the financial information company famous for its S&P 500 stock index, provides extensive company information. **www2.standardandpoors. com/**

Vault has information on industries and companies, including message boards where you can view others' comments on companies. Some information is free; some requires a paid membership. Reports on various industries such as law, finance, and health care are sold individually. **vault.com**

Wetfeet publishes various guides to industries, companies, and regions. **wetfeet.com**

Two places in the Google Directory list many more sites:

directory.google.com/Top/Business/Major_Companies/Company_ Information/

directory.google.com/Top/Business/Major_Companies/Company_ Rankings/

Networking Groups

BNI (Business Network International) has chapters around the world. Focused on building business, its techniques are also effective for job networking. A BNI meeting can be very structured and efficient—a welcome framework for newcomers who "don't know how to network."
bni.com

ExecuNet is a paid-membership group that offers information, coaching, and networking at meetings around the country.
execunet.com

The Five O'Clock Club, organized in various cities, focuses on job networking.
fiveoclockclub.com

Directories

These two directories are available in book form. The first rates online job sites, and the second is a comprehensive guide to executive search firms. These and many other directories are available in libraries and career centers.

CareerXRoads—A Guide to Internet Career Sites
by Gerry Crispin and Mark Mehler
Available online at **careerXroads.com**

The Directory of Executive Recruiters
by Kennedy Information Systems
Available online at **kennedyinfo.com**

Salary/Compensation Research

bls.gov/ncs/ocs/
content.salary.monster.com/ (**S**alary.com in partnership with Monster)
salaryexpert.com

In the "guide to guides" category, JobStar (**jobstar.org**) is a gateway to industry- and profession-specific salary surveys.

Wageweb (**wageweb.com**) and Realrates (**realrates.com**) are survey-based sites with less comprehensive but still useful data.

SERVICES

Career Assessment

There are many tests available online and offline. They differ in their focus (personality, skills, interests, values) and in their methods. Some can be taken and the results understood alone; others require a career counselor's interpretation. Some are free and some require payment.

Online Assessments
Career interest assessments:
- Campbell Interest and Skills Survey
  assessments.ncspearson.com/
  assessments/tests/ciss.htm
- Career Directions Inventory
  careerinventory.com
- Kuder Personal Preference Record—National Career Assessment Services, Inc.
  kuder.com/
- Self-Directed Search
  self-directed-search.com/

- Strong Interest Inventory (different versions, with or without counselor's interpretation)
  cpp-db.com/products/strong/index.asp

Personality (or combined personality and interest) assessments:

- CareerLeader
  careerdiscovery.com/
- Cash-Lehman Pathfinder
  cashlehman.com/pathfinder/
- Enneagram
  enneagraminstitute.com/
- Keirsey Temperament Sorter (based on MBTI)
  advisorteam.com/user/ktsintro1.asp
- Myers-Briggs Type Indicator (MBTI)
  knowyourtype.com/
- Personalitytype.com
  personalitytype.com/quiz/html
- Rockport Institute's Pathfinder
  rockportinstitute.com/

Assessments Not Fully Available Online

- ASVAB (Armed Services Vocational Aptitude Battery) tests knowledge and abilities in eight categories such as word knowledge, general science, and mechanical comprehension. It's administered by schools. More information is available at **todaysmilitary.com/explore_asvab.shtml**
- C.A.P.S. (Career Ability Placement Survey) tests abilities in eight categories, such as mechanical ability and spatial relationships: not online. More information is available at **edits.net/caps.html**
- Johnson-O'Conner tests aptitudes such as manual dexterity and musical ability. More information is available at **members.aol.com/JOCRF19/**

Career Counselors

The International Coach Federation maintains a detailed "Coach Finder" service on its Web site.
   coachfederation.org

The National Board for Certified Counselors "Counselorfind" directory is a less-detailed but easy-to-use search engine to locate certified career counselors.
   nbcc.org/cfind/

The Directory of Executive Recruiters, published yearly by Kennedy Information, contains information on thousands of executive recruitment firms. It can also be found in many libraries and career centers.

> **kennedyinfo.com**

Resume-Writing Services

You can find a resume-writing service on Monster. The service is a partnership with CareerPerfect, Inc.

> **resume.monster.com/writingservices**

Monster's resume expert, Kim Isaacs, is president of ResumePower.com, a resume-writing service. (There's more information in "Contributors," below.)

> **resumepower.com**

Resume-writing services can also be found locally by using the indexes of the two largest associations for resume writers:

> National Resume Writers Association
> **nrwa.com/**

> The Professional Association of Resume Writers & Career Coaches
> **parw.com**

CONTRIBUTORS

The following experts contributed to the content of this book, and offer various services to individuals and businesses. They have provided the information below.

Lou Adler
The Adler Group
Advanced Hiring Concepts
17852 17th Street, Suite 209
Tustin, CA 92780
Phone: (714) 731-3403
Web site: **adlerconcepts.com**

Rebecca Barnett
President, Winning Your Way, Inc.
Author of *Winning Without Losing Your Way: Character-Centered Leadership*
Offering speeches, seminars, and consulting on character-centered leadership
Toll-free: (866) 843-9294
Web site: **winningyourway.com**

Gail Blanke
President & CEO, Gail Blanke's Lifedesigns

Author of *In My Wildest Dreams, Living the Life You Long For*
Motivational speaker, executive coach, committed to providing people with the
tools and courage to live an exuberant life
Toll-free: (800) 752-7314
E-mail: GBLD97@aol.com

Gerry Crispin
Coauthor of *CareerXroads,* a popular career reference guide
More of his ideas can be found at **careerxroads.com**. He can be reached at
mmc@careerxroads.co (he promises to respond).

Bruce Dorskind
Dorskind Group
525 East 72nd Street
New York, NY 10021
Strategic consulting on recruitment, mergers and acquisitions, and recruitment
advertising

Therese Droste
Career counselor and journalist
2737 Devonshire Place
Washington, DC 20008
Phone: (202) 483-3548
E-mail: tdroste@erols.com

Rob Galford
Managing Partner
The Center for Executive Development
420 Boylston Street, Suite 408
Boston, MA 02116-4002
Phone: (617) 369-7614
E-mail: rgalford@cedinc.com

James C. Gonyea
Internet Career Connection
Extensive line of career guidance services and information available free to the
general public
Web site: **iccweb.com**

Chuck Hughes
Steve Pemberton
Road to College
95 Main Street
Maynard, MA 01754
Phone: (1-888) 835-4620
E-mail: chughes@roadtocollege.com
        spemberton@roadtocollege.com
Web site: **roadtocollege.com**

Kim Isaacs
Director of ResumePower.com

4695 Watson Drive
Doylestown, PA 18901
ResumePower.com offers resume and career services for job seekers worldwide, including resume preparation, interview coaching, salary negotiation training, job search assistance, and resume distribution services
Toll-free: (800) 203-0551
Phone: (215) 794-9527
E-mail: Info@ResumePower.com
Web site: **ResumePower.com**

Deborah Knox

Life Transitions
Relocation, re-employment, and renewal
Seminars, coaching, workshop facilitator, and author
Coauthor with Sandra S. Butzel, *Life Work Transitions.com: Putting Your Spirit Online,* and the companion Web site **lifeworktransitions.com**
E-mail: dlkcoach@aol.com
Web site: **deborahknox.com**

Heidi LaFleche

Freelance Editorial Services
Providing writing, editing, proofreading, and project management to businesses, schools, and individuals
Voice mail: (617) 429-8722
E-fax: (443) 596-2325
E-mail: heidilaf@yahoo.com
Web site: **home.attbi.com/~hlafleche/index.htm**

Carole Martin

The Interview Coach
Coaching by an expert on the subject of interviewing
Toll-free: (877) 647-5627
Web site: **interviewcoach.com**

Michael R. Neece

President & CEO
Interview Mastery™/Caseridus, Inc.
22 Ash Street, Suite 300
Hopkinton, MA 01748-1808
Phone: (508) 435-2647 (USA)
E-mail: mneece@interviewmastery.com
Web site: **interviewmastery.com**

Kiki Peppard

Empowerment Advocate
1621 Starry Lane
Effort, PA 18330
Phone: (570) 629-6793
E-mail: kpeppard@ptd.net

Nina Pickell
Advisor, Core Allies
85 Poplar Street
Watertown, MA 02472
Phone: (617) 513-9631
E-mail: information@coreallies.com
Web site: **coreallies.com**

Ginny Rehberg
Rehberg Management Group
Career consulting, executive coaching, outplacement services
Phone: (617) 435-6622, (617) 964-5858
E-mail: career_doc@usa.net

Dr. Barbara Reinhold
Career counseling/transitions and performance coaching
Western Massachusetts
Available in person or by phone
Phone: (413) 529-9884
Web site: **barbara-reinhold.com**

Alison Rosenblum
Hudson River Career Resources
P.O. Box 38159
Albany, NY 12203
Phone: (518) 482-5909
Fax: (518) 482-5051
E-mail: Alison@hudsonrivercareers.com
         arosen@nycap.rr.com

John Rossheim
President, Rossheim.com Inc.
An independent journalist and Monster senior contributing writer, John offers customized research services to executive job seekers, human resources departments, and search firms. Rossheim produces research briefs and white papers on topics ranging from industry-specific employment trends to hiring issues such as pre-employment background checks.
E-mail: john@rossheim.com
Web site: **rossheim.com**

Peter Vogt, M.S.
President, Career Planning Resources
2400 Ivy Lane
Bloomington, MN 55431-2830
A professional career counselor specializing in new and recent college graduates, as well as current college students.
Phone: (952) 884-7235
Fax: (952) 884-7234
E-mail: peter@careerplanningresources.com
Web site: **careerplanningresources.com**

395

A

Accelerated salary review, 349
Achievement stories, 127–30
 in job interview, 305, 312–13
Achievements
 in cover letter, 213–14
 key messages about, 119–20
 recasting military, 372–73
Action, following through with, 23–25
Action phrases, 173
"Add another day" plan, 100–101
Advertised jobs. *See* Jobs, advertised
Affiliations, on resume, 179
Age
 job searches and, 370–71
 job security and, 5
Age discrimination, 6, 370
Aggressive interviews, 322–23
Agricultural industries, changes in, 4
Alumni, networking with, 225, 364
Appearance, at interviews, 306–7
Applications. *See also* Resumes
 checklist for, 269–70
 customizing for advertised jobs, 265–69
 following up on, 270
 including salary information in, 269
 job searches and, 99
 tailoring strategies to job ads, 263–65
 for unadvertised jobs, 271–77
 unprofessional, 270

B

Backup plans, 111–12
Behavior-based interviews, 321–22
Benefits, 348
Body language, interview, 326–27
Book resources, 381–83
Budget worksheet, 103
Business contacts, developing, 65–66

C

Career assessment, resources for, 390–91
Career centers, researching employers in, 242–43
Career coaches, 62–63
Career counselors, 62–63, 391
Career Fit Indicator, 75–77
Career Guide to Industries, 243
Career management, 10–12

Assessments
 exercises, 84–91
 professional career, 82–83
 self-, 72–82
Athletic training attitude, 17–19, 380
 competing with cover messages, 209–19
 confidence through, 145–55
 power of research, 229–52
 preparing for negotiations, 341–51
Attitude. *See also* F.A.M.E. attitudes
 at job interviews, 324–27

creating broad career vision, 36–37
Career summary, 165–66
Career transitions, 368–69
 out of the military, 372–74
Case-based interviews, 322
Certifications, 142
 on resume, 178
Closing, networking meetings, 292
College degrees, lack of, 366
Community, personal network and, 66–68
Company culture, 32–33
 matching candidates to, 47–48
Company loyalty, old-fashion, 3
Company Web sites. *See also* Internet
 advertised jobs on, 262–63
 researching jobs on, 238–39
Compensation
 establishing common expectations regarding, 343–44
 including information in application, 269
 interview discussions about, 315–16
 negotiating nonsalary, 347–49
 negotiating salary, 344–46
 researching, 250–51
 resources for, 390
Competition
 job search, 19
 using cover messages for, 209–19
Confidence
 during interviews, 327

Confidence (*cont.*)
  at job interviews, 303–4
  training and, 18–19, 145–55
Contingency search firms, 59
Contract agencies, 58
Contract recruiters, 58
Contributors, 392–95
Cover letters. *See* Cover messages
Cover messages, 209–10
  canned, 211
  closing, 214–17
  common mistakes in, 219–20
  creating opportunity through, 273–76
  customizing, 265–69
  explaining employment gaps, 375
  inadequate, 215–16
  openers, 211–12
  sample, 221–23
  stating case in, 213–14
  styles for, 217–19
Cover reasons for, 210
Criminal record, 375–76
Culture. *See* Company culture
Culture match, 46, 47–48
Customers, researching employers with, 245–46

D

Direct approach
  creating opportunity with, 271–77
  networking using, 289
Discrimination, 371. *See also* Age discrimination

E

E-business, 6
E-mail
  applications, 266–67, 275
  contacting referrals with, 287
  cover message format, 219
  direct approach for introverts with, 277
  resume format, 160
E-Recruitment firms, 59
Earn, Learn, and Yearn cycle, 7–8
Earnings, education and, 6
Economy, understanding, 365
Education. *See also* Learning
  earnings and, 6
  lack of formal, 366
  on resumes, 176–78
Ego, *versus* passion, 29

Emotion, negotiation and, 347
Employee cycle, 7–8
Employees, changes favoring, 4–7
Employer cycle, 8–9
Employer Web sites. *See* Company Web sites
Employers. *See also* Target employers
  focusing on, 21
  job interview objectives, 304
  learning to approach, 256
  potential opportunities with, 256–57
  researching, 239–46
Employment history, 125–26. *See also* Work experience
  on resume, 169–72
  uneven, 374–76
Entrepreneurial attitude, 22–26, 380
  finding/creating opportunity, 255–77
  preparing for interview, 303–40
  taking action, 97–113
Ethics, job offers and, 351
Executive recruiters, 392
Executive search firms, 59, 60–62
Exit reviews, 354–55
Expenses, budgeting for job search, 102–4

F

F.A.M.E. attitudes, 13–14, 379–80. *See also* Athletic training attitude; Entrepreneurial attitude; Free agent attitude; Marketing attitude
  incorporating into new job, 356–57
  making habits of, 26–27
Family, personal network and, 66–68
Federal government jobs, 371–72
Feedback
  after interviews, 319
  during interviews, 315
Follow-up interviews, 323
Follow-ups
  in cover message, 216–17
  importance of, 270
  on job interviews, 316–18
  for job search assistance, 356

for unadvertised jobs, 276–77
Free agent attitude, 11, 14–17, 380
  building networks and, 53–70, 279–97
  finding true job satisfaction and, 29–41
  resume as sales tool, 157–208
  transitioning with new skills, 353–60
Free career counseling exercise, 86
Friends, personal network and, 66–68
Functional resumes, 183–87

G

Gatekeepers
  dealing with, 270–71
  respecting, 310–11
Government resources, 64–65

H

Habits
  creating for new job, 358–60
  creating new, for job searches, 26–27
  incorporating into new job, 356–57
Headhunters. *See* Recruiters
Heroes exercise, 88
Hiring
  difficulties of, 43–44
  key messages about, 120–21
Hiring cycle, 51
Hiring managers, 56–57. *See also* Recruiters
How much is enough exercise, 90
Human resources department, 54–55

I

I-AM exercises. *See* Interactive Assessment Materials
Illegal interview questions, 324
Informational interviews
  networking with, 294
  as research tool, 246–48
  setting up, 248–50
Inside recruiters, 58
Interactive Assessment Materials, 83
  free career counseling exercise, 86

heroes exercise, 88
how much is enough exercise, 90
overcoming objections exercise, 91
shower exercise, 84
signature exercise, 85
twenty questions exercise, 89
what did you want to be exercise, 87
Interests, assessing, 78–80
Internet. *See also* Company Web sites
finding advertised jobs on, 258
networking on, 224, 295–96
researching employers on, 240, 243–45
researching jobs on, 231–39
resources, 384–92
safety on, 262
searching for jobs on, 259–62
Internet researching employers on, 242
Internships, building work experience with, 362
Interviewers
possible, 309
questions to ask, 337–38
Interviews. *See* Informational interviews; Job interviews
Introverts, direct approach for, 277

J

Job advertisements, using well, 263–65
Job fairs, 365
Job hopping, 375
versus free agent attitude, 379
Job interviews, 301
aggressive, 322–23
appearance for, 306–7
attitude and behavior and, 324–27
behavior-based, 321–22
behavior-based questions and answers for, 331–33
candidates' objectives at, 305
case-based, 322
closing, 314–15
common mistakes in, 339
compensation discussions at, 315–16

as conversation, 303–4, 312–14
decision curve, 45–46
employers' objectives at, 304
first impressions, 310–12
follow-up, 323
following up on, 316–18
general questions and answers for, 327–29
illegal questions, 324
informational interviews disguised as, 249
items to bring to, 309
long-distance, 367–68
networking disguised as, 280
off-the-wall, 323–24
phone, 320–21
position-specific questions and answers for, 330–31
possible interviewers at, 309
preparation for, 306–9
props for, 308
questions to ask interviewers, 337–38
references and, 316
secret of, 45
stressful questions and answers for, 333–37
structured, 322
types of, 320–24
using achievement stories/key messages in, 312–13
using job ads for, 264–65
Job market
entering, 227
personal, potential opportunities with, 256–57
Job matching
company culture and, 46, 47–48
interests and, 78–80
motivation and, 46, 48
personality and, 74–76
self-assessment and, 73–74
skills and, 46, 47, 77–78
work values and, 80–82
Job objective, 167–68
Job offers
considering, 341–42
employers' compensation criteria, 344–46
evaluating, 342–243
multiple, 350–51
negotiating, 343–50
Job satisfaction, 30–31
finding daily, 35
work values and, 80–82

Job search portfolio, 115–16
achievement stories, 127–30
adding to sales pitch, 150–52
certifications, 142
employment history, 125–26
key messages, 116–22
keywords, 123–25
personal story, 135–36, 139
positive messages, 136–38
references, 138–41
skills inventory, 131–35
Job searches. *See also* F.A.M.E. attitudes
application time, 99
backup plans for, 111–12
budgeting expenses for, 102–4
competition of, 19
creating new habits for, 26–27
creating plans for, 97–98
creating routines for, 108
establishing workspace, 104–5
innovative plans for, 24–25
law of supply and demand and, 10
long-distance, 367–68
long employment gaps and, 374–75
maintaining productivity, 106–8
managing time for, 101–2
managing work and, 100–101
from military to civilian sector, 372–74
physical needs for, 104–5
preparation time, 98
preparing for, 95–96
in public service, 371–72
pursuing opportunities time, 99–100
recordkeeping, 106
reviewing plans for, 224, 297–98, 377
setting priorities for, 109–10
student, 362–66
wrapping up, 355–56
Job security
decline in, 4, 5
then *versus* now, 3
Job switching, 5
Job tenure, 4, 5
Job transition, 301, 353
leaving current job, 353–56
Jobs. *See also* Work
advertised, 257–58
applying for, 265–69
finding, 258–59
searching online for, 259–62

Jobs (*cont.*)
  creating habits for new,
    358–60
  evaluating new, 360
  federal government, 371–72
  ideal, 119
  incorporating F.A.M.E.
    attitudes into new,
    356–57
  leaving current, 353–56
  researching, 231–39
  starting new, 357–58
  temporary, 14–15, 112
  unadvertised, 256–57
    applying for, 271–77
    following up on, 276–77

K

Key messages, 116–22
  in job interview, 305, 312–
    13
  mature job searches and,
    371
Keywords, 123–25
  on resume, 179–80
"Knowledge Marketplace," 6

L

Leadership, seizing, 25–26
Learning. *See also* Education
  pushing, 33–34
Libraries, researching employ-
    ers in, 242–43
Life mission, 38–39
Listening skills, 305
Loose ends, tying up, 354

M

Manufacturing industries,
    changes in, 4
Marketing attitude, 19–22,
    380
  defining personal brands,
    71–91
  delivering memorable mes-
    sages, 115–43
    in special search situa-
      tions, 361–76
  understanding recruiting
    process, 43–52
Marketplace. *See* Job market
Military, transitioning out of,
    372–74
Mission. *See* Life mission
Money
  job satisfaction and, 30–31
  talking about, 344–46
Monster, researching jobs on,
    234

Monster Salary Center, 234
  salary wizard, 250
MonsterLearning, 34
Monster's Resume Builder, 161
MonsterTrak's Major to Career
  Converter, 80
Motivation, demonstrating,
    317
Motivation match, 46, 48

N

Negotiation, 301, 343
  common mistakes in, 350
  establishing common expec-
    tations, 343–44
  multiple job offers and,
    350–51
  nonsalary compensation,
    347–49
  talking about money, 344–
    46
Nervousness, at job interviews,
    303–4
Networking, 279–80
  groups, 389
  long-distance, 292
  meeting agenda for, 290–92
  students, 364
  into target employers, 293
  using referrals, 287–89
  without referrals, 289
  workings of, 281–82
Networking grid, 68–70
Networking groups, 296
Networking Log, 284–85, 286
Networks. *See also* Relation-
    ships
  building, 282–85
  contracting hiring managers
    through, 56
  expanding, 293–96
  friends, family, and commu-
    nity and, 66–68
  importance of, 15–16
  keeping active, 296–97

O

Objectives, job interview, 304–
    5
Obtain, Train, and Retain
  cycle, 8–9
Occupational Information
  Network. *See* O*Net
*Occupational Outlook Hand-
  book*, 234
Off-the-wall interviews, 323–
    24
O*Net, 232–34
Opportunity
  advertised jobs, 257–71

creating, 271–77
creating to networking,
    281–82
grabbing, 23
networking and, 280
potential, 256–57
pursuing, 99–100
window of, 255–56
Outplacement services, 63
Outside recruiters, 57–60
Overcoming objections exer-
    cise, 91

P

Passion, work and, 29–30
Perquisites, 349
Personal brand
  defining, 20–21, 71–72
    interests, 78–80
    personality, 74–76
    skills, 77–78
    work values, 80–82
  self-assessment, 72–73
Personal growth, learning and,
    33–34
Personal story, 135–36, 139
Personality, matching jobs to,
    74–76
Phone interviews, 320–21
  long-distance job searches
    and, 367
Physical cues, interview, 326–
    27
Pitch, 145–46
  adding job search portfolio
    to, 150–52
  networking with, 282–83,
    290–91
  summary for, 146–50
  training with, 152–54
  value of, 154–55
Positive messages, 136–38
Power verbs, 173–76
Pre-interview checklist, 306
Prep time, job searches and,
    98
Priorities, setting, 109–10
Problem-Action-Result
  method
    answering behavior-based
      questions with, 331–33
    preparing achievement sto-
      ries with, 127
Productivity
  maintaining, 106–8
  time management and,
    106–8
Professional career assess-
    ments, 82–83
Professional networking
  groups, 66

Professional reputation, 20
Promotions, timetable for, 359
Props, for job interviews, 308
Public service, finding jobs in, 371–72
Publication resources, 383–84

Q

Qualifications
   in cover letter, 213–14
   emphasizing at job interviews, 312–14
Questions
   answering interview, 326
   to ask interviewers, 337–38
   asking at job interviews, 313–15
   behavior-based interview, 331–33
   general job interview, 327–29
   illegal interview, 224
   position-specific interview, 330–31
   stressful interview, 333–37

R

Raises, timetable for, 359
Rapport, creating interview, 311–12
Recordkeeping, importance of, 106
Recruiters. *See also* Outside recruiters
   discomfort of, 43–44
   facts about, 48–49
   preventing bad tricks of, 61
   quality sought by, 46–48
   types of, 58–59
Recruiting process
   changes in, 51–52
   effects of technology on, 50–51
References, 138–41
   at job interviews, 316
   on resumes, 176
Referrals
   acquiring, 282–85
   asking for, 292
   networking with, 287–89
Rejection, 319
Relationships
   building healthy work, 37–38
   creating personal network, 15–16
   with hiring managers, 56–57

with human resources department people, 54–55
   using for job search, 53–54
Relocating, job searches and, 367–68
Relocation assistance, 349
Research
   compensation, 250–51
   employers, 239–46
   informational interviews and, 246–50
   job and company resources, 387–89
   jobs, 231–39
   organizing, 230–31
   value of, 229–30, 252
Resources
   books, 381–83
   contributors, 392–95
   Internet, 384–92
   publications, 383–84
Resume-writing services, 192–93, 392
Resumes, 157. *See also* Applications
   action phrases/power verbs for, 173–76
   additional information on, 181
   affiliations, 179
   appropriate length, 182–83
   building, 160–61
   for career changes, 369
   career summary, 164–66
   certifications, 178
   common mistakes in, 188–91
   contact information, 161–62
   cover messages and, 210–11
   for criminal record, 375–76
   delivering memorable, 22
   durability of, 158–59
   education, 176–78
   employment history on, 169–72
   formatting, 159–60
   functional, 183–87
   headline for, 163–64
   for job hopping, 375
   in job interview, 313
   job objective on, 166–68
   long-term employment on, 376
   networking with, 288
   proofreading, 191–92
   references on, 176
   for returning to workforce, 370
   as sales tool, 16–17
   samples, 194–208
   skills/keywords, 179–80

student, 362–63
   styles, 181–82
   targets, 168–69
   transitioning from military and, 373
   updating, 355
   work status on, 169
Retained search firms, 59, 60–62
Retirement, job openings and, 4–5
Retirement savings, rolling over, 355
Routines, creating for job searches, 108
Running with an applicant, 57–58

S

Second interviews, 323
Securities and Exchange Commission (SEC), researching employers with, 243–44
Self-assessment, 72–73
   interest, 78–80
   job matches and, 73–74
   personality, 74–76
   skills, 77–78
   work values, 80–82
Self-discovery, 71–72
   key messages and, 117–18
Service industries
   changes in, 4
   employment in, 6
Shower exercise, 84
Signature exercise, 85
Silence, in job interviews, 313–14
Skill-based resumes, 183–87
Skill categories, 132
Skill match, 46, 47, 77–78
Skilled workers, long-term shortages of, 5–6
Skills
   assessing, 77–78
   emphasizing at job interviews, 312–14
   job search, incorporating into new job, 356–57
   key messages and, 118–19
   listening, 305
   personal value and, 15
   on resume, 179–80
   types of, 77
Skills inventory, 131–35
Skills shortage, 5–6
Staffing firms, 58
Start dates, 348
Stress interviews, 322–23

Stressful interview questions, 333–37
Structured interviews, 322
Students, 362–66
Summary
    resume, 165–66
    sales pitch, 146–50
Supply and demand, job searches and, 10

T

Target customers, focusing on, 21
Target Employer form, 241
Target employers. *See also* Employers
    creating opportunity with, 271–77
    networking into, 293
Target employers file, 231
    keeping customized cover messages in, 275–76
Target Job form, 233, 237, 253
Target jobs file, 230
Targets, resumes, 168–69
Technology, affecting recruiting process, 50–51
Temporary agencies, 58
Thank-you notes, following up with, 316–18
Third interviews, 323
Third-party recruiters, 58

Time management
    job searches and, 101–2
    productivity and, 108–9
Timetable, for raises and promotions, 359
Training, 17–19
Transferable skills, 77
    from job search to employment, 113
Tuition assistance, 349
Twenty questions exercise, 89

U

Unadvertised jobs. *See* Jobs, unadvertised
Unemployment benefits, 104
U.S. Bureau of Labor Statistics
    Career Guide to Industries, 243
    Occupational Outlook Handbook, 234
U.S. Department of Labor, O*Net, 232–34

V

Values
    listing personal, 40
    living by, 41
    work, 30–31
Vision, creating broad, 36–37

W

What did you want to be exercise, 87
What's Important to Me form, 40
Window of opportunity, 255–56
Words
    action phrases/power verbs, 173–76
    appropriate cover message, 217–18
Work. *See also* Jobs
    bringing passion to, 29–30
    valuing elements of, 30–31
Work experience. *See also* Employment history
    internships and, 362
Work status, 169
Work values, matching jobs to, 80–82
Workforce, returning to, 370
Working, job seeking and, 100–101
Working conditions, 349
Workplace changes
    decline in job security and, 4
    favoring employees, 4–7
Workspace, establishing for job search, 104–5